I HEART POLITICS

'If you want to find out why we're in the political position we're in right now, this is the book for you. Andrews breaks down the last few years in politics in an accessible and fun way. A must-read.'
Mollie Goodfellow, journalist and comedy writer

'Andrews' writing is illuminating, educational and a whole lot of fun. What can I say? It'll make you a fan.'
Kieron Gillen, co-writer of *The Wicked + The Divine*

'This is an important book, by turns deeply serious and darkly funny. Andrews takes the tools of cultural analysis and in a personal, accessible yet analytical tone, uses them to explain why the kaleidoscope of our politics seems so broken.'
Glen O'Hara, Professor of Modern and Contemporary History, Oxford Brookes University

'Andrews adopts an unusual lateral view on the tribalism and loyalties of parliamentary politics. *I Heart Politics* is equal parts fascinating and funny, insightful and infuriating. I'm a fan.'
Ally Fogg, journalist

Phoenix Andrews is a journalist, writer, broadcaster and researcher. His expertise in politics, fandom, popular culture and digital culture has seen him published in *The Times*, *Independent*, *Prospect*, *New Statesman,* Slate and other publications, and interviewed by BBC World Service and Times Radio.

I HEART POLITICS

HOW PEOPLE POWER TOOK OVER THE WORLD

PHOENIX ANDREWS

Atlantic Books
London

First published in trade paperback in Great Britain in 2024 by Atlantic Books, an imprint of Atlantic Books Ltd.

10 9 8 7 6 5 4 3 2 1

A CIP catalogue record for this book is available from the British Library.

Trade paperback ISBN: 978 1 83895 422 2
E-book ISBN: 978 1 83895 423 9

Printed in Great Britain by TJ Books Ltd, Padstow, Cornwall

Atlantic Books
An imprint of Atlantic Books Ltd
Ormond House
26–27 Boswell Street
London
WC1N 3JZ

www.atlantic-books.co.uk

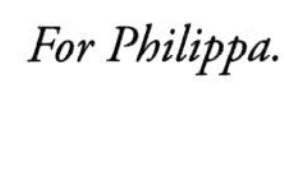

For Philippa.

CONTENTS

INTRODUCTION

'The lettuce has won!'

A week is, as Harold Wilson said, a long time in politics. History is made – JFK is assassinated, and suspect Lee Harvey Oswald is arrested then shot by nightclub owner Jack Ruby. Change is in the air – Thatcher protégé Michael Portillo loses his seat as Tony Blair pronounces that 'a new dawn has broken – has it not?', making way for the 1997 Labour landslide. Something unexpected happens – the 2010 General Election, coalition negotiations and David Cameron and Nick Clegg in the Downing Street rose garden. A ridiculous story comes out – Cameron and Piggate in 2015. The most exciting weeks combine all these things – the final days and resignation of Liz Truss as Prime Minister in 2022. History was made: Truss became the shortest-serving PM in UK history. Change was in the air: it seemed constant, as Truss and her Chancellor Kwasi Kwarteng scrambled to manage the impact of their economic announcements and everything fell apart. As for a funny story, they flooded in. The lettuce. The jokes. The day-collar truthers (a theory that a necklace worn regularly by Truss indicated that she was a submissive in a BDSM relationship). At those times, being a fan of politics comes into its own. Everybody knows something about the important days and the funny ones, but only the truly committed feel the benefit of those years of politics-watching and frustrating factional rows: deep, absurd joy at every new revelation. When other people get into the topic, you feel like your knowledge and time in the trenches pays off because friends and colleagues ask you for insight and are interested in what you have to say.

The casual viewer in October 2022 enjoyed the idea of a Prime Minister being outlasted by an iceberg lettuce, but there was an extra level of entertainment to be had in understanding the references in the *Daily Star* livestream of 'Liz vs Lettuce' and the steady trickle of MPs making manoeuvres against Truss. Fans know the names and backgrounds of the minor players. We know the context for every allegation and innuendo. We knew why the lettuce had been served tofu (a line in a Suella Braverman anti-woke speech, hours before she was sacked as Home Secretary). Fans were aware that Ed Miliband had waited seven whole years to mock David Cameron's 'stability and strong Government with me, or chaos with Ed Miliband' tweet by using a single emoji of a clown, and that Miliband had been the one to call the fracking debate that precipitated the collapse of Truss. It was delicious.

Who said the lettuce had won? Social media. Politics Twitter (a loose community of journalists, people who work in politics, activists and fans on the platform now known as X) added both entertainment and insight to proceedings. Westminster's most seasoned lobby hacks, wonks and parliamentarians saw their veneer of reason and respectability peel away in real time while live reports came in from the field of a Conservative Party in ruins. Fans followed the action ball by ball like they were listening to *Test Match Special*, and then some. However, those reliant on broadcast news and articles published after the madness was over missed out on both detail and fun.

Online fandom is more intense in every way. Part of the joy of

'Liz vs Lettuce' was that everyone lost their cool. Celebrities like H from pop superstars Steps and double act Dick & Dom, of noughties children's programme *In Da Bungalow*, called for Truss to resign. Fans had the fun of witnessing both those outbursts and the visible discomfort of Truss's many right-wing libertarian backers. They also enjoyed piecing together news stories as they came out, including illicit photographs taken by a Labour MP during a voting lobby skirmish, conflicting statements issued by ministerial aides and interviews with exasperated senior Tories. The pace was thrilling.

If a week is a long time in politics, the past decade has felt like a whole generation. We've had more weekly crises than hot dinners: financial, political, social and personal. While I understand the sanity-preserving impulse to avoid all news and current affairs, if you're reading this book then you probably haven't managed that. In that case, you've seen the rocky nature of the political landscape over this period. There have been multiple populist movements – Brexit, Trump, Corbynism/left populism and the big anti-woke/culture war/ conspiracy theory mess that has glommed up many countries in what is left of the West. Nationalism has mixed itself into that soup, both Scottish and English. The Queen died. We had a pandemic. Somehow the UK has engineered a cost of living crisis worse than most rival countries, leading to economic hardship across the board and endless headlines about inflation and industrial action. Political loyalties are fragmented and public services fractured. Interest and enthusiasm have moved from barely there to the passionate backing of political parties, individual leaders and campaigns – and then back to nihilistic apathy. Trust in elites, the media and organizations has gone, according to the polling, and they've crumbled.

There's been much chat about polarization, with the assumption that the left and right have moved away from the centre at equal rates. However, though the right have moved a long way to the right, especially in the UK, Europe and the US, the left have barely shifted – they're losing the argument.[1] The real story is affective polarization: where people's feelings about their own views and communities become more positive and opposing ones more negative. Similarly, while freedom of speech has been a big topic across party lines and international borders, it isn't being suppressed as many would have you believe. Those with reactionary views are regularly seen in newspapers and on broadcast media complaining about being silenced and cancelled, whereas people from the minority groups they criticize do not have that mainstream media or political power so are not heard at all. There are no transgender newspaper columnists or regular panel show guests, but no shortage of people voicing their opposition to trans rights. You can fit the all-time total of Black Westminster MPs on a single-decker bus (thirty-nine, at the time of writing), but many white people complain that their views on race have made them feel excluded.[2] The rise of social media has meant more voices have been heard, but it hasn't all been welcome. What is reasonable criticism to one person should be shut down to preserve free speech for another.

Politicians and commentators ask us to 'pay no attention to that man behind the curtain', as the Great and Powerful Oz told Dorothy, but as politics stops working, more and more people start to see the problems with politics and the media. While political parties – most notably Labour – have always 'purged' members, removed the whip (party backing) from MPs and blocked candidates seen as a threat to the leadership of the day, these moves have become more urgent and more obvious in recent years as leaders' authority within their parties and with the general public has waned.

Over the years we've had post-war consensus and (neo)liberal consensus, but now we are somewhere else entirely. With my academic hat on, I call this period in time the 'digital dissensus': rather than consensus, where everyone broadly agrees on how things are, there is an abundance of conflicting and dissenting views. The loudest voices aren't necessarily the most representative, even of their particular brand of politics. Fandom is one of many explanations for why politics has become so unstable. People in fandoms might notice these patterns of behaviour, but those outside of fandoms, quite reasonably, don't understand why people are behaving the way they are. Someone ranting to you about the ECHR (European Convention on Human Rights) or Just Stop Oil or US President Joe Biden with the same passion they'd normally reserve for talking about their family or James Bond films? This is fandom behaviour crossing over into political issues and personalities.

This period began with the financial crash of 2008, whose fallout continues and intensifies online.[3] The initial fragments of coherent ideologies – of big groups such as Remainers and Leavers, Populists and Liberals, Internationalists and Nationalists, Corbynites and Blairites – are fracturing further, falling out with each other and forming smaller groups with ever more distinct characteristics and concerns. It's noisy, it's chaotic and it's difficult to navigate.

Friends joke that I see everything as fandom, and it's kind of true. I'm obsessed with it. Why did that woman ring a radio station to defend the Prime Minister as if someone had slagged off her mum?

Why is my friend's dad acting like wanting to stay in the European Union is a personality trait? Their behaviour looks the same as when Taylor Swift fans kick off at anyone who gives her a bad review, or when people a bit too into gin post pictures of it all over Facebook. Oh. Yeah. They're acting just like fans. I'd seen those patterns before, of enthusiasm and defensiveness and weird behaviour. Once I'd worked out what was going on, I started to see it everywhere. There's an old football song that England fans would sing at games against Germany, to the tune of 'Camptown Races': 'Two World Wars and One World Cup, doo-dah, doo-dah'. New Labour fans have their own version, which they use to mock the left: 'Lose, lose, lose, lose, Blair, Blair, Blair, lose-lose, lose-lose' (Peter Mandelson) or 'Lost, lost, lost, lost, Blair, Blair, Blair, lost-lost, lost-lost' (Alastair Campbell).

While people understood that supporters of Jeremy Corbyn and Donald Trump were 'fans', what with the chants and the t-shirts and the hats and the screaming rows with dissenters, it was obvious to me – as someone who knew fandom inside out – that there was more to it than the celebration of individual politicians and a desire to defend them from criticism. Fandom had seeped into every aspect of politics and public life. Brexit cracked that wide open like a rift in space and time. The elite, the establishment, whatever you want to call it, were caught on the hop. The people who had always won without trying had lost. Oof.

Nobody other than Liberal Democrats, Eurosceptic Tories and bureaucracy nerds had cared that much about the European Union before. All of a sudden, a person's views on Brexit said everything about who they were, and they were determined to find like-minded people and have a good moan. Instead of going to the pub, they went where everyone goes these days: social media. Before they knew it, half of them were wearing EU flags as capes, the other half were doing the same with Union Jacks, and both discovered that they had a Lot of Feelings about it. The memo about never discussing money, religion or politics in polite society had been set on fire. People now had Very Strong Views about everything and had joined more groups to talk about them than an over-caffeinated student at a freshers' fair.

When you are a fan, it's not just what you like. Your fandom is part of your identity, like your name and where you come from. That's why football fans take it so personally when their team loses: they lost too. Their team is 'us'. When staying up late on election nights, people say the same sorts of things. 'We've got no chance in Scotland.' It's not ownership. It's not even membership. It's family.

The word 'fan' originated in nineteenth-century baseball journalism and was popularized by Ren Mulford Jr of the *Cincinnati Times-Star*. As baseball became a national sport, journalists needed to find an alternative to derogatory terms like 'crank' (obsessive), 'bug' (stats nerd) and 'rooter' (casual supporter). Mulford Jr wrote in 1888: 'Do you know what a "fan" is? A crank. A fiend. An enthusiast.'[4] Lots of people who are passionate don't consider themselves to be fans, and the word itself can be a barrier. The stigma of the term hangs on the idea that fan = fanatic = irrational, or at least not serious. One of entrepreneur (and political figure) Elon Musk's most dedicated supporters, illustrator Salina Marie Gomez, told the *Verge* that 'I wouldn't consider myself a fan because [the word] implies a kind of a blind obsession with a celebrity.'[5] She doesn't want to imply that she is uncritical or unthinking.

A fanbase is the collective name for the fans of someone or something. 'Fanbase' is roughly equivalent to 'supporters': everyone who supports a political party is a supporter of that party, and everyone who likes something is a fan and part of the fanbase. Just as being a supporter doesn't imply that you are a paid-up party member or regular campaigner, being part of a fanbase doesn't imply that you interact with other fans. People can be fans while enjoying their interest on their own or with friends and family. What makes a fan part of a narrower *fandom* rather than the broader *fanbase* is the sense of community and identity that comes from joining in.[6]

Fans use their shared interest to find their people: the people who get where they're coming from and share their values as well as enthusiasms. There have always been people with strong political affiliations and people who argue for particular positions when political debate dominates the news, usually during an election or crisis or scandal. What tips this behaviour into fandom is when their politics becomes part of their identity and they find people to talk to who understand what they're talking about: their community. Voting the same way every election or joining in a workplace conversation isn't the same as making friends and debating politics online with strangers, or getting upset if someone criticizes a politician who shares their views.

A fandom builds a community around a shared interest. Fandoms are broader and more intense than just liking something. Someone who is part of the *Doctor Who* fandom, for example, will probably collect merchandise, know about all the spin-offs, engage with debates within the fandom, maybe attend *Doctor Who* conventions and talk to other fans on- or offline. They might also write articles, make videos or art or write stories relating to *Doctor Who*. I'm a *Doctor Who* fan who knows a lot of other *Doctor Who* fans, reads the *Doctor Who Magazine* and chats to other fans regularly. I co-wrote a *Doctor Who* book! It's an important part of who I am. Football fans are similar – there are those who watch major competitions and vaguely follow a team, and there are those whose lives are full of significant moments connected to their football club. You know as soon as you meet a committed Gooner (Arsenal fan), even if they aren't wearing a football shirt, and it's rare for them not to spend time with other fans at matches, in the pub and online.

A fandom is a collective identity. It's more than the sum of its parts. When you join a fandom, you're suddenly part of a network of people who understand and will discuss the things you're interested in, which is better than just enjoying something on your own. Anti-fans – think of the passionate opponents of Donald Trump or Jeremy Corbyn – get a similar sense of purpose, identity and even joy from despising someone or something and finding others who feel the same way.

I've been 'in fandom' since I was tiny, asking for music albums for presents and begging copies of pop magazines off my cousin Mark (a decade older than me). My room was plastered with posters and press cuttings of my favourite bands. I made my own fan collages, recorded 'radio shows' discussing my favourite bands on cassette and wrote bad *Grease* fanfiction before I left primary school. My first homemade pop magazine was put together with friends when I was twelve, and then I learned about fanzines via flyers in the local record shops. I made and traded zines as a teenager and twenty-something who hung around gigs and comedy shows, then upgraded to a website and podcast. Fandoms came and went but *Doctor Who* persisted.

The first election I remember was in 1987 and I was six years old. I watched *Newsround* and didn't like Mrs Thatcher, even though my parents did. My mum had campaigned for her as a young Conservative and my nana enjoyed explaining the call 'Number 10 – Maggie's Den!' when we played bingo together in Scarborough. I fervently followed Thatcher's decline and sneakily watched *Spitting Image*, reading books about politics from the mobile library that visited our road in holidays. When the time came for Thatcher to be replaced, I discussed the runners and riders with our regular supply teacher at my primary school. She liked Douglas Hurd for a sensible choice. I favoured John Major – he was younger and seemed to have less baggage – but thought Michael Heseltine's hair would win the day. It took a little longer for my passion for politics to match my passion for pop music, but I was 'up for Portillo' (awake when Michael Portillo lost his seat in 1997), even though I wasn't old enough to vote.

My first political party conference looked a lot like a fan convention or comic con, and it basically was. Instead of queueing to get a poster signed by Peter Capaldi, I was queueing to get into a tiny fringe event with Ed Miliband. Panels about monster prosthetics were replaced with panels about housing policy. Diane Abbott walked past me and everyone was trying to grab a selfie. The twenty-something potential candidates hoping for a safe seat all looked like they were doing Wes Streeting cosplay: identical blue suits, shiny shoes, red ties and crisp white shirts. I found it funny when old New Labour MPs were mocking Jeremy Corbyn supporters for being fans, because people too young to have been born when Tony Blair became leader were going mad for 'Things Can Only Get Better' (Labour's theme song of the 1997 election, very much a fannish choice) at the Labour Students disco.

Fandom has always been with us and goes back to ancient times. We have always been political; we have always been passionate. Political graffiti in ancient Greece and Rome were the fan social media of their time. When leaders gave money to citizens who were struggling, the people's gratitude also made it into Pompeii's graffiti: 'When Caesar came to most holy Venus – when your heavenly feet carried you, Augustus – there were thousands of thousands of gold pieces.' There are no half-measures in their praise. It's reminiscent of the brown-nosing replies under Elon Musk's posts. The printing press, brought to England in the fifteenth century, enabled politicians and fans to share ideas, have arguments and issue threats via pamphlets (like today's meme wars, where rival groups of fans share visual and text-based jokes). History books are full of contemporary references to the 'cults' (fandoms) of Oliver Cromwell, Napoleon, Ferdinand Lassalle and more. In the nineteenth century, celebrity authors like Benjamin Disraeli became politicians, and politicians became celebrities. Heroes and villains alike spoke to mass rallies and sold merchandise to their supporters. Fan mail poured in.

Fandom is being taken more seriously *now* because it's getting harder to ignore. Social media, DIY politics and newer forms of activism have changed who can be heard in politics and what they want to say. At the turn of the millennium, election turnout had dropped on both sides of the Atlantic. Voters thought politicians were all the same. For over a decade it didn't matter to many people who won, as you would either keep being okay or keep being screwed over no matter who was in power. Elections were being won from the centre, but eventually that centre collapsed in on itself. Gordon Brown and Al Gore seemed stale. Politicians had become smug. The centre ground was so hollow that it didn't mean anything anymore. There were no new ideas.

Over time, however, culture wars and important single issues pushed people into more emotional and active involvement on politics. Like other institutions, parties didn't mean what they used to. Personalities did. Outsider politicians, influencers and thinkers on the left and right pulled in fans across the world. When Corbyn, Brexit and Trump disrupted everything, the UK and the US had to stop pretending that only developing countries had problems with democracy.

Social media brought new forms of criticism, activism, new ways to organize supporters and new ways for people to get involved as politicians, commentators or fans. Traditional forms of networking and campaigning excluded people who couldn't physically access them, didn't feel welcome or had different kinds of skills. Grassroots political group chats, video, memes, polls, analysis, GIFs, graphic design and crowdfunders are everywhere. Fans make their own content rather than just sharing official party materials. Some of it is serious and some is very silly. There is fun to be had.

We have a human need to make sense of the world, but currently there is uncertainty in politics on every level and in every country. Climate crisis, economic challenges, wars and the impact of the Covid-19 pandemic have affected local and national governments and changed how people feel about politics and politicians. At the same time, because of economic and social change, many people feel uncertain about their status and identity. The old ways people used to bolster these things were via their work, which is less stable now, or in institutions that aren't as important these days. Football matches and gigs are so expensive that many fans are priced out. Fandom is becoming more mainstream for other enthusiasms outside sport. Marvel fandom used to be cult, but now you can buy Marvel-branded clothing everywhere. Gaming is normal for all ages – even cryptofinance and billionaires have fandoms online. Talking to a wider range of people on social media, not just family and friends and colleagues, encourages shared experiences and interests of a different kind.

The appetite for more knowledge and engagement with politics is exemplified by the popularity of political podcasts like *The Rest Is Politics*, which regularly tops the podcast charts and holds sold-out live events. If its listeners aren't fans of politics the same way the listeners of *The Rest Is Football* and the *Gary Neville Podcast* are football fans, something very strange is going on. I can see people engaging with presenters Rory Stewart and Alastair Campbell on social media every day, between episodes, and getting stuck into online debates about politics. Online fandom moves more quickly than offline. The range of people involved in the cut and thrust of social media is broader than that seen at political events, because it fits more easily into busy lives. The online experience can be richer, because fans have access to more information and social contact, but seeing behind the curtain of politics can burst an idealist's bubble. Offline fans – or realistically, fans who just spend less time online – don't see how badly politicians and activists can behave and have the narrative curated for them by whatever news sources they consume and their limited connections in real life.

I can't just observe fandom in a detached way, because I'm inside it. I'm all over it, grinning at the chaos of it all and asking awkward questions – like the Cheshire Cat. I've been to rallies and launches and marches and hustings and fundraising dinners and karaoke nights for all sorts of parties and campaigns. I've chatted to people dressed up as chickens or Michael Gove. I even accidentally stumble on politicians and fans in the wild. I spotted a glowing homemade Bernie Sanders sign as I was walking to the Tube in 2019 and I joined in the march rallying overseas voters in the Democratic primary, talking to Bernie fans and those of Elizabeth Warren. Paid reps for Mike Bloomberg gave me stickers. One time in Ottawa I walked up Parliament Hill to go to a shopping centre and saw a stage with TV cameras and lights. I stuck around and ended up seeing Justin Trudeau and indigenous Canadians give speeches. Trudeau's famously objectified 'bubble butt'[7] was just a few feet away from me as he walked back to his office. My replies on social media were full of insults. . . and swooning.

If Lord Byron could get away with writing the equivalent of stan (super-fan) posts about Napoleon – who he also saw as a version of himself because that lad was never *not* a narcissist – it's okay to be a fan of politics. Byron openly adored Napoleon, buying his merchandise and willing him to win. Here are my favourite Byron posts:

> Napoleon! – this week will decide his fate. All seems against him; but I believe and hope he will win – at least, beat back the invaders. What right have we to prescribe sovereigns to France? Oh for a Republic! 'Brutus, thou sleepest.'

> Sent my fine print of Napoleon to be framed. It is framed; and the Emperor becomes his robes as if he had been hatched in them.[8]

People's politics don't come out of nowhere. Just like musicians are fans of other musicians, politicians and activists got into politics because they are fans of politics, as well as wanting power or change. Just look at how US presidents decorate the Oval Office with paintings and statues of politicians they admire. The relationship between politicians and fans is more complicated than between leaders and followers, because what fans say and do, enjoy or despise feeds back into how politicians think and act. It's more like a chain of influence – influence is about taking elements from someone else's work and building on it, rather than being given something. It's active rather than passive. Someone's politics are a mixture of what has gone before and ideas of their own, and being a fan doesn't mean sharing the same views on everything. Fans can also influence politicians. They share a deep interest, after all.

People who aren't fans of politics aren't that bothered about political parties, politicians, policy, activism or campaigns most of the time. Even those who are passionately engaged in current affairs can't all be called fans (and of course, many would reject the very idea), because politics isn't that important to who they are. The inactive public aren't well informed on, say, the minutiae of policy.[9] They're not thinking about it, they're not buying books about it, they're not reading long articles about it and they're not talking about it with people they've never met before on the internet or in person. That doesn't mean they don't care about certain issues. They're partisan about those things.

It's just not 'politics' or 'politicians' or 'activism' or 'campaigns' or even 'current affairs' or 'my community'. They want things to get better in their lives, or otherwise just make it (the noise about politics, the news) stop. When Theresa May used the slogan 'strong and stable' in the 2017 election, the appeal to the public was supposed to be an end to all the turmoil around Brexit and personality politics. Only around 15–20 per cent of people follow politics closely or at all.[10] In one study of 3,000 Americans, only 27 per cent said that they discuss politics frequently and a majority considered themselves to be 'moderates'.[11] Out of that group, 70 per cent believed that a typical member of the other party can't stop talking about politics and holds extreme views. People who are into politics are not great at judging what's normal, because they are overrepresented in the media but in reality they are only a small group of voters.

Politics fandom isn't just about electoral politics and winning elections. Activists, campaigners, thinkers, commentators and influencers can inspire people to think differently about politics. Their support often comes from regular voters, especially if they talk about specific parties and politicians, but those with no connection to party politics can pick up a following from non-voters and previously apathetic people. Fans are a diverse bunch.

While treating all online spaces like fandoms (niche spaces where most of the audience understand the context of each post) is particularly prominent in under-twenty-fives, people much older learned how to act online from the places they first hung out when they got the internet. For some people, socializing and discussing topics online with people they also met online (as opposed to family members, work colleagues and communities initially established offline) is a recent development – even if they have had access to the internet for a long time. I'm in my forties and I was interacting with strangers in a range of different contexts, including fandoms, from my earliest days online in the late 1990s. I learned how to negotiate different norms, use of slang and assumptions about culture.

Being ignorant of the dynamics of fandom and internet cultures makes it more likely that someone will copy these behaviours without recognizing their own involvement in the toxicity. These behaviours might be making inflammatory comments, driving followers to mock individuals and not understanding the broader audience in online spaces who will read their words out of context.

The problems of fandom are perpetuated and compounded in political spaces whenever people say that fans are the problem with politics. Most of the people who say this are fans themselves in politics-based fandoms that they don't think of as fandoms. A prominent political journalist or celebrity might say or post something flippant and foolish about a politician (positive or negative) – for example, claiming that Boris Johnson will be remembered as one of the greatest Prime Ministers of all time for saving the UK from communist Corbyn – and then complain about the reaction from fans and anti-fans. A British YouTuber who goes by the mononym Shaun made a post on Twitter in January 2020, and it regularly goes viral during political arguments online: Shaun's post simply states: 'brigaded by the vile trolls again, simply for deliberately provoking them with lies and insults'.[12]

Politics is about more than political parties and winning elections, internal or public. There are other reasons for being a fan than protecting your team, excluding other people or beating the one you hate the most, and the happiest fans know this. It's about moments of tenderness and understanding within a community, and even joy.

Fandom is an acknowledgement that our politics are built on collective understandings and emotional attachments. There is such a thing as a society (contradicting Margaret Thatcher), and what we believe, who we share that with and where we belong is important to who we are. What fandom offers is a way of looking at the world with empathy, explanations for things that seem inexplicable and tools that enable more people to get interested in politics without losing their principles or losing hope.

The opposite of democratizing political engagement is asking for top-down intervention to save us from bad decisions by the public or elected politicians. After Liz Truss resigned, former flamboyant pop star and current centrist broadcaster Reverend Richard Coles tweeted: 'Could the King, within his powers of course, FIRMLY ENCOURAGE the calling of a General Election, for the good of the country?'[13] While Plato argued that the ideal state would be run by philosopher kings, leaving the people (*demos*) out of it, the call from the so-called sensible grownups like Coles was for Charles III – a sometime philosopher and literal king – to actually step in and save them from the messy business of politics. Convention has it that the British monarch follows Westminster politics closely, but does not intervene. However, the maelstrom of Brexit saw the wardrobe choices (such as a blue and yellow hat resembling the EU flag, or brooches with historical significance) and rubber-stamping role (Royal Assent) of the King's mother, Queen Elizabeth II, wildly interpreted by a subset of fans of remaining in the European Union. They strongly desired for her to use the powers she had on paper to make all the things they didn't like stop at once. They especially wanted the Queen to use any royal tricks she could to stop Brexit itself. These sensible sorts started to resemble the noisiest fans of Harry Styles and wildly popular K-pop group BTS, desperate for their idol and other fans to notice them, and that wasn't even the maddest thing that happened in the Brexit wars and the years that followed.

Every iteration of the UK government further escalates its fannish tendencies among both politicians and supporters, while the Opposition is also in hock to icons of the past. From campaign song 'It's Maggie For Me' and Margaret Thatcher treasuring framed flattery from Enoch Powell to 'Things Can Only Get Better' and Tony Blair claiming that 'Putting me in No 10 was like letting a fan take over Manchester United'. From Boris Johnson namedropping Churchill and Pericles to 'Boris Or Bust'. Liz Truss cosplayed Thatcher's most iconic outfits while stanning for Ronald Reagan, followed by the 'In Liz We Truss' mugs being swiftly withdrawn from the Conservative Party online store as her stock began to fall. Keir Starmer sent out posters of his own face to Labour Party members during his leadership bid and peppers his speeches with Thatcher, Wilson and Kinnock hits.

While many of the goings-on in the House of Commons – not least weekly Prime Minister's Questions (PMQs) – owe a lot to the brash British style of music hall culture, politics fandom has a lot in common with music hall too. Historian Peter Bailey claims that music hall, by combining elements of the theatre and the pub, was the first real attempt to combine an indulgent and carnivalesque good time with 'orderly consumption' – or to put it more simply, sell riotous entertainment as if it were any other commodity.[14] Bailey also points out that music hall let the crowd try out different styles and identities, though they were mostly working class, because the interactive performances on stage satirized and celebrated all kinds of different people and complicated the relationships between insiders and outsiders and performers and audiences. Music hall crowds, Bailey reckons, can be thought of as 'producers as much as consumers'. It is the same with fans of politics, especially since social media blurred the boundaries between professional and amateur and private and public for politicians, journalists, celebrities and activists. Fans contribute to what politics is as much as follow what it does.

Note on X/Twitter: In this book the name 'Twitter' is used when it refers to events that occurred prior to the platform's rebranding as X in July 2023.

1

HISTORY

Fandom has always existed. Of course, it has changed over time. New technologies and the emergence of the 'celebrity' shaped the evolution of fandom, along with the media and politics, which have been intertwined for as long as they've existed. More people gained voting rights as access to information and campaigning abilities grew, at first through growing literacy and the printing press, later by broadcast media and the internet. From the populism of the ancient world to the memorabilia explosion of the twentieth century, history tells us a lot about politics fandom and how it became the phenomenon it is today.

The ancient world is where politics fandom began. Greek philosopher and historian Plutarch documented the Trump-like relationship between populist politician Clodius and his fans, whom he called 'a rabble of the lewdest and most arrogant ruffians'. Clodius, while harassing the great Roman statesman Pompey (for planning to bring back his enemy, Cicero, from exile), stood in a prominent place and called out to the crowd:

> 'Who is a licentious imperator?'

'What man seeks for a man?'

'Who scratches his head with one finger?'

And they, like a chorus trained in responsive song, as he shook his toga, would answer each question by shouting out 'Pompey.'[1]

Much of the language of politics comes from the Greeks and Romans: 'democracy', 'partisan', 'faction'. So too does the political myth. We never really know everything about a politician or political movement, and what we do know is heavily influenced by the stories they tell about themselves and those that are told about them. This kind of storytelling didn't start with the modern media. Narrative and emotions drive voting patterns more than policy and principles, and likely have done since before someone scratched this message into a wall in Pompeii: 'I ask that you elect Gaius Iulius Polybius as aedile. He bakes good bread.'[2] Many people aren't that interested in politics or its players in the time between elections, but political fans both keep political myths alive and even develop them.

Perhaps the most beloved figure in political history is Pericles, the great ancient Athenian orator and statesman, who has been cited as inspirational to politicians past and present. But why is he so admired, by Hitler and Boris Johnson alike? Perhaps because historians are fans, too – and they themselves have fans, who support their authority as experts. History is shaped by the people who write and share it. Their choices of what information to include in their writing and how they frame the facts persuade us, intentionally or not, to view politicians as heroes or villains.

In the case of Pericles, his reputation comes from ancient Greek historian Thucydides. Thucydides himself has modern-day fans and is still widely studied because he writes insightfully about politics, social behaviour and communication. He also rewrote accounts of historical figures to make them appear more noble and articulate. Pericles' most famous speech is the Funeral Oration (given after a battle, not at an actual funeral), which Thucydides recounted from his own memory and that of others. It is likely not a verbatim transcript, but rather an attempt to capture a sense of Pericles' ideas and ideals and an invitation to readers to compare the vision Pericles outlined in his speech with the reality of the period.

The following excerpt from the opening of the Funeral Oration shows that the speech was eloquent and admirable, and it made fans of many who love politics and democracy:

> Our constitution does not copy the laws of neighbouring states; we are rather a pattern to others than imitators ourselves. Its administration favours the many instead of the few; this is why it is called a democracy. If we look to the laws, they afford equal justice to all in their private differences; if no social standing, advancement in public life falls to reputation for capacity, class considerations not being allowed to interfere with merit; nor again does poverty bar the way, if a man is able to serve the state, he is not hindered by the obscurity of his condition.[3]

But how much of this writing is a true reflection of Pericles, and how much is myth created by a fanboy and excellent writer?

Beyond grand battles and noble speeches, things got messier when the general public started to become involved in politics. There were no elections in the Byzantine Empire, which was the continuation of the Roman Empire in eastern provinces during Late Antiquity and the Middle Ages. *Curiae*, or city councils, usually only appointed the wealthy landowning elite. Ordinary people could only voice their opinions on social and political issues through shouting and booing at public events. Well-organized fan clubs (*demes*) that supported sports factions or teams ('faction' comes from *factione*, the name for a company of charioteers) were the main outlet for their enthusiasms and frustrations, acting like a mixture of football hooligan gangs and political parties. Sports and politics have long been linked, from chariot racing fans booing the emperor at the Hippodrome in Constantinople to Liverpool fans cheering the death of Margaret Thatcher. The name for a fan of a faction? *Partisan*, a word often used as a slur in modern politics for those seen as mindlessly tribal. The emperor and his officials looked out for signs of public unrest across the Byzantine Empire, which often flared up among the partisans at chariot races. Fans shouted their political demands between races. The imperial forces and guards in the city needed the co-operation of the factions to maintain law and order.

There were initially four major factions in chariot racing, named for the colours of charioteers' uniforms. These were the Blues (*Veneti*), the Greens (*Prasini*), the Reds (*Russati*) and the Whites (*Albati*). Fans wore their faction's colours. By the sixth century the only teams with any influence were the Blues and Greens, and that's when things got spicy. The Nika Riots against Emperor Justinian took place in Constantinople during one week in AD 532.[4] Nearly half of

Constantinople was burned or destroyed, and tens of thousands of people were killed.

It began with a fight that broke out during a chariot racing event at the Hippodrome. The fight was between fans of the Blues and Greens. It ended badly, and seven partisans involved in the violence were found guilty of murder. However, one Green and one Blue fan escaped hanging because the scaffold holding the noose broke, and they sought sanctuary in a church. The crowd who were watching the hanging called upon the emperor to pardon the pair. But Emperor Justinian didn't give in to their request and refused to respond to the demands, so a riot kicked off.

By the time there were only two races left of the season Justinian still refused to respond, and the factions united to oppose him. It didn't matter who they supported; it mattered that they, as fans, won. Partisans stopped yelling 'Blue!' or 'Green!' and started chanting 'Nika!': the 'Victory!' chant. Justinian still wouldn't respond to partisan demands at the Hippodrome, so they burned down the praetorium and the crowd freed the prisoners. The emperor tried to restart the games, but the partisans set fire to the Hippodrome itself and demanded three officials were fired. Justinian finally responded by dismissing the officials, but then he sent in troops to try to stop the partisans.

The partisans set alight more civic buildings; Justinian sent in more troops from the garrison. He eventually suppressed the riot. Much of the violence and unrest may have been avoided if Justinian (a fan of the Blues) had understood how far the partisans were prepared to go and if the public had more of a voice in local and imperial politics.

The next snapshot of history I want to explore involves a

technological development that changed fandom and politics forever, so we will have to travel forwards about a thousand years. Charles Babbage, the mathematician credited with inventing the computer, reportedly said that 'the modern world commences with the printing press'. With the printing press, literacy and learning became available to ordinary people. They also now had an affordable and widely available method to read and express political views: the pamphlet. These printed tracts were used to argue points of religious doctrine, report news and express political dissent. By the 1580s, during the Reformation period, pamphlets had begun to replace broadsheet ballads as the main means for communicating information to and influencing the views of the general public. The printing press also made it possible to be a fan nationally and internationally. Pamphlets were very much the social media of their time, with interpersonal complaints playing out as well as ideas spreading between their pages. Thus began what became known as the 'pamphlet wars'.[5] [6]

During this time, both Protestants and Catholics engaged in the pamphlet wars, which might be viewed as the first battle for the popular mind in Western history. Now *that's* politics. People often draw a parallel between fandom and religious fervour, and associate popular political figures with a cult of personality. The Reformation saw what might be called the first battle for the popular mind in Western history, when Protestants and Catholics engaged in a vicious and highly personal pamphlet war. For example, theologian Martin Luther himself, far from being above the fray, got stuck into the nastier end of the pamphlet wars when he wrote *Against the Murderous, Thieving Hordes of Peasants* (1525) – a rant about radical Luther fans who he thought made him look bad when they got out of hand and began the German Peasants' War. His original title was 'Against the Rioting Peasants', but the tabloid-headline writers of the day (printers in other cities) harshened it without his permission. Luther rebuking his own fans in print might be seen as a precursor to Labour MP John McDonnell rebuking fans of Jeremy Corbyn's Labour Party for perpetuating 'antisemitic stereotypes' and undermining the cause.[7]

You might think that Martin Luther's main beef would have been with the Catholic Church, but he also found time to squabble about religion with a fellow reformer, the up-and-coming John Calvin. While Luther managed to fit in being a priest, academic, composer and author (and a former monk), Calvin juggled writing with being a theologian, pastor and religious reformer – having given up his career as a lawyer. Both were what we now call Protestant, but they had major disagreements.

Luther and Calvin attracted passionate fans; at the time religion was very much like politics is today. Church courts had huge jurisdiction over your life – they could impose penalties for adultery and fornication, for example. The Church was also a massive landowner and might be your landlord. Challenges to the Church's power were unwelcome to the Church authorities, and Luther was made an outcast for heresy. Among other things, Luther claimed that the Bible was the only source of divinely revealed knowledge, which challenged the authority of the Pope.

Calvin and Luther fans still have it out on the talk pages of Wikipedia (where edits to entries are discussed), and there is a wealth of Reformation-flavoured stories hosted by fanfiction (or 'fic') repository Archive of Our Own. Fanfiction is known for its racy parings of characters from popular fictional worlds such as *The Lord of the Rings* and *Doctor Who*, but in reality only some fic involves pop culture, and only some involves sex. Luther is more popular in the talk pages and features more often in fanfic. This might be explained by the fact that, as a 'living saint', as he was viewed at the time, he was keen on signing autographs,[8] and the printing press helped him go viral,[9] picking up fans not only in Europe, but across the world.

The first martyr of the Scottish Reformation was Patrick Hamilton, a twenty-four-year-old member of the University of St Andrews, a preacher and a huge Luther fan. While Hamilton was studying in Paris,[10] Luther's ideas became a sensation, and his fans and anti-fans engaged in fiery debate. The Sorbonne damned Luther and said his work should be burned. Philip Melanchthon from Wittenberg published a defence of Luther that was an immediate sensation. It inspired Hamilton, who went on a nerdy and fannish trip to Leuven to study with Erasmus, the Dutch scholar and humanist. He then returned to Scotland to preach Luther's ideas. He was accused of heresy – Scottish Lutherans were seen in Catholic Scotland as foreign insurgents – and he knew the punishment was death by burning. Hamilton would eventually be willing to die for his Luther fandom (though not yet). Being a Lutheran was a big part of who he was and where he felt he belonged.

Hamilton fled to Germany and got to know Luther himself. Later he moved to the new university at Marburg and published his own arguments. Then he moved back to Scotland ready to die for his views. His old colleagues at St Andrews testified against him.[11] He was called up in front of the Archbishop, convicted as a heretic, stripped of all his worldly goods and sentenced to death. Hamilton was bound to the stake with an iron chain and burned for six hours in front of St Salvator's College (there was a strong easterly wind and even gunpowder just burned his head and hands while he remained conscious). Someone in the crowd watching asked Hamilton if he still believed in Luther's ideas, and Hamilton raised three fingers before finally dying. Unsurprisingly, Patrick Hamilton's martyrdom and the poor handling of Lutheran enthusiasm just drew new and more passionate fans to both Hamilton and Protestantism. The whole affair was hugely disruptive to both Scottish and European religion, royalty and politics, which were pretty much one and the same at the time. Martyring fans just for supporting a theological stance shifted public opinion on the need for political freedom.

Calvin's ideas have persisted, and his approach to Christian humanism had a lasting influence, particularly in US politics and religion.[12] To be a Calvinist is, ostensibly, to have high moral standards. However, his fans were more into his ideas than the man himself, which made them less passionate than Lutherans. He was what popular culture would now call a 'problematic fave':[13] someone you admire, despite despising their views or actions. There is a reason for that. He didn't just have the usual sort of unpleasant views for his time. He was a bit too keen on the torture and death of his enemies, and he justified these actions as the will of God. Michael Servetus was an acquaintance of John Calvin who upset him by sending him critical comments on his work. The next time Servetus went to see Calvin preach, Calvin had Servetus arrested and charged with heresy. He was burned alive, slowly, with a theology book tied to his chest, and died while screaming for mercy. Calvin said that Servetus had been punished for his arrogance. When several other heretics were tortured and killed, he wrote to his friend Farel: 'I am persuaded that it is not without the special will of God that, apart from any verdict of the judges, the criminals have endured protracted torment at the hands of the executioner.'[14] In short, he (almost) made Donald Trump look like a calm and reasonable man.

Along with his supporters, Luther himself was threatened with being burned to death, and his books and thesis were publicly burned by his enemies as a threat. An effigy of Luther was burned in Rome, and in a separate incident a puppet of Luther was tried and condemned to the stake. In response, Lutherans claimed that Luther may be mortal, but his ideas would never die (a slogan commonly appended to images of the man). However, they went further and said that his portrait literally *couldn't* burn – supposedly a painting of Luther among a burning of some of his books in 1521 stayed intact. The burning took place a full twenty-five years before Luther's actual death, during a period where a medallion was made (Luther memorabilia created in his lifetime) that had his portrait on the front and a phoenix rising from the ashes on the reverse. Those fans went hard, treating the living Protestant Luther with the reverence normally reserved for (long dead) Catholic saints.

The legend of the man whose portrait wouldn't burn became truly established two centuries later as the 'Incombustible Luther'[15] (new band name just dropped), thanks to the popular press spreading the stories of incidents in Artern (a copper engraving) and Eisleben (painting on wood) where images of Luther unexpectedly survived house fires. Mass media was vital to the continued celebrity and fandom of Martin Luther.

Let's hop in the TARDIS and time travel once more to investigate another important phenomenon in the development of politics fandom: celebrity. I'm going to borrow my definition here from historian Greg Jenner, who wrote probably the best book you could read on the topic – *Dead Famous*:[16]

> **CELEBRITY** (noun): A unique persona made widely known to the public via media coverage, and whose life is publicly consumed as dramatic entertainment, and whose commercial brand is profitable for those who exploit their popularity, and perhaps also for themselves.

Early politics fandom intertwined with graffiti, history and sports. The printing press brought media, literacy and internationalism to politics and fandom. Then the newspapers and magazines needed celebrity to fill their pages, and as a result the public demanded more personality and relatability from their politicians and leaders. They wanted to consume the lives of all prominent figures as entertainment, in the form of gossip and interviews, and politicians became celebrities in their own right. The expectations of media and celebrity culture meant politicians had to share more of themselves and have more of a 'hinterland' (life and enthusiasms outside politics). In return, their relationship with some of their supporters would deepen into real fandom.

Even with the help of a TARDIS, it is impossible to travel in time without at some point landing in Victorian Britain – a period mythologized almost as much as antiquity. There is an oft-repeated 'statistic' (all references to it in other works cite the same source quoted below, a 1964 reprint of a 1938 book) that says for every portrait of anyone else in working-class houses, there were ten of Gladstone. This led to some amusement on social media, from people who were snarkily imagining a house with a couple of family pictures and otherwise entirely wallpapered with Gladstone paintings. As you can see from the quotation, it was more hyperbole about the Gladstone fandom than a quantitative study:

> Yet he held in the affections of the mass of the working-classes a place deeper and higher than either Shaftesbury or Chamberlain. It is safe to say that for one portrait of anybody else in working-class houses in the 'eighties of last century there were ten of Gladstone.[17]

Gladstone's rival, Benjamin Disraeli, was a celebrity novelist before he was ever Prime Minister, with a big bag of fan mail to prove it.[18] He received fan letters from Queen Victoria because he was her favourite Prime Minister, and they formed a close friendship that lasted until his death. By contrast, Victoria didn't at all like Gladstone and his liberal concerns for the electoral franchise.

Upon Disraeli's party's defeat in 1880, Victoria wrote to him:

> Very grateful for your kindness. What your loss to me as a Minister would be is impossible to estimate but I trust you will always remain my friend to whom I can turn and on whom I can rely. Hope you will come to Windsor on Sunday in the forenoon and stop all day and dine and sleep.

In another letter, she said that 'none of her Ministers have ever shown her more consideration & kindness than he [Disraeli] has!'[19]

Disraeli was so beloved that the anniversary of his death on 19 April 1881 became a national day of commemoration, named after his favourite flower: the primrose. Primrose Day was marked each year into the 1920s, with primroses left at his tomb and statue, and fans celebrated their hero by wearing primroses as buttonholes, garlands and hat decorations. There is a surviving Pathé news clip from 1916, depicting a Primrose Day memorial ceremony and a woman selling primroses to a young soldier in uniform.[20] Disraeli fandom was incorporated into the Primrose League (an organization founded in 1883 to spread Conservative principles), which welcomed women and other new members into the Conservative Party, and published pamphlets, held meetings, created some jazzy badges and other merchandise and were generally the Momentum (the faction that grew out of Jeremy Corbyn's leadership campaign) of their day.[21] [22] [23] They were a canvassing and campaigning powerhouse.

After their glory days of the late nineteenth century, it all went south for the Primrose League. During the 1920s, they used Disraeli's Jewish heritage (he converted to Christianity as a child) and their non-political community and cultural activities as a shield for their 'anti-alien' (racist) rhetoric. The League, using the Aliens Act 1905 (which introduced immigration registration and controls for the first time) onwards, blamed Jews, immigrants and foreign influences (mostly communists) for the Great Depression and political unrest.[24] They also employed their reach, local knowledge and large membership in a similar vein to former chief strategist to Donald Trump Steve Bannon's 'precinct strategy'; taking over administrative processes and making sure that their people were registered to vote as voting rights expanded – and others were not.

The Primrose League used their citizenship and the trust that came from their association with a much-loved figure, Disraeli, as a weapon.[25] They guided the new women voters on how to use their votes effectively and held public speaking lessons. They opposed the General Strike by influencing restrictive trade union policies and declared that citizenship rights came with the responsibility to support the British Empire (fannish attachment to the positive aspects of Empire being key to many Conservatives' identity, then and now). Further expansion of voting rights and mass democracy in 1928 posed a threat to the League that fandom built, with both Conservative and Liberal MPs worried that men's votes would be 'swamped'[26] by those of women. The form of Conservatism promoted by the League advocated leadership and Empire, but not the rights of women.

You wouldn't know it now given how the term is used, but 'suffragette' was originally an insult coined by the *Daily Mail* in 1906 to mock suffragists (anyone campaigning for voting rights) who focused on women's right to vote. Suffragettes laughed and embraced the term for marketing purposes, and marketing and merchandise were their contribution to the evolution of politics fandom. They were happy to get arrested, loved a bit of violence and knew how to do uniforms[27] and memorabilia. The suffragettes' Women's Social and Political Union had campaign shops everywhere, showing future capitalist feminists how to promote themselves and extract money from their fans.[28] They had official colours, ribbons and publications to raise money, allow supporters to parade their politics and help them to find fellow fans. The Museum of London has an excellent collection of suffragette ephemera.

Christabel and Emmeline Pankhurst used their suffragette magazine *Britannia* (edited by Christabel) for patriotic propaganda supporting the war effort during World War I. Sylvia Pankhurst had split off from her sisters by then to take her own radical socialist path, and their other sister Adela had given up activism. Sylvia's magazine *The Woman's Dreadnought* promoted pacifism. Her fandom had started to eclipse that of the other two, and her publication continued as a serious feminist and socialist publication.[29] The history of suffrage was somewhat rewritten in the 1920s and 1930s by former suffragettes (and later their fans), likening the struggle for the vote with the bloodbath that was World War I and focusing on either the militancy of Emmeline and Christabel or the agency and comradeship of women as if there had been no disagreements.[30] [31] [32]

Soon another technological change was on the horizon: radio. Churchill's famous oratory was delivered to fans across the nation directly into their living rooms. He could speak without being filtered through the commentary of the press. Churchill is a bit like *Doctor Who* in that he had many eras (including the present-day fantasy version, as typified by the fictional scene in biopic *Darkest Hour* where Churchill takes the Tube and asks citizens if he should stand against tyranny[33]), and while there are fans of every incarnation, there is one that towers above them all. The World War II British Bulldog Churchill is his Tom Baker (the most popular of the original Doctors), if you will, and he is yet to be matched by a David Tennant (the most popular modern Doctor) of politics. Despite well-founded criticism and a complex history, Winston Churchill is the most popular UK Prime Minister of all time.[34]

Once Churchill was made Prime Minister, he became the first British politician to be able to speak to the people frequently without them having to leave their homes. Churchill's fondness for giving speeches, his rich and warm vocal tone and theatrical style of delivery did his domestic image no end of good. He received large volumes of post throughout his career. Delia Morton was hired by Churchill's secretary to deal with the backlog of fan mail that arrived daily, even after his resignation as Prime Minister. Churchill's demands led to some interesting filing decisions:

> communications from 'pottykins' – another of Churchill's invented words, this one for incoherent correspondents – were filed under 'P'. Churchill was in the habit of stopping by her desk and asking to see the pottykins letters, which it turned out, included scribbles from Ezra Pound, filed of course under 'P' in bins called 'pottykins'.[35]

As a boy, Churchill himself was a fan, a behaviour that continued through his life. He wrote fan letters to the adventure writer Henry Rider Haggard when he was young.[36] He became an accomplished amateur artist and friend of painters such as Walter Sickert. He took a great interest in literature, always viewing it through a political lens and often writing critiques of writers he was friends with such as George Bernard Shaw and W. Somerset Maugham.[37] Indeed, he became a journalist and prolific author of non-fiction (along with one novel) before he was a politician. He wrote a fan letter to film star Vivien Leigh and was friends with her for over twenty years. Churchill first met H.G. Wells in 1902 and was deeply influenced by his fiction.[38] [39] The pair often fell out over politics but remained regular correspondents until Churchill's death.

If you want to learn about the influences on Churchill's politics and presentation, look no further than his creative and cultural enthusiasms. Great Men of History (an approach popularized in the nineteenth century claiming that history can be explained by the outsized impact of great men or heroes that can be traced back to Plutarch's biographies of Noble Greeks and Romans) accounts tend to assume that popular culture references are always an embarrassing and inauthentic attempt at leaders trying to seem relevant to the general public. For example, see Gordon Brown's professed interest in the Arctic Monkeys or Rishi Sunak's love of 'bonkbuster' author Jilly Cooper.[40] Great Men of History accounts insist that leaders' politics must be shaped by history, events and highbrow expertise. However, politicians aren't for the most part influenced by academic theory or philosophy, as Churchill expert Richard Toye says:

> What we forget is that Churchill and others were probably not interested in reading that stuff when they got home after a hard day in the House of Commons. They wanted to read a book that was full of ideas but was also going to be fun. H.G. Wells was perfect for that. Churchill was definitely a closet science-fiction fan. In fact, one of his criticisms of *A Modern Utopia* was that there was too much thought-provoking stuff and not enough action.[41]

Knowing that Churchill was a fannish sort and happy to write both effusive and scathing letters to and commentary about his favourites makes sense of his political instincts and broad appeal beyond just 'he beat the Nazis and won the war'. He understood how to be an exciting politician. He was his own historian, writing himself into legend through his own books and speeches. It took Churchill a long time to get there – he was sixty-five when he became an unlikely Prime Minister in 1940 – but he created a character and mode of politics that fans could get behind. Churchill's eccentricities and bold rhetorical style played out differently in each of his adult eras: with the army as a war correspondent and soldier; his first stint in politics as a left-wing liberal (elected at twenty-five as a Conservative MP, he crossed the floor to be a Liberal MP and minister); losing his seat at forty in 1915 (became very right-wing and anti-communist); the wilderness years pre-war (nobody is a fan of that period); Prime Minister 1940–45 (glory years); his second premiership 1951–55 (desperate to hang on); later life and decline of Empire (quite popular with Americans); and retirement (lots of fan mail, particularly from said Americans, but coasting on past glories).

The World at War documentary series really cemented Churchill's legend for the generations that followed. At school, I had to watch clips of the 1970s TV epic, narrated by Laurence Olivier, in history lessons. Its popularity may have been due to Jock Colville's anecdotes about Winston's obsession with building and bricklaying:

> although he was sixty-five years old he vaulted over a brick wall, a traverse which had been built at his instruction, and landed feet first in a pool of liquid cement and with

> impertinence, in retrospect, I said to him, 'Well, I think you've met your Waterloo,' because he was stuck in the cement. And he turned to me and said, 'How dare you! Anyhow, try Blenheim' – his energy was indeed remarkable at this time.

Churchill fans are the biggest historical fandom in the UK: writing and buying books about him, making and watching movies about him, buying mugs and tea towels with his face on, defending his Westminster statue as if it were their first-born, bringing snacks and drinks for said statue when drunk and so on. The fans pretty much all focus on the World War II Winston. They don't respond that well to criticism of their man.

Part of Churchill's appeal, then and now, was that he was a fan, and so he knew what fans needed in order to feel satisfied with a narrative. His speeches and broadcasts cannot be separated from his theatricality and passions. Churchill's mythical status is rooted in his awareness of and love for art and fiction and his ability to exploit the new technology of radio as a broadcaster and storyteller, not just a politician. He reshaped expectations of what a political leader looked like, for Britain and the world, and with it built a lasting fandom.

Into the later twentieth century, mass access to photography and then video made fandom more visual. Politicians didn't just have to sound good: they had to look good. Mass Observation (a social research project that recruited observers and volunteer writers to document everyday life in Britain) diaries show us the popularity of politicians at events in the twentieth century and how much ordinary people valued their access to lawmakers, particularly once they could see what they looked like, and leaders became absorbed into the category of media celebrity.[42] Harold Wilson and John F. Kennedy were often surrounded by adoring crowds. Admittedly much of the Kennedy myth was invented by his wife Jackie after his death, in an article where she turned his brief presidency into a glittering fairytale of 'Camelot': a pioneering and progressive hero cut down in his prime.[43] Nevertheless, JFK was idealized from the day he was selected as the Democratic candidate for president. His youthful good looks, famous mistresses and photo-perfect family made Kennedy the ideal politician – and celebrity of the gossip magazines – for a new media age. JFK's support for civil rights was initially lukewarm, tempered by what he saw as the militancy of the movement, but his famous speech in 1963 shaped both his legacy and the direction of travel on segregation.

People still believe that there was an audience split in the first of the televised 1960 presidential debates against Richard Nixon, where radio audiences favoured Nixon's resonant voice, and television audiences preferred handsome JFK's sharp appearance. It is true that Nixon had presentation issues – an ugly and ill-fitting suit, sweaty brow, bad shave and general sense of discomfort – but there is no evidence from contemporary surveys to indicate that Nixon won over radio audiences (where none of this was visible).[44] That would have required a significant polling shift from previous Kennedy supporters, convinced by Nixon's arguments. The real impact of the series of debates was more speculation about the effect of visual cues on voters now the genie was out of the bottle and poor TV performers could no longer escape the cameras. Personality in politics had become more important than ever.

Film director Oliver Stone distorted cultural history and influenced public opinion and public policy via his controversial 1991 movie *JFK*, which combined real footage with staged scenes and speculation. What he called his 'magnetic attachment to the idea that it had to be powerful people' behind Kennedy's death was his fandom for a conspiracy theory that continues to fascinate the public.[45] Stone blurred the lines between fact and fiction, memory and narrative, and in 2021 released a two-hour documentary in defence of his original feature and his counterfactual stories of JFK's future politics, had he lived. In the opening minutes of the documentary, Stone states: 'Conspiracy theories are now conspiracy facts.' The ability of the media to shape our image and understanding of politicians, policies and campaigns past and present is not just exploited by politicians and their teams, or fans taking things into their own hands, but also by their opponents in both politics and the media. Broadcasters and newspapers have portrayed Rishi Sunak as a superhero and an angel with a literal halo. An image of Jeremy Corbyn, digitally altered to invite associations with Russia and the Cold War, was used as a *Newsnight* backdrop. The conspiratorial rabbit holes and 'post-truth' of our current legacy and social media landscape were present in and encouraged by Stone's film.

Kennedy was a politician who became a celebrity with fans. Soon enough, Hollywood brought us celebrities with fans who became politicians. Into the later twentieth century, mass access to photography and then video made fandom ever more visual. The image of a saviour riding in on a white horse (originally Christ in the book of Revelation) wasn't too on the nose for movie actor and president Ronald Reagan, who as Governor of California rode out into the Sierra Nevada mountains on a horse to support conservationists and halt highway construction and had a favourite 'grey' (white) horse called El Alamein at his ranch near Santa Barbara.

Despite once leading Hollywood actors in a strike, Reagan saw young people who disagreed with him the same way that conservative voters and many generations of right-wing politicians and journalists have since: too disruptive, uncivil, and illegitimate in their demands, and he found free speech in universities to be a productive issue for stirring up his fans in the late 1960s. On NBC in 1968 he called protesters a 'small group of criminal anarchists and latter-day fascists' who 'seek to close down the campuses, our universities, and even our high schools' and were 'not in any way to be confused with the traditional and generally acceptable activities of students who seek change through proper and constructive channels'. The protesters responded in kind when he next visited Berkeley campus by chanting 'Fuck Reagan!'[46] And so Reagan anti-fandom was born.

Ronald Reagan was a celebrity president: he was famous as an actor before he was a politician and became one of the most globally well-known politicians even by US presidential standards. That status brought with it both fandom and anti-fandom, in a decade where America was the dominant force in popular culture and world politics. Margaret Thatcher and Ronald Reagan forged a productive partnership that installed neoliberalism (deregulation of finance and markets with reduced state intervention) as the new ideology, and their image was reproduced by both fans and antis in the form of merchandise galore. The big boom in contemporary political t-shirts, dolls, badges, keyrings, books and more started here.

Satirical programmes like Britain's *Spitting Image* confused the issue, with as many people who loved Thatcher and Reagan buying keyrings, dolls and mugs based on their image as those who despised them. I spoke to one woman, Emma, who had been obsessed with

Thatcher as a child and had posters and figurines of her *Spitting Image* puppet. Emma knew nothing of Thatcher's politics at the time, she was just the funny strong woman on telly. Her parents were Conservative voters and big fans of Maggie T. Depending on whether you believe former Tory minister Edwina Currie (who enjoyed the publicity boost from her own depiction) or Thatcher's chief press secretary Bernard Ingham (who found his puppet cruel and pathetic),[47] 'THATCHA!' either loved her masculine and misogynistic comic portrayal and played up to it or viewed it with disdain.[48]

Margaret Thatcher bears some responsibility for modern politics fandom. Not just her own fans, but the way she viewed the world and the policies she pursued encouraged the public to move away from working collectively and as part of civil society and towards pursuing personal ambitions. Viewed through the lens of massive Thatcher fan Michael Portillo, it seems benign and even empowering:

> it was always this 'they' that was responsible for what was happening in people's lives. And what Margaret Thatcher was trying to do was to change the 'they' to a 'we'. You know, 'We can do something.' Or I can. I may not be a very substantial figure but I'll have responsibilities in my family, I'll have a position in my community and I can make a difference.[49]

Margaret Thatcher set out her idea of the relationship between the people and government in a speech in 1968 called 'What's wrong with politics?' She believed that 'the way to get personal involvement and participation is not for people to take part in more and more government decisions' but to have a smaller state with fewer services. She had no time for the 'personalities' of American politics or for consensus, which 'could be an attempt to satisfy people holding no particular views about anything. . . No great party can survive except on the basis of firm beliefs about what it wants to do.' She did believe that fans needed to want what she was offering. 'It is not enough to have reluctant support. We want people's enthusiasm as well.'[50]

The Conservatives have struggled to find a central 'I' to inspire them or their voters since, which is one of the reasons Thatcher fandom hasn't faded and Boris Johnson was seized on as a potential solution. Claims to be her heir (or her nightmare, in the case of Labour) remain part of every leadership campaign. References to what Thatcher would or would not have done were a big part of the Brexit years, and Liz Truss cosplayed Thatcher for photoshoots before she became Prime Minister.

In France, Charles de Gaulle is the leader they can't let go. The Gaullist fandom's 'résistancialisme' myth pretends most of France backed the Resistance during World War II. It is a black-and-white history of the heroic *real* France against the villains of Germany, the traitor Pétain and 'le père la défaite' (father of defeat) of Vichy France. Workers, artists and young people rejected de Gaulle in the uprising of May 1968. They saw him as a pathetic symbol of the boring, oppressive, nationalist version of France that was economically successful but culturally dead. The 1968 rebellion was crushed, but de Gaulle resigned as president a year later. French historian Pierre Nora promoted a state-led version of Paul Ricoeur's 'devoir de mémoire' – the duty not to forget – that was pluralist, incorporated different groups and couldn't be captured by nationalists. This vision was backed by former French president Jacques Chirac as he rejected 'résistancialist' views. Populists on the left and right reacted against the multicultural nuance of a history that doesn't make minorities assimilate into their version of the past.[51] [52] Now that the present feels uncertain again, every politician in France claims to be a fan of de Gaulle.[53] France 'no longer believes in Socialism, in liberalism, in Christianism or in Communism', said Nora. 'The country is wracked by disunity. Gaullism is the only appeal that means anything.'[54]

We're still dealing with the aftershocks from the 1960s and 1970s, which continue to drive all kinds of fandoms and anti-fandoms: in Europe, the wars over history and culture; in the US, the roles of anti-communism and racism in shaping their view of civil rights and foreign policy; in Latin America and the Philippines, the consequences of colonialism and US interventionism for their politics and lives.

Several aspects of 1968, the year of student protests, youth movements and activism, point us to the present day. The story of current unrest and impulses driving fandoms today could be tracked back to how that period was handled and dissent suppressed. Social movements seeking change were built from the bottom up, often based on Marxist ideals and using uncivil means to seek civil rights. The status quo (no, not the band) rushed to reassert its top-down authority. Communism was seen as the greatest threat to democracy, not right-wing extremism or military dictatorships (many of which Western governments had a hand in installing and then supporting). The mass of people protesting were ignored (or massacred) and police brutality soared, while charismatic figures like Martin Luther King Jr and West Germany's Rudi Dutschke became stars. The music was great and many found their political voice for the first time. But just as every major French politician still claims to be a Gaullist and Enoch Powell won the argument for a long time on race and immigration, the grassroots politics of the '68 radicals never went away. Nor did their ability to draw a fandom as well as an army of activists.

The final innovation of late twentieth-century fandom and media, in the wake of the success of the Beatles and Beatlemania: mass-produced merchandise. It can be fan-made, like Maggie jumpers at Conservative Party conferences. It can be official, like the button badges and bumper stickers sold by the Reagan campaign. Or merchandise production can be opportunist, like the thousands of posters and t-shirts turning 1960s revolutionary Che Guevara into a student staple and character in a Broadway musical. Arguably it's this aspect of fandom, allowing fans to wear and display their allegiances, that most depoliticizes political characters and makes them more icon than ideology. The proliferation of colourful inspirational memes and officially licensed 'Fridamania'[55] products featuring Mexican painter Frida Kahlo, who was also a communist and Mexicayotl activist, are a good example of the mythologizing and flattening effect of this kind of fandom and the commercial attempts to serve or even create its demands.

Celebrity politicians like Donald Trump and Volodymyr Zelenskyy; politicians who openly wear their fannish allegiances, like Boris Johnson and Liz Truss; political movements who brand themselves, like Extinction Rebellion and Just Stop Oil: none of this is new. The internet has had consequences much like the advent of the printing press but on an exponential scale, expanding reach and accessibility for political engagement and fan activity. Fans are louder and more creative than ever, because they are playing on a bigger stage.

2

THE HOWS AND WHYS OF FANDOM

Harry Fairchild, the world's first table tennis coach with Down's Syndrome, was excited when the then Labour leader turned up to his club during the 2017 party conference.[1] A big Corbyn fan, he began singing the 'Oh, Jeremy Corbyn!' chant (to the tune of 'Seven Nation Army' by the White Stripes). Brighton Table Tennis Club offers sessions to young people, those aged fifty-plus, adults with learning disabilities and children in care. Corbyn had stopped by for a few rallies with some of the club members. Not to be outdone, Corbyn then sang right back: 'Oh, Harry Fairchild!' Fairchild ran straight over to give him a hug.

If you flip through a newspaper or magazine article on the topic of fandom, you'll see something about 'parasocial' (one-sided) relationships, 'fanatics', maybe some outrageous examples of fan culture and some references to teenage girls, embarrassment and screaming. What those articles don't tell you is what people get out of being a fan nor how many perfectly ordinary people are in fandoms yet don't always realize it.

'I was into politics at a young age,' says actor Martin Freeman, in an interview for the *Guardian*. 'It's not like at 10 I was recording

Question Time on the VHS. It was more the music I was listening to. I loved two-tone – politics via Linton Kwesi Johnson. I was a little lefty, but with more passion than rigour, more into the T-shirts and badges than trying to think up a transport policy.'[2]

This chapter explains why fandoms happen and how being a 'supporter' works today. What's *really* happening isn't people losing their minds over politics, but rather people trying to make sense of the world and all its uncertainties. By building relationships with other people, gaining a stronger sense of who they are and how they fit in, and fighting for the things they care about. *That's* what fandom does. Fan is no more of a dirty word than politics itself.

Being involved in politics is meant to be serious and boring. But in reality, we know that – throughout history – citizens have always enjoyed forging strong (and strongly pleasurable!) emotional connections with their rulers. So, what's so fun about politics? And why is it fun to be a fan?

Politics is fun because it's unpredictable and thrilling, like a sport, and is full of wild characters and wilder ideas, like fiction. There is always something happening, constant shifts in the public mood. You can compare the present with your knowledge of the past and the people involved to try to work out where it's going next. It's fun because if you care about the world, campaigning and persuading people to make it a better place is exciting. Being a politics fan is fun because you can share all the information, analysis and memes that fill your head with people who understand, appreciate it and have something to say about it. It has all the scurrilous gossip of celebrity fandom, rewards for insider knowledge of music fandom and constant stats updates of sports fandom. All that and a sense of purpose.

Psychology researchers Samantha Groene and Vanessa Hettinger quizzed Harry Potter fans on general knowledge questions and questions relating to their fandom.[3] Participants were then asked to write a creative essay with a Harry Potter prompt. Fans who did well on the Potter part of the quiz, affirming their fandom, put in more effort and performed better on the essay task than fans who did badly on the quiz. Their identity as Harry Potter fans was threatened and it affected their motivation to 'perform' as fans. Priding yourself on your knowledge is a big part of fandom, and it's rewarding when that is recognized by others.

Fans grow as people through fandom, developing their personal and social identities through interaction and self-expression. It's fun because shared experiences are fun – waiting for an exit poll to drop or going on mad trips around the country to events. There's joy in seeing your favourites in person and being recognized by your heroes, taking silly selfies, sharing in-jokes, being part of a big crowd and feeling hopeful about the future, making placards and turning a moment into a GIF or meme. It's fun to ironically sing 'Things Can Only Get Better' with your gang as you run around the streets of a strange town, gathering information for a campaign. It's heartwarming to eat a meal with a group of passionate people who want the same thing as you and laugh at your jokes before working on a policy brief.

There's a weird assumption that people who have fun in and around politics and joke around with politicians don't care about the issues. It's also ahistorical. 'People want to have a good time when they come and listen to a political speech,' said Margaret Thatcher in 1987. She hired people to make sure that they did.

PR consultant and conference producer Harvey Thomas learned his trade producing big evangelical meetings and worked on Conservative events from 1978 to 1991. His job was to get the fans going and make sure there were exciting bits that could be filmed for the news. In 1983, Thatcher's entrance music was Lulu singing 'Hello, Maggie', the comperes were popular TV comics Bob Monkhouse and Jimmy Tarbuck and the crowd wore 'I love Maggie' t-shirts. By the late 1980s, there was even dry ice. Instructions to audience members placed on each seat at a Conservative election rally in 1992 stated:

> Tonight's rally is the last before election day and we need your help to ensure its success. This envelope contains a skip hat, Union Jack and party popper. Please keep this with you and do not use any of the contents until the end of the rally. Immediately after the prime minister's speech he will be joined on stage by Mrs Major. By this time you will very likely be on your feet applauding and at this stage please put on your hat, wave your flag and explode your party popper.[4]

I went to a Conservative Progress conference during the 2019 Tory leadership contest and they had put a Union flag on every seat, to echo those glory days. The crowd gave their best pantomime boos every time Priti Patel or Esther McVey said 'Marxist' or 'Tony Blair', and waved their flags while cheering for 'proud Thatcherite' and 'taking back control'. Part of the fun for the audience was the full immersion in this simple tale of good and evil. As at pro wrestling matches, they revelled in the kayfabe – suspension of disbelief – the interaction and a jolly good time spent with a group of like-minded fans. Fun and belonging – what's not to enjoy?

An ingroup in social identity theory is a social group whose members identify with each other based on shared interests or characteristics, and show each other loyalty and respect – in this instance that's the right-leaning Brexiteers making up the majority of the audience. An ingroup is usually defined in opposition to one or more outgroups: a social group with whom an individual doesn't identify. In studies, ingroups discriminate against outgroups, even if the groups are randomly assigned and there is no personal advantage gained by doing so. The ingroup of fans at this Conservative event, or 'us', gained extra pleasure from speakers attacking the outgroup, or 'them' – other political parties, left-wingers, centrists and Remainers who didn't share their views.

Us vs Them or ingroup vs outgroup isn't a sign of polarization. It's how politics has always worked. The outgroup losing in a research experiment[5] becomes more important for participants than benefits for fellow members of their ingroup. That is very 'Anyone but the Tories' or 'Anyone but Trump' or 'Keep out the Left': it doesn't matter what the ingroup winner does in power, as long as they stop the outgroup from having it.

Diehard Labour fans of a certain age are known to trade lines from a memorable speech by former leader Neil Kinnock. You know the one:

> I'll tell you what happens with impossible promises. You start with far-fetched resolutions. They are then pickled into a rigid dogma, a code, and you go through the years sticking to

> that, out-dated, mis-placed, irrelevant to the real needs, and you end up in the grotesque chaos of a Labour council – a LABOUR COUNCIL – hiring taxis to scuttle round a city handing out redundancy notices to its own workers.[6]

Somehow centrist nostalgists have turned Kinnock into New Labour's John the Baptist, instead of the guy who lost two elections and fell over on Brighton beach, but part of the fun is knowing that some of the people chanting along with you think he's a hero and some think he was a loser. We can all enjoy the meme. Then you can show your fellow fans the really bad song from the Red Rose election rally in April 1989 on YouTube (a rousing/nauseating number called 'Meet the Challenge, Make the Change'[7]) and everybody has learned something. 'It was just like an American convention,' Tony Benn wrote in his diary later that year. 'The Conference has been disastrous for the Left.'[8]

Benn banged the same drum against New Labour, claiming the party conference in 2007 was the last real one before it would become 'an annual meeting for the fan club of the parliamentary bigwigs and their business friends'.[9] He was obsessed with calling the other factions fan clubs. Back in 1980 he told historian Eric Hobsbawm:

> I can cite as evidence, confirming the wisdom of that strategy, that the National Executive, which had been widely ignored for years as a rather powerless fan club of the parliamentary leadership, came to be seen by the Tory press and by the establishment, from 1975 onwards, as a serious centre of

> socialist thought and criticism loyal to the government but critical of some of its policies.[10]

He was reliant on the fervent support of his fans on the left, until he retired from frontline politics and found that those with whom he politically disagreed also thought of him warmly and enjoyed his company – even his great rival, Denis Healey. Benn toured successfully as the nation's favourite granddad, bringing joy through readings from his diaries and rousing speeches.

Politics is also fun because you can be transgressive. You're also not meant to answer politicians back, make filthy innuendos about unfortunate headlines or edit images to make other fans laugh. Deference is gone from politics, and that's part of what makes fandom work. Traditional political support required strong leaders and factional organizers who directed their followers to undertake conventional campaigning activities, usually tied to internal and external elections. Now, in addition to this, popular support can come from grassroots demand and fans decide among themselves the best course of action – for good or ill. Some political movements, like Extinction Rebellion or anti-fracking group Frack Off, have leaders and spokespeople but most campaigns are planned and carried out by individual members and local interest groups working autonomously. Looser groupings of fans, attached to politicians like Jeremy Corbyn or Bernie Sanders, follow the spirit and political 'line' of their heroes but don't look to them for leadership or direction. They enjoy political and social activities outside the demands of party bureaucracy, electoral politics and the personal campaigns of those politicians.

Fans are free to say and do things elected politicians can't officially support – like negative campaigning against rivals, funny memes or attention-grabbing stunts – and this can be useful to their heroes in extending their reach and range of activity. Musician Stormzy could chant 'Fuck the government and fuck Boris' as part of his track 'Vossi Bop' in 2019, while backing the youth-focused #GrimeForCorbyn campaign. However, politicians have little control or influence over their fans when they say and do things that damage their reputations by association, such as online bullying or spreading misinformation. Asking them to stop just draws more attention to the problem and is not always met with agreement. Later, we'll look more closely at the ways fans are used in politics. It is a big shift for established political parties, lobbying groups and movements, who are accustomed to being able to marshal supporters and shape the media narrative in a particular way.

Politics has changed so much that researchers who just used to study party members now have to look at the demographic profiles and partisan activities of party supporters.[11] All party memberships look similar in the UK: dominated by middle-class white men over fifty, many living in London and the South East.[12] [13] Even though party membership has grown in recent years, the public identify with political parties less than they used to. According to the House of Commons Library, membership of the Conservative, Labour and Liberal Democrat parties increased to around 1.5 per cent of the electorate in 2022, compared to a historic low of 0.8 per cent in 2013.[14] Membership peaked for both the Conservatives and Labour in the early 1950s. In 1953 the Conservative Party had a reported membership of 2.8 million. In the same year, Labour claimed over a million members. Both figures were likely to have been inflated by the parties, but mass party membership was real for a while. Being a 'partisan' to researchers means supporting one party consistently. People who don't identify with parties are less likely to vote at all.

Lea Ypi, Professor of Political Theory at the London School of Economics, argues that partisans are vital for healthy democracy.[15] It means you are committed to your politics and want to use your vote effectively by casting it consistently for the same party. Parties rely on consistent and committed support (members, supporters, voters, volunteers, funders like unions) to be able to stand in elections and run campaigns. If nobody was a partisan, or too many voters changed their mind all the time about who to support, the only politics we'd have would be those appealing to rich donors. That's unethical and unsustainable.

Voters like parties that they believe have consistent and coherent policies, but they don't pay that much attention to the policies themselves. It's the vibe (aura, energy, gut feeling about something) that parties give off, which comes from distinctive ideology. The ideology motivates support – being too similar to or reacting against the other party isn't generally popular with voters.[16] At times when politicians are seen as being 'all the same', people are less enthusiastic about voting for anyone and election turnout drops. Simple messages like 'Get Brexit Done' and 'Yes We Can' do work to help voters understand the vibe a party wants to create, especially if the message is hopeful and upbeat, but be wary of simple stories about elections. New Labour's landslide victory in 1997 was as much about getting rid of a moribund Conservative Party as it was enthusiasm for Tony Blair or modernization of Labour. Most of the UK population became indifferent towards Labour and the Tories as the parties converged towards the centre after 1994. Despite what we are told, hearts and minds aren't always won from the centre.[17]

Fans can be part of the winning picture, as can positive campaigns for hope and change, but they aren't the whole narrative. Nor is it inevitable that a tired and unpopular government will be voted out. Getting the electorate to vote at all is half the battle. While the debate still rages about the effect of a 'youthquake'[18] of young voters' enthusiasm for the Labour Party in preventing Theresa May from keeping her majority in 2017, voter turnout was up on previous elections. Some of that story was social. If other people in your household share your politics, you're more likely to vote.[19] People are also more likely to vote if their friends and family talk about voting, whether it's in enthusiasm or anger. Shockingly, the income gap for political engagement is set long before people hit voting age and doesn't change if their own income rises.[20] If your parents were low earners, you are less likely to vote or get involved in other political activity for the rest of your life.

As voters started to feel less connected to parties, they became more motivated to vote based on the personality of party leaders instead.[21] Members also join and leave parties based on how they feel about the leadership. For voters to cast a ballot, they need a clear idea of what a party stands for, a leader that they like and a community around them that shares their politics and values voting. A fandom can provide this structure: people keen to vote, people who know what they are voting for, clear affection for the leader, and regular information that reinforces the values and politics of the party.

It can be comforting to think that ideological differences between left- and right-wing voters are linked to strongly held principles. But people tend to use morals to *justify* their existing political positions, rather than inform them. Emotions, social connections and general vibes brought most people to their views and voting records, not cool rationality or persistent moral concerns. Received wisdom says that people tend to avoid publicly sharing views and identities that are marginalized or stigmatized, because they want to present a positive and acceptable story to others. That doesn't apply to everyone. Rejection can make someone identify even more strongly with what is being rejected, whether it is as a member of a minority group, supporter of a fringe policy or fan of someone embarrassing.

People use emotions to help them process information effectively and that makes them more likely to think deeply and meaningfully about their political decisions. The anthropologist George E. Marcus and the political scientist Michael MacKuen found that enthusiasm (fun!) makes people get more involved in politics and anxiety (fear!) makes them think more critically. When voters don't feel anxious, they rely on their existing partisan instincts and respond enthusiastically to positive campaigning. When they are worried or scared, they pay more attention to the issues and negative campaigning. People 'rely on their internal emotional states to signal when to abandon their predispositions and begin conscious political choice'.[22] You can't be rational without listening to your feelings.

Vibes are extremely important in politics, for good and bad. When even a single word has the wrong vibes, it's over – or is at least going to get a lot of anti-fan noise. Margaret Thatcher couldn't use 'progressive' in a speech because head of Number 10's Policy Unit Ferdinand Mount told Robin Butler, her Principal Private Secretary, that it did not have the right 'vibes' – and yes, he did say 'vibes'. He thought it was too associated with the left.[23] 'Progressive' has a long and complicated history,[24] but has ended up mostly used by 'sensible' centrist technocrats in the UK.

'If politics really is mostly vibes,' writes journalist and Labour Party expert Morgan Jones, 'then Blair and Rowling were the king and queen of a certain kind of hazy millennium not-very-cool Britannia, a political vibe very assured of its own righteousness. . . Good politicians have their fingers to a pulse that most of us never even know is there. They have the capacity to make wildly disparate people, with wildly disparate beliefs, think that behind whatever lines are being spoken, in their heart of hearts, the politician ultimately believes what they do. The truly effective politician can convince you that they are, actually, thinking what you're thinking.'[25]

Voters' judgement of the overall competence of the rival political parties is called 'valence'. Vibe controls valence, not objective data. Politicians who were celebrities or journalists before they were elected understand that vibe is now more important than action or delivery of policy. This has been enabled by the tendency of the press (who guide the public) to have a goldfish memory when it comes to politicians' records and the close connections between politicians, the media and other celebrities. Some of any given politician's vibe comes from marketing, some from the media, some from their mistakes and some is what they bring to the table in the form of their personality, style and charisma. But fans can also influence the vibe, as can anti-fans, either from the grassroots or from positions of power. Vibe is a feeling people have that isn't always linked to presentation or reputation, unlike a brand, and can change quickly. A brand is more persistent.

Vibes are about framing, active emotion shaping and intangible things that are impossible to describe.

The truly effective politician described by Jones has knowledge of what fans and other voters bring to a vibe, tapping into their latent concerns but also their latent instincts. Nigel Farage is brilliant at it. He picks up on the mood of his fans and quickly makes social media videos and public appearances talking about an issue, even before it makes general public consciousness. The overall brand of a politician or party may not change during an election campaign or period of polling, but to win they only have to edge it on vibes. The voter will say that it was valence. 'I just trust them more on the economy' is not knowledge of their competence, it is vibe. Charisma isn't enough. Authenticity isn't enough. Competent isn't enough. To win, the vibes have to be right. Fans can help or hinder that. In 2017, Jeremy Corbyn's vibe was fresh and exciting and his fans seen as youthful and passionate. By 2019, Corbyn was seen as grumpy and unable to deliver and his fans as threatening and unpleasant. Boris Johnson's many failings still had better vibes than those of Corbyn by the time of the election in December that year. The first Conservative Party leadership contest of 2022 offered a range of personality types to tempt the selectorate. Perceived competence and a break with Johnsonism, the sell for a number of candidates, mattered a whole lot less than feelings and vibes when Liz Truss took the crown.

Margaret Thatcher was interviewed by the *Sun* about her diet and beauty tips in 1979.[26] 'You can't indulge. It will sit on your hips,' she said. Keen not to appear dull, she later added, 'There really is a limit to the number of lettuce leaves a person can eat, especially in the winter.' Less Iron Lady than *Woman's Realm* in vibe, this attempt to make Thatcher seem more relatable to working-class women meant engaging with a female journalist (Katherine Hadley) who wrote the immortal line: 'Yet who would want a dowdy female fatty for Prime Minister?' The consensus on what makes for a Prime Ministerial vibe has not altered a great deal over time, even if the misogyny aimed at Theresa May and Liz Truss was usually more carefully phrased. May's election as Prime Minister was met by the *Sun* headline 'Heel, Boys!' and the sexualized line 'She is expected to whip feuding male Cabinet colleagues into line in the no-nonsense style of Maggie Thatcher.'[27] Former Conservative Party chair Jake Berry told TalkTV after Truss's downfall, 'I think I'm suggesting that interventions by prime ministers should be like sex in a long and happy relationship – infrequent but always anticipated with glee.'[28]

Tony Blair also used beauty – he spent a lot of money on cosmetics and make-up artists as Prime Minister[29] – and foodstuffs to communicate his vibe to voters. Having shared early in his career that his favourite food was then-exotic fettuccine, this was later revised to the more down-to-earth fish and chips. It could have been a damascene conversion to skin-on haddock, or more likely he was trying to sound less elitist. Blair finally settled on a choice focus groups deemed most likely to appeal across class and income lines: a bacon, lettuce and tomato sandwich (BLT).[30] This is awkward given that one of the key contributions to Ed Miliband's non-PM image was his seeming inability to eat a bacon sandwich. The reality is that nobody looks good being photographed or filmed eating, especially not busy politicians, and bacon jibes had unpleasant undertones of antisemitism for the secular Jewish MP. That weird photos of Blair eating chips exist didn't harm him at all. His vibe was handsome, suave and confident. However, Miliband's vibes had already been declared to be Off. Geeky, awkward, can't eat like a normal person, can't lead.

If a person, policy or word has good vibes, it's got legs and fans will surely follow. What, you thought it was policy? Or principles? Or personality? Nope, just pure vibes. There's no fixed path to electability. A stylist and vocal coach can help, but they only contribute to what is really a vibe. On your side, vibe. Authentic, vibe. Sassy, vibe. Normal, vibe. Weird, vibe. Scary, vibe. Perhaps worst of all is NO vibes, which has more or less been Keir Starmer's unfortunate position, much like Theresa May. Just nothing. Focus groups of voters don't know what vibe-free politicians stand for, even if they like his image or dislike her opponent. If a politician or party is scared of altering valence with people who will never shift their views of brand, they leave themselves vibe-less. They could win the election but have no mandate to do anything because their vibe is missing. Labour MP Wes Streeting said in 2023 that 'The only thing worse than no hope is false hope. It will disappoint some of our friends that we are not pledging support for every cause they believe in.'[31] The problem is, the vibe coming off the Labour Party is that voters don't deserve any hope or change and Labour don't support any causes.

One anonymous MP observed in October 2022 that 'Any PM is currently just "vibes", because [in reality] the Treasury is in charge'.[32] That was explicit recognition that the Prime Minister was just there to set a tone that would give the right impression to the media and not scare the financial markets, rather than make consequential decisions.

Rishi Sunak advocating for 'policies not personalities' as he became Prime Minister was disingenuous, as it always is when anyone in politics says it.[33] It was precisely his vibes and not his politics that saw him replacing Truss as Prime Minister, just as it was hers that convinced party members of their original choice. Former *Financial Times* editor Lionel Barber's bizarre proclamation that Sunak's coronation was Britain's 'Obama moment' made clear from its jolly schoolboy context – 'pukka', 'Let's give him a break' – that his analogy was about more than a non-white man taking the country's top job for the first time.[34] Especially as Obama was the voters' choice in a presidential election. The public did not get a say in Sunak's victory. They were just sold reasons why they should celebrate. Rishi's ride through fandom was bumpy, from topping members' polls and portrayal by the BBC as a superhero during Covid's peak, to the heart of Boris Johnson's betrayal or stab-in-the-back myth and losing to fan favourite Liz Truss. He reached Prime Minister without ever building a solid base of support outside the media, and that made him seem inauthentic and weak.

Sunak was seen as the glamorous, pragmatic and urbane choice. While he was Chancellor, the press made much of the battle between the Treasury and Number 10 for pandemic policy and spending. Furlough payments and business Bounce Back loans might have been seen as 'socialism' by some of the Conservative Party faithful, but they went down well with the general public. The Eat Out To Help Out restaurant discount scheme was popular at the time, despite some mocking online, and was only fully critiqued long after its impact on the spread of the virus could be seen from Covid-19 data. We even suffered the indignity of Amber Rudd's journalist daughter, Flora Gill, writing for *GQ* that 'there are worse people to flick your bean or stroke your sausage to than Dishy Rishi'. Sunak was considered to be well dressed[35] and attractive with good taste, at least until menswear commentator Derek Guy pointed out all the problems with the beleaguered Prime Minister's short-trousered suits.[36] Within days of taking office as Prime Minister, the Ready For Rishi campaign enthusiasm deflated. All the hot air escaped, leaving a boring near-billionaire who was tanking in the polls. Flying everywhere during a period (summer 2023) where climate crisis was driving much of the news agenda, and once again associated with the scandal of Partygate (attending parties in Downing Street during lockdowns), he seemed to exemplify 'there's one rule for them and one rule for the rest of us'.

A lot of politics – and indeed life! – is about 'Us and Them'. 'Us' is ourselves, our families and friends, the people who are aligned with us and think roughly like we do, maybe live in similar houses and earn similar money. We are biased towards people like us, because we understand how they work and want them to do well. 'Them' are the people who are different from us in ways we don't like, and we often highlight those differences while helping our own group to get ahead. Sociologists and psychologists would call 'us' the ingroup and 'them' the outgroup. But the ingroup is how someone identifies, not how they would be classified by academics or marketing departments. Voters might feel like they have more in common with people they go to the gym with or meet online than the people who live in their street. When you know you are a member of a group and that group is important to who you are and what you do, it makes you more socially confident. CrossFitters, crafters, cousins. Remainers, runners, rockers. Fan communities totally play into social identity, but in the past it would have been family, local, work or religious affiliations that seemed more authentic.[37]

Authenticity matters, even when it is manufactured. The internet has fed our obsession with *knowing stuff* about politicians: whether that's their personal life or their voting records. The internet has encouraged certain kinds of intimacy and accountability within current politician/voter relationships. Conservative MP Tobias Ellwood's social media posts are of course regularly met with left-wing criticism, but when his own fans as well as colleagues took him to task for posting a video praising the Taliban then he had to admit they had a point.[38] It's much harder for a politician or commentator to quietly change their mind on an issue on which they have previously loudly opined, without owning up to it and apologizing first. The public don't have the power to make the brazen feel shame, but they can post a screenshot or clip that proves their hypocrisy – what social media users call 'receipts'.

Voters are looking for strong direction and consistency to persuade them to turn out. While we may think that populists like Trump and Johnson have been bad at this, given how often they twist the facts to suit their agenda, they're a lot better at the job of *seeming* consistent and authentic in their personalities (if not their political views) than other politicians. They speak with what the American comedian Stephen Colbert calls 'truthiness', something that *feels* true and fits with their existing assumptions. These guys come across to their supporters as straightforward people who don't judge them for holding the 'wrong' views. Even out of power, they stay popular with their fans for this reason.

Our relationships with people we only know online aren't inauthentic. Even the famous people. A parasocial relationship is where someone develops an emotional connection with a media figure that isn't reciprocated. That sounds deluded – or sad, like unrequited love – but many people have these relationships. How do you know if you 'like' your favourite newsreader? The relationship is imagined but it's based on what you know about the real person and how they come across through the media. With politicians, sharing their hinterlands of interests outside politics helps us to see them in a more human way and get to know what they stand for.

The internet has changed interactions with well-known people from one-sided relationships to something more complicated. Social media creates opportunities for celebrities to reply to their fans and get to know who they are, because they are members of the same online community. The celebrity and their fandom are more present in the everyday lives of fans via their phones, and it feels direct and intimate.[39]

US Democratic Congresswoman Alexandria Ocasio-Cortez, or AOC to her fans and antis,[40] has used Instagram to livestream cooking dinner, showing people around her apartment and applying make-up while taking questions from the public. She's also played Animal Crossing and Among Us with fans, while campaigning for voter registration, and talked about her traumatic experiences of sexual assault and the Capitol Riot on 6 January 2021. She's faced backlash from Republicans and conservative media for her openness, but seeming approachable and relatable has won her support from progressive young people.[41] [42] [43] In a Harvard poll in April 2021, 36 per cent of young Americans (aged 18–29) considered themselves to be politically active – an increase of 12 points from 2009.[44]

The authenticity of a *fandom* comes from all the time, money, thoughts and feelings that fans have collectively invested in the community.[45] Fans feel more like they're contributing to their community by 'being there': showing up financially and physically, not just saying they're fans. Like families and close-knit groups of friends, authentic fandoms develop a shared language and in-jokes. They have their own hashtags, memes and emojis. Some fandoms crowdfund to support charities, like K-pop and Tom Hiddleston fans, or to cover legal and medical costs for prominent fans. Their support is mediated via literal receipts.

'I've often said that finding a fandom is like falling in love,' says Nat Guest, a serial fan, 'in that you can't force yourself to "feel" it – you just suddenly get bitten by a particular show or a particular pairing. And when that happens, the chemical function in your brain does feel similar to the early days of being enraptured by a new partner. You're obsessed with spending as much time with it as you can, you want to learn every piece of minutiae and trivia, you're almost on a high. That's a hard thing to explain if someone hasn't experienced it.'

It's late 2016. Ed Balls is dancing on TV in a white, glittery suit. He is playing a mad scientist. He used to be the Shadow Chancellor. People say, 'Oh I knew you were a politician – but I never knew you were human as well.' He hasn't changed. He's always been like this. It's just now you notice: because to win, he knows he needs to have fun. In this competition, *Strictly Come Dancing*, having fun is what will draw you in to support him. He shakes his booty, spins, trots. He's the People's Champion.

As he twirls his way through the cha cha cha, Ed's inner Beyoncé comes to the fore. Instead of grabbing his crotch, he finds himself rubbing his tits. The crowd – and the internet – goes wild. . .

In 2015, Ed Balls was seen as a rather dour, bullying beast of a politician and a drag on Labour's polling numbers. People were urging Ed Miliband, then Labour leader, to get rid of him. They fell out. Then he signed up to *Strictly*. Now? According to YouGov, he's consistently ranked as one of the most popular Labour politicians and most popular politicians in the country. He isn't even a politician anymore.

Since leaving politics, Ed Balls often talks about that inner Beyoncé – directly, in those exact terms. He signed up to *Strictly* hoping to dance to Carly Rae Jepsen. His paso doble was the campest the show has ever seen. He has sung 'Shout Out to My Ex' by Little Mix live on television twice, and I've sung 'Georgy Girl' with him to a brass band at a barbecue. This is all great fun. The problem is, this only happened after his last political role, in May 2015. While all of the signs of his fun side were there in his Westminster days, the need to be serious and argumentative overshadowed the piano playing and the Santa suit and the love of musical theatre. And that's the problem. . .

The Ed Balls I love is out of politics. When he was an MP he wasn't allowed to be human or likeable. The legend of Balls, the fun-loving fan favourite, was only born once he left the fray.

French philosopher Jules Michelet argued that the heroes of antiquity were created by 'the thought of nations' because people inherently need stories to anchor themselves. As embodied beings, we can't deal with abstract thoughts as separate from ourselves; we have to put them into the bodies and personalities of human figures so that we can understand them. Characters like Hercules and Romulus were created as 'historic fictions', to express both the people's views and the idea of The People (the general public, the non-elite). To make national myths and to understand politics itself, we had to make mythical heroes and build our nations based on their fandoms.

As with the enduring debate about Winston Churchill, the reality matters less than our need to create versions of these figures and align ourselves with them to tell our stories of who and what we are and what matters to us.

Politics fandom can be a giant collective act of participatory storytelling sometimes, like interactive theatre or a multiplayer game. The moments where something is happening but nobody quite knows what or how it will play out let fans wargame different outcomes, sincerely and satirically, and impress each other with analysis (and jokes, and memes). At crucial points during the Brexit debate, the BBC Parliament channel picked up record numbers of viewers (averaging 293,000 watching daily, from a usual peak of 120,000 during Prime Minister's Questions[46]) who were following it like a cricket match and seizing on snippets of data and process to inform their commentary at home and online. When governments have started to fall, similar things have happened, with rolling news and social media providing the focus for a rich and exciting collective experience. The gaps in information spark all kinds of interventions, as the journalists and politicians aren't always ahead of the fans in working out where the story will go next.

Philosopher Emile Durkheim had a theory of religion based on something he called 'collective effervescence': what we feel when we are excited as individuals and united as a group. He saw society's need for collective acts of social ritual and religious worship as a rational response to the banalities of everyday life and work. These 'sacred' collective experiences, which stand out from the ordinary and 'profane', were 'not incoherent or fantastical'. He didn't see it as heretical or strange that people were transferring the energy, joy and numinous feelings of sacred togetherness onto symbols, physical objects or individuals. For Durkheim, the sacred was entirely social, the group worshipping itself, even if it was directed at a god or gods. In his account, 'the collective consciousness is the highest form of the psychic life, since it is the consciousness of the consciousnesses'.[47] It is not coincidental that so many of the early accounts of fans, whether documenting the fevered atmosphere of football matches or the screams and fainting of Beatlemania, compare fandom and religion. It's not the dedication to an object, it's about what fans get from being together and sharing the experience.

Fans sharing a moment are not irrational, deluded, silly or horrifying. Collective effervescence, fizzing with the energy of being together, is one of the oldest forms of social organization. It is entirely natural that the sacred would move from its focus on religion to other collective events in sport, popular culture and politics – and that brings us back to the fans of chariot racing, who gave us so many of the words we use for fandom and politics. They were enjoying themselves at the races, using colours to show their allegiance to a shared identity, and chanting and demonstrating for the imprisoned partisans to be freed. Their loyalty to their community and the sacred experience of watching their team led them to make a political demand of the city.

Terms like 'crowd' or 'mob' or 'public' or 'masked protesters' aren't neutral descriptions, but they reflect wider social worries and biases: fuel protesters blocking roads in 2000 were portrayed as normal working people with concerns, whereas Just Stop Oil protesters using the same tactics in 2023 were framed as out of touch and disruptive. That's why people don't want to think of politics as 'fandom', another term like those above, because it is a word and a way of looking at things that seems frivolous or for people who are out of control. Even 'partisan', with its long history, has always been resisted, because it seems irrational to some. At least writer J.B. Priestley, criticizing football fans, saw some of the appeal of being part of a partisan crowd: 'I never see them at a match without disliking their stupid partisanship, their dogmatism that has no foundation in knowledge of the game. . . but it is still good, when the right side has scored a goal, to see that wave of happiness break over their ranked faces, to see that quick comradeship engendered by the game's sudden disasters and triumphs.'[48]

Crowds of fans are not automatically unthinking, conformist or inauthentic (the general conclusion of mid-twentieth-century accounts of crowds) or falling in opposition to authenticity (the position of philosopher Hegel). Kierkegaard thought the individual was crucial for forming communities,[49] even though he hated crowds ('the crowd is untruth'[50]) and set them in opposition to individuals realizing their own selfhood. He also called friends 'superfluous', so he's not our pal here for working out what's going on. Gustave Le Bon wrote one of the first major works on the psychology of crowds,[51] and lots of people writing about popular culture and politics seize on and enthusiastically misapply his main ideas of 'submergence' and 'contagion' to anything they dislike that picks up popularity.

In submergence, says Le Bon, a person loses their sense of self and responsibility due to their anonymity, which is the same thing Kierkegaard worried about, and that makes them more susceptible to social contagion, where they follow the ideas and actions most popular with the rest of the crowd. The emotions and behaviours spread like a virus. It's so intoxicating, according to Le Bon, that individuals in the crowd overcome their personal barriers to transgressing social, legal and moral norms. Anyway, it's nonsense. All those popular crowd theorists that pop science and lazy opinion writers admire were making it up. There is no good data to support what they say: it was all theory and not empirical studies.

Most events involving crowds happen without incident. There is no empirically observable reason to treat crowds and collective behaviour as synonymous. This notion just fits with our prejudices, based on reels of Nazi rallies and football hooligans. As Clark McPhail says, 'gatherings merely provide opportunities for various sequences of collective behavior to occur'.[52] Collective behaviour, a group of people saying or doing the same thing, doesn't always or even often happen whenever a crowd assembles. You know that from your own experiences of being in a group of people. It's rare for all or most of the crowd to join in with any collective behaviour, for the collective behaviour to be simple (unless the crowd is very big, then it can be a 'Mexican wave' at the football or the Live Aid audience stomping to 'Radio Gaga') or for it to involve conflict between participants. Collective violence or harmful activity is rarer still, even when participants are intoxicated.

McPhail also usefully categorized the types of collective behaviour that usually occur at political demonstrations, all of which have been mocked or feared by people who either don't like the political views expressed or any kind of physical acts of protest or both: rally (big group listening to speeches), vigil (quiet and usually solemn presence), picket (blocking entry to a building or event), march or civil disobedience (in various forms, some more benign than others).

Rival fandoms in politics comment on the relative size of marches, rallies and vigils, and the acceptability and perceived civility of acts of civil disobedience to the public also partially depends on partisan attachment or lack of it.[53] Are they my allies or are they pathetic agitators? Peaceful protesters holding authority to account or violent insurgents?

Mass society theory, a popular concept that emerged in the 1930s, put forward the idea that as countries industrialized and traditional group ties weakened, 'the masses' emerged: a population liberated from group constraints and shared morality.[54] Thinkers on the left and right claimed that the public were alienated by social change and, once separated from institutions and communities, easily manipulated by bad actors. That's why the voters keep getting it wrong and high culture has been replaced by mass media. Historian and philosopher Hannah Arendt said in *The Origins of Totalitarianism* that both the Nazis and the communist movements 'recruited their members from this mass of apparently indifferent people whom all the parties had given up as too apathetic or too stupid for their attention'.[55] The excluded many are tragically vulnerable to totalitarianism, or so mass society theory tells us.

Arendt, decontextualized in 'inspiration meme'-sized chunks (a quotation in block letters on a coloured or photographic background, shared on social media), became hugely popular again with the rise of populism in the past decade. It was comforting to think that individuals weren't really supporters of Brexit or Trump or anti-vaccination conspiracy theories, it was the poor deluded and left-behind masses who were, and if they just had the right information then the threat would be neutralized. That individuals didn't storm the Capitol or send bomb threats to hospitals, the mob did and they can be cut out like a tumour while we inoculate those susceptible to these ideas with media literacy. It was the group's fault, went the rallying cry. Groups are bad. Groupthink is bad. The masses are bad. The mob are evil. Let the grownups come back to sort it all out; the people have got it wrong.

Group identities at any level, be it fandom communities or political movements or national affiliations, can indeed be very powerful. Grassroots movements and fandoms may emerge simultaneously to demand change, like social theorist George Katsiaficas suggests in his idea of the *eros* effect, when citizens are tired of injustice and want liberty.[56] That's why we see the same things happening globally and concurrently, with both socially liberal and reactionary movements in multiple countries. However, political groups and mass movements – good and bad – don't take away individual agency. It's comforting to think that they do, because then we can fix everything by taking out the fan-favourite leaders – 'lock him/her up!' – or proscribing the groups they join. In itself, responding to bad politics and risks to democracy with a ban, incarceration or assassination is an authoritarian move that doesn't fix the problem.

Thinking we can just block bad politicians, make people less emotional about politics and legislate against types of protest activity isn't going to change why those things happen and why people get something out of supporting them. Fans of aggression and authoritarianism can't be mollified by fans of technocracy. Fans of social justice and civil rights can't be suppressed with fans of incrementalism. Put simply, sending Trump to jail still wouldn't stop half of America wanting him in power. Biden being elected didn't render US politics more stable and normal. Things just don't work the way they used to, and the devotion and communities of fandom are part of why the old solutions don't work either. Those in charge will keep trying to make us think that they do. When ordinary people and their enthusiasms and frustrations come into politics, it makes things messy and uncomfortable. The establishment were much more comfortable with the early 2000s, when voter turnout was suppressed but the status quo chugged along with little trouble, than all the troublesome feelings and protest movements that exist now. Their reaction to Jeremy Corbyn, Donald Trump and Brexit showed that these events were seen as causes of problems rather than symptoms of ones that had existed for a long time.

How a protest or campaign is talked about by organizers, broadcasters, newspapers and social media affects who will take part and whether the public will object. For example, Just Stop Oil are near-universally slammed by the media, despite polls showing climate issues are important to the UK public across demographics. Protesters can be legitimized, delegitimized, promoted as the voice of the majority, or treated as anarchic troublemakers. A protest event can be portrayed as a confrontation, spectacle/circus, riot or debate[57] [58] – or a mixture of these 'frames' or ways of presenting information. The Center for Media Engagement at the University of Texas in Austin found that coverage of protests is often negative about both the cause and the protest itself and underrepresented groups are harmed most of all. Humanizing and legitimizing the protesters and the purpose of the protest helps people to understand what is happening and makes the story more credible to most audiences, other than strong partisans against the cause.[59]

Framing a protest as a riot, like the Kill the Bill protests in Bristol in 2022 against the Police, Crime, Sentencing and Courts Bill,[60] highlights conflict between protesters and 'normal' society, focuses on damage to property and portrays protesters as deviants with strong emotions. Framing protest as a confrontation emphasizes the conflict between police and security and protesters, and reporters will also highlight any conflicts with journalists or insults aimed at the media. The spectacle frame (presenting political events as entertainment) has been very common in large Brexit, QAnon, Trump, anti-politics and anti-vaccination protests where journalists and social media users focused on the dramatic, strange, emotional and spectacular aspects of the event and its numerous participants. The breathless accounts of the Capitol Riot seemed more fascinated with describing the outlandish outfits of people like Jake Angeli, the 'QAnon Shaman', than explaining the threat to democracy presented by this event and those that followed it.

Debate is the only framing to treat the protest as legitimate by emphasizing the reasons for the protest and focusing on protesters' viewpoints and demands.[61] [62] The Women's March, People's Vote, anti-CRT (critical race theory) and anti-GRA (Gender Recognition Act) protests and events tend to be given this kind of respect and it is no coincidence that these movements pose no threat to the establishment as their views align with those of senior politicians and journalists. Government ministers and MPs across Parliament have spoken out against critical race theory, gender recognition and Brexit. It is not destabilizing to support positions that have entered the Westminster mainstream and are debated on political talk shows and in newspaper columns every week.

Political liberals often call for debate. They claim that all sides of a debate need to be heard,[63] [64] while in practice portraying extreme views that they themselves hold or are adjacent to as valid and mildly radical or even formerly widely accepted progressive views as extreme in presentation if not in content. For example, liberal American journalist Matthew Yglesias[65] wrote an article about the need for 'progressives' to be less rigid in their views of fundamental human rights. He said that his 'old-fashioned view is that nothing is beyond compromise'. It quickly becomes apparent from the article and subsequent posts on social media that it is LGBTQ+ rights where compromise must be found, even though in the US the fight is to protect existing rights from new legislation that rolls back current protections. It is not a case of reducing demands in the meantime with the hope of making greater gains later. Another example is the reaction of some liberals to the first uterus transplant in the UK. Many of the arguments being made against this medical breakthrough, coloured by fear that trans women or cis men will demand access to wombs, apply to mainstream organ donation. The same liberal commentators are far less exercised about living kidney donors and the ethics of this.

What makes protesters most responsive to organizers, feel most like something needs to be done and believe that they really should join in action is talking about familiar issues and occurrences that relate to their daily lives.[66] Abstract ideas are harder for activists to relate to and for the public to support. Some recent approaches to climate activism, framed around time running out to save the Earth from burning and save the future for your family, have been backed by a broader range of people (participants and supporters) than direct action protests or traditional campaigns about either climate change in general or companies causing environmental damage. This urgent-yet-fun approach can also attract high-profile speakers and supporters who have fans of their own, such as Greta Thunberg, which draws visibility to the issue and drives public interest.

The other main factor that makes protesters want to join in depends on who gets the blame for the thing they are being asked to do something about. Making a protest all about specific individuals, organizations and institutions makes protesters more responsive than abstract concepts like 'capitalism' or 'freedom'[67] and stoking fear or using catastrophizing rhetoric makes the action seem more urgent to protesters.[68] Individual targets motivate protesters most of all, which is very human and lends itself to harnessing the power of fandom and anti-fandom, but this approach to campaigning also draws a negative response from people who see politics directed at a single person or small group as bullying, rude or unfair. The media can draw on that sense of incivility[69][70] to scrutinize and delegitimize elements of the protest, even if the cause is widely supported, and political opponents can do the same. Informal and crude campaign messages can be framed as serious threats, clothing and imagery deliberately misconstrued as an attack. Incivility and making the dominant groups feel uncomfortable is still worth it, as Martin Luther King made clear in 1963 in his letter from Birmingham Jail, criticizing those 'white moderates' who deplored civil rights protests for their violence and yet not the conditions Black people faced that made them necessary.[71]

Fun, enthusiasm and hope persuade people to become politically active, but so do anger and fear. The three main motivations for joining collective action are moral outrage (anger at perceived injustice), social identification (strong sense of group belonging and shared interests), and group efficacy (confidence that the group are more likely to succeed than fail). People are more drawn to motivational and emotional messages and information about politics that they have discovered via their social networks.[72]

Fandoms based on positive solidarity are motivated by love and empathy. The connection between positive solidarity and political responsibility makes them angry about structural injustice and passionate about addressing inequality. Hannah Arendt said that technology had united the world in a kind of solidarity, but that solidarity was negative because it was based on fear of nuclear war and the world ending. Fandoms based on negative solidarity tend to be driven by fear and the grievances of their own demographic – that's the 'us' again, the ingroup. Negative solidarity is associated with reactionary politicians and movements. Fear and uncertainty are linked to the core concern of political conservatives – to resist change and justify inequality.[73]

Politicians and campaigners have tried and failed to make fandom happen from the top down, annoyed that telling the public to like someone doesn't always work. Perhaps some of the arguments here will help them to understand the complex reasons why people became fans in the first place. They're also going to find out how others have successfully picked up fans and what they do with them when they have them – both good and bad.

3

THE USES (AND ABUSES) OF FANDOM

Politicians and activists don't always know how fandom works or what draws people to politics. They aren't sure why people need it, or the real reasons why they have fans themselves. However, more and more grasp the benefits of having fans as a new form of political engagement, and want to secure that loyal and active support. One thing we do know is that once they realize a fandom exists, people in politics will exploit fans to their advantage. This chapter is an investigation into the power of fandom, its uses and abuses and where fans fit into the wider conversation around politics.

Political movements can attract positive fans by making people feel hopeful and attract negative fans by making people feel angry and scared. Politicians can use the power of fans to help them to bring about change or exploit the loyalty and excitement of the fans for abuse. The quickest way to generate a fandom in politics is to build on a negative: convince people who feel neglected or invisible that another group is swamping them. The second quickest is to be a charismatic presence during a crisis, for good or ill.

The power of fandom is evident from what politicians and campaigns making full use of fandom have managed to achieve.

From Brexit to Just Stop Oil, grassroots activists with a passion for their causes and leaders have steered the political conversation in recent years – albeit sometimes aided and abetted by professional provocateurs. Fandom has enabled political parties and environmental campaigns to broaden and increase their activist bases, a fact key to the case studies in this chapter. Candidates could evade electoral spending and transparency and civility limitations (the need to be polite) by having fans work autonomously, freed from party HQ and official campaigns.

The Republican Party didn't cut ties with Trump and his fans, even after the Capitol Riot in January 2021. Quite the reverse: anyone who didn't question the legitimacy of the 2020 presidential election was left out in the cold and many midterm election candidates for the GOP in 2022 backed Trump's claim that the election was stolen.[1] The GOP were no longer just playing to the extreme fringes of their party to excite their base or opportunistically get elected. Many had become true believers in reactionary right extremist politics. Even after Trump's 2023 indictment, the only limiting factor for Republican supporters was whether or not he could run for president from jail.

What Donald Trump offered his fans, and still does, is the chance to tell a new story about America and the world. One where America is great because of people like them, where they are the winners and anyone they don't like is not a 'patriot'. Their enemies are not really American. Trump doesn't just tell them what they want to hear or what they already think. Plenty of politicians do that. He co-creates this new story with his fans, who were unhappy with the world, and having a say is part of the appeal. It empowers fans.

Fans of those who followed in Trump's footsteps saw real results from their participation in rallies and online fandom. The Florida governor Ron DeSantis, Trump's protégé and then bitter rival, was able to sign bills to turn his fans' obsessions into laws like the Stop W.O.K.E. Act (a Florida law regulating what can be taught in schools and workplaces). Their loathing of immigrants led to a political stunt where DeSantis transported fifty Venezuelan asylum seekers overnight from Texas to New England, two states that had nothing to do with the state he governs, on the grounds that they might have ended up in Florida. Anecdotes and infographics created by fans of DeSantis and others like Marjorie Taylor Greene would be repeated by their favourites on stages and in the media. The politicians gained authenticity and colour for their arguments by including these nuggets from supporters and the fans felt powerful and valuable as a part of the story.

As with any political or marketing campaign, these fandoms need to be fed with regular interaction and fresh ideas to keep them active, engaged and motivated. Fandoms can get this from either their leaders or fellow fans. Many movements thrive on crowdsourced information, analysis, jokes and memes to back up their arguments and recruit new fans. As well as recognition from their idols, fans get a rush from the reaction to their contributions. They collaborate on projects and compete among each other to find new data points and correlations, develop new theories and advance their positions. This bottom-up approach to research and communication has some similarities with the open-source intelligence (OSINT) framework, where activists and journalists use openly available tools and resources to gather and analyse information and create usable intelligence. Perhaps the best-known example of OSINT is the citizen investigation site Bellingcat, which identified the two key suspects in the poisoning of the former Russian spy Sergei Skripal in Salisbury in 2018. When unethical people use the same techniques, it can do more harm than good. In the more conspiracy-minded fandoms like the radicalized Republicans and QAnon, the further someone takes an idea or connection or pattern, the more attention they receive from other fans. The lore, or traditions and knowledge of the fandom community, deepens and so does their attachment to the cause. After Trump's mugshot was published in August 2023 and he returned to X, QAnon fans were quick to point out that the three letters at the start of each line spelled out 'END'.[2] They linked this to a message posted by Q (leader of QAnon) in 2019 that reads: 'There is no step five. End.' It was, to them, a secret code and sign that they were right all along.

In pop culture fandoms, 'fan service' is material added intentionally to fictional content to please the most committed audience (rather than serve the characters, plot, broader audience). The term originated in anime and manga aimed at adults, where the fan service took the form of nudity and sexualized content, but is now broader. A good example would be passing mentions of old monsters (the Macra) or planets (Metebelis 3) in *Doctor Who*, which make the fans yelp with excitement – while the casual viewer misses nothing if they don't pick up the reference. When fan service goes too far, the creators direct too much attention towards pandering to the fans and not enough to servicing the story.

Fan service now happens in politics all the time. Often, it's harmless enough – a bit of red meat thrown to the base as part of an internal election or big event. It is rational to offer some crowd-pleasing announcements to reward the most loyal supporters and keep them in the fandom. But when it comes to real policy that gets enacted, rather than just floated to the papers or suggested during a campaign, fan service can become quite dangerous. The chain of influence that saw Reagan and Thatcher fans Liz Truss and Kwasi Kwarteng try to please their biggest fans inside and outside the Conservative Party – and crucially, also the libertarian think tanks and donors who had bankrolled them – came at the expense of the national interest and, indeed, common sense. Their mini-budget in September 2022 wiped billions off the stock market and crashed the value of the pound, with lasting consequences. Truss had built her base in the party via traditional means: endless drinks receptions for the elite, the fundraising dinner circuit for ordinary members. However, when she became Prime Minister attention to the politics of how to make and announce economic policy was ditched in favour of sassy captions for her Instagram followers like 'Growth is the best way to make everyone's life better'.[3]

Fellow Conservative MP Kemi Badenoch has shown an eye for fan service throughout her time in politics, gaining support from right-wingers and feeding them policy announcements. She was recognized early in her career as a rising star by associating herself with conservative think tanks the Adam Smith Institute and Policy Exchange, and building relationships with right-wing media figures and campaign groups who object to social justice and culture change.[4] Her persona combines a focus on traditional right-wing issues (small state, social conservatism), Johnsonesque patriotic boosterism, contrarian positioning on topical issues, media charisma and Modern Tory aesthetics (academic parent, market town safe seat, non-white, second generation immigrant). High-profile endorsement from Michael Gove in her failed leadership bid of summer 2022 was a surprise. Badenoch's message to fellow Conservatives in her speeches, leaked comments and articles has focused on what others are doing wrong – an appeal to negativity – more than a push for a positive programme of government. During her initial appointment as Equalities Minister, her most significant interventions blocked support for transgender rights[5] and anti-racist education policies,[6] appealing to the desire for a scapegoat that helps politicians build a support base among the angry and isolated.

Politicians without fans in the 2020s are much more reliant on fragile factional support and have less control over their policies and personnel than stronger leaders with a solid base. To keep their parties together, their authority comes from supporting those with internal popularity rather than existing loyalties. Rishi Sunak and Keir Starmer have both suffered from the need to please the right of their parties and the lack of genuine grassroots enthusiasm for their political projects, which seem to lack ideas and coherence. Before Sunak (and their brief experiment with Liz Truss), the Conservative Party looked to Boris Johnson and his popularity as their last hope for winning elections – even as many of them despised the personality that supposedly made him a winner.

Being the most recognizable face of the campaign to leave the European Union and regular television appearances on the likes of satirical news quiz *Have I Got News For You* made Boris Johnson one of the best-known political figures in the UK before he became Prime Minister. The mononym 'Boris' was used consistently across the newspapers, regardless of their partisan affiliation, where other leaders are usually known by their surnames or full names. Political commentators acted like he had unassailable support. Having fans was the only thing that made him valuable to many of the Conservative Party's MPs, who found his regular gaffes and other unprofessional behaviour difficult to tolerate.

There is a tendency to overstate Boris Johnson's popularity, especially given that he polarized the public. Theresa May's net likeability rating peaked at 60 per cent in 2016 whereas Johnson never got higher than 46 per cent. However, Conservative supporters were 76 per cent satisfied and 20 per cent dissatisfied with Johnson as Prime Minister between July 2019 and September 2021.

Johnson was less popular at every stage of the 2019 General Election campaign in 2019 than Theresa May was in the 2017 campaign, according to Ipsos Political Monitor.[7] His ratings fell steadily. He didn't win an eighty-seat majority because his support was so strong, in the Red Wall or anywhere else. According to analysis from political scientists, Johnson was just lucky that he had a particularly unpopular opponent (Jeremy Corbyn) and that Brexit was a key issue for many voters – with its own fandoms on each side, of course.[8] His approval ratings rose in the early part of his premiership, thanks to his Brexit deal, and peaked in April 2020 at the highpoint of public anxiety about the Covid crisis and during his own hospitalization. Once Brexit and Covid faded in importance, his character and behaviour became more of a problem for the public and only his consistent support for Ukraine kept his worst rating with Ipsos MORI 5 points ahead of the lowest point for Liz Truss.[9] Shortly before he left office, YouGov found over three-quarters (76 per cent) of people thought that Johnson was untrustworthy.

Yes, a leader with a lot of fans can do well in elections (Corbyn 2017, Johnson 2019) – and a leader with no fans will struggle to keep their party and its supporters onside. However, what appeals to fans can be viscerally off-putting to others, and the Conservatives overlooked that aspect of Johnsonism. They could have learned other lessons from the case study of Nigel Farage, who has tried multiple times to secure election as a Member of Parliament and failed. His charisma and strong base of support have scared the big parties into taking on his policy positions, but opposition to Farage is stronger than his appeal. He just has a better understanding of the power of fandom and how to nourish his fans than most politicians: making regular videos for social media, running his own subscription club for supporters and swiftly responding to their concerns with new announcements. Other leaders have taken on his tactics of using fans as media 'outriders' (people who support a politician and can talk them up without the restrictions of an official role), advancing and defending political positions on television. Post-Brexit, other campaigns and politicians have learned the value of fans in high places manufacturing support or making public backing seem stronger for an idea than it really is.

Political actors (politicians, activists, staffers) really benefit from the passion of fans. They are often among the most hardworking volunteers on the campaign trail, working long hours in terrible conditions. Their passion, desire for knowledge and belief in the politician, party and campaign help attract other supporters and explain to the public why the cause is so important. The community of fans gives a politician support outside the bureaucracy of the party machine, which can feel more genuine and boost their morale. Fans sometimes do the 'dirty' work that would be harmful for a politician or official campaign to undertake directly, defending their politician when criticized or attacking their opponents.

'We act modern, cool and sophisticated,' said Robin Lakoff, a linguistics professor at the University of California, in 1992. 'But underneath, we want a daddy, a king, a god, a hero. We'll take the heel if we can get Achilles, a champion who will carry that lance and that sword into the field and fight for us. We're not as rational as we think. It's sort of scary.'[10] In a crisis, the daddy/hero gives fans faith that someone is willing and able to fix the problem and they don't have to worry anymore. The scale of neglect and crisis varies, and each can be stoked for the benefit of the object of fandom, but a hero can address an anxious population's feelings of status threat and uncertainty. The objects of their fandom say 1) you matter and 2) it will all be okay in the end. This reassurance shores up their sense of self – identity politics, if you will, how secure they feel in who and what they are – and gives them something to cling to and believe in when all seems lost.

Volodymyr Zelenskyy was just that actor and comedian who played the Ukrainian Prime Minister on TV and then got elected for real. A pub quiz answer. He became a household name internationally in February 2022, when Russia invaded Ukraine. Like Winston Churchill, war was the making of his legend at home and abroad. His fandom was swiftly established, global and positive. Everybody loves an underdog, and the handsome guy in a khaki t-shirt standing up to Putin and recording video messages using his phone's front camera – giving the impression of being intimate, authentic and charmingly amateurish – was what the world was waiting for.

Around the same time the RMT union's General Secretary Mick Lynch became a star in 2022. He captured the public mood while speaking on behalf of striking railway workers, with polling for YouGov rating Lynch more positively that December than the government's Transport Minister.[11] Britain's cost of living crisis increased the appeal of his no-nonsense way of speaking, media criticism and political commentary, but Lynch pressed his new admirers to follow the RMT's social media accounts instead of his own. He understood what he needed to do and who he was doing it for – the workers: 'You've got to get people to identify with you, through values. . . We're going to need the support of the community and the whole of Britain's public opinion. It's got to be bigger than my trade union, because we're not able to do this on our own.'[12]

'Now everybody, it's NIGEL FARAGE!' 'The Final Countdown' played like a wrestler's theme tune, as the audience rose to their feet in a standing ovation. They all waved flimsy blue placards, emblazoned with 'I'm Ready' (for Brexit). 18 October 2019 – I remember that Brexit Party rally at the QEII conference centre in London like it was yesterday. Or rather, I still have the video on my phone. It took over a minute for Farage to walk through the crowd, making his entrance via a sort of catwalk like the other speakers. The fans bloody loved it.

Not all charismatic figures building fandoms in a crisis are heroes or reluctant celebrities. They want to be famous, and they give the public someone or something to blame for their problems while claiming to be the solution. Nigel Farage is a master at capitalizing on events that can be framed to support his arguments. A surge in asylum seekers dying trying to cross the Channel in little boats? A news story about someone refusing to be vaccinated and losing out in some way? Farage is there, stoking his negative fandom and drawing in new recruits. He's a master storyteller, who pretends to be a man of the people. Farage is a privately educated former banker with reactionary and sometimes extreme politics, but he sells the 'authenticity' of beer, straight-talking and common sense to people who would previously never have voted for parties of the right.

For contrast, how about another case study: a storyteller of the left? Faiza Shaheen is portrayed by her detractors as an out-of-touch academic, despite being a state-educated working-class woman who grew up in the constituency where she has stood for Parliament (Chingford and Wood Green). Her topic of study is economic inequality. Only six seats swung towards Labour in (otherwise disastrous) 2019, and hers was one of them. She lost by just 1,262 votes. She wasn't going to run again, and then changed her mind: 'I just couldn't let it go. I don't know if it's hope or a sense that we don't have any choice. We either accept this world or we try to do something. And how can you accept this?'[13]

While still a parliamentary candidate, Shaheen wrote: 'These activists have become my family, they look out for me, give me support and generously give their ideas and time. They knock on doors and talk about me with so much enthusiasm it's as if I'm their family. It's beautiful.'[14]

How did she do so well in the 2019 election when nearly every other Labour candidate struggled? Her nickname as the 'Chingford Corbynite' should have sunk her, given Jeremy Corbyn's unpopularity at that point. Obviously, there were multiple reasons why Shaheen bucked the trend, including a local agreement with the Green Party not to run against her. 'I had a sit down with two senior members of the party,' she said. 'I'd met one before, I knocked on his door when campaigning. I've done a lot on green issues so we had common interests. Good on them, they are doing it in lots of places.'[15] While the efficiency of Labour's ground game (ability to attract activists to help with canvassing and getting out the vote) was mocked, Shaheen's support was broad and genuine and her crowds large and consistent. They believed in her story as a woman with strong local connections, including her former teachers, and passionate values. They went out and told it for her, and people turned out to vote. In other words, she had fans and knew how to use them.

My favourite Faiza Shaheen story is this one: one of her first jobs was at Greggs in Chingford Mount and the branch kept selling out of vegan sausage rolls during her 2019 campaign due to the sheer number of activists out canvassing in the seat and the Shaheen connection making a stop-off for pastry-based snacks a campaign ritual. It was reported that 200 Labour activists a day converged on Chingford at weekends, with about ninety campaigners a day showing up on weekdays.[16] Hugh Grant and Billy Bragg turned up for rallies, both eager to kick former minister Iain Duncan Smith out of Parliament. But neither of them could outdo the legend of selling out of vegan sausage rolls three times in one day. That's the sort of tale that warms you to a fandom.

Shaheen and Farage both built fandoms from demographics experiencing crisis, real or perceived, and both lost elections. However, Shaheen encourages positive solidarity among her fans: communities coming together in the hope of things getting better in future, joining with others in the shared goal of improving circumstances for the worst-off in society. Farage encourages negative solidarity among his: competitive individuals united in their opposition to those they blame for society's decline.

Some crisis fandoms will be very short-term and fall as quickly as they rise, as you would expect. Nobody can live up to being the god of the moment, however good they are, and continue to inspire such intense interest and passion from fans once the situation loses its urgency. Those who picked up very engaged fans at the peaks of tensions around Brexit and Covid, for example, will have experienced a big drop in interest in their work and opinions once those issues became less salient to their audience. Problems can also arise once the good will extended to many people during difficult times wears off: past misdeeds are dredged up, bad decisions have consequences and a person's current or general inadequacy is exposed.

The media also make use of fans to explain a new candidate's appeal, though more often they see fandom as a way to delegitimize a politician or viewpoint. Most party members in the UK are white, middle class, educated and over fifty.[17] Most activists are too. Within political parties, both the people and the activities they take part in aren't very diverse, whereas outside parties there is more variety in activism and activists.[18] Those in either group who turn up as 'ordinary people' or representatives of a profession (doctors, nurses, lorry drivers) on television or at a protest are quickly 'exposed' online and in the media as not ordinary people at all, but instead a 'party hack' or 'activist' whose motives must be dubious. If there are any social media posts or photographs showing they support a particular politician, the activist is dubbed a 'Corbynista' or 'Greta fan' and it is strongly implied that they approve of the worst behaviour that can be linked to that identity.

More seriously, fans can be abused by politicians and others working in politics. Their attachment to politics as a whole, their party or heroes in their movement makes them both slow to spot exploitation and unlikely to report it – in case they cause harm to something they love. Stories about activists, MPs and senior party officials bullying, harassing and assaulting staff, volunteers and party members do not just call into question the management of HR processes and complaints in Westminster and beyond. Politics and activism rely strongly on enthusiasm and loyalty over decent pay and conditions. The opportunity to meet well-known politicians is not just a perk for election volunteers or rich party donors, but has also been used to attract vulnerable fans who are exploited.

Like other high-profile industries such as music and film, politics can get away with low wages, dubious employment practices and poor treatment of staff and volunteers because of its proximity to power and wealth. Those elements attract people who want those things for themselves, but also those who are fans of those who already have it. People work long hours in politics and keep quiet about sexual harassment and bullying to be able to stick with their dream. They can be so awed by working in their dream job with people they've always admired that they don't even realize they're being exploited or abused.

Two examples from the past decade show the abuse of fans in the UK context: the RoadTrip campaign for the Conservative Party in 2015 and 'Pestminster' – Westminster's cross-party 'Me Too' scandal of sexual harassment and assault.

RoadTrip was a slick campaigning operation with serious consequences. Young people were used by a group of men in their thirties and older, who took a battle bus of activists around the country during the 2015 General Election to campaign in key marginal seats. They were promised close contact with leading lights of the Conservative Party. One of the activists told *Vice* that there was a 'half joking, half serious way that people were being told to keep their eyes on certain MPs'.[19] The campaign allegedly disguised the breaking of election spending rules by omitting the thousands of pounds spent on the battle bus in their accounting, and drove an expenses row.[20] Most importantly, RoadTrip culminated in the death of a campaigner and ardent fan of the Tories called Elliott Johnson.

RoadTrip wasn't originally the official election campaign. Mark Clarke, a failed parliamentary candidate, ran an alternative grassroots scheme, successfully organizing teams of volunteers to campaign for the previous year's by-elections – most impressively in Newark, securing the election of MP Robert Jenrick and then support from Conservative Campaign Headquarters and Grant Shapps. Clarke's offer was simple, in his own words: 'The days have two campaigning sessions, followed by a sponsored bar, a free curry and drinks into the night. We facilitate accommodation, and we arrange transport for those travelling long distances. We want people's time, not to make them pay to campaign.'[21] He also talked up the MPs and grandees that would be joining the volunteers on tour, including Theresa May and Robert Halfon, knowing the young activists he wanted were fans of both politics and the big Tory names.

A school friend of Elliott Johnson's described how 'He wanted to be a politician in the Conservative Party. He would come to sixth form with four things: a waistcoat, a pocket-watch, his favourite book on Maggie Thatcher and a briefcase'.[22] Johnson was a Tory blogger and Clarke quickly seized on him to become his spokesman, writing for RoadTrip. A tape made by Johnson purported to show that Clarke had bullied and threatened Johnson and that fellow Conservative Andre Walker had compared him to a Nazi collaborator.[23] Elliott Johnson was later found dead next to a railway track, aged just twenty-one. His Thatcher fandom and love for the party appear to have been exploited by those who shared his enthusiasms, but not his values. Both Clarke and Walker have always denied the allegations made against them.

As with RoadTrip, the system of employing aides in Parliament relies on exploiting the fandom and enthusiasm of young people who love politics and are awed by power. While not volunteers, the roles are low paid and the activists work long hours. MPs are individual employers, with very little oversight, and this plus the tendency of those high up in political parties to protect their own has enabled a culture of bullying and abuse in Westminster. Once #MeToo scandals started to be exposed in other industries, it was inevitable that 'Pestminster' would hit the headlines too. Both women and gay men have reported sexual harassment and assault by MPs, peers and senior parliamentary managers. The culture of drinking, favours and feelings of loyalty means that young politics fans find it hard to say no or speak up.

Defending the MP Chris Pincher brought down Boris Johnson. In the Carlton Club bar, witnessed by fellow MPs, Pincher sexually harassed and groped two men. Their complaints became well known and Pincher resigned from the government the next day. Boris Johnson had been warned about Pincher's behaviour while still Foreign Secretary, but feigned ignorance of his character. He himself resigned a few days later. At the time of writing, forty MPs had been investigated for sexual misbehaviour, with two on bail and two currently imprisoned for their actions.

In the words of a young man assaulted by Pincher:

> Parliament is unfortunately not safe. A lot of people talk about these sorts of things happening to them by MPs and they are scared to come forward. . . I'd only just started in Westminster and it was my first time in the Carlton Club. I was excited about being there, and then this happens from someone in a position of responsibility and power. It's the birthplace of the Conservative Party. It's a place where you want to go to meet people and because you want to build your standing.[24]

It's fair to want to moderate how fans behave when they are acting like bullies and harming the cause, but policing their exuberance is a quick way to lose their support. Patric Cunnane was one of the Labour supporters celebrating in Downing Street in 1997, as he told the *Guardian*: 'I tried to start a chorus of "We stuffed those Tory bastards", but I was told very firmly by a party organizer that wasn't the attitude to take. I thought after 18 years at least we should be allowed to say that.'[25] It is easy to forget that grassroots fandom is all about joy, social connections and getting involved in politics and not just about what politicians and campaigns want and need from fans. Fans don't just do what they're asked to do by their idols. There's a bit more give and take in politics fandom. Fans often have minds and ideas of their own. Let people have hopes and dreams and enough constructive ambiguity to project something to believe in. Early Corbyn got that right, before it went sour, asking people to vote for 'hope over fear' and being positively received.[26] Hence the unexpectedly large turnout in 2017 and Theresa May being robbed of her majority. That was a positive fandom that gave the fans space to imagine something better.

Way back in the nineteenth century the French politician and thinker Alexis de Tocqueville warned of the 'tyranny of the majority' – the tendency to suppress unpopular minorities in favour of representing the interests, prejudices and even whims of the dominant and powerful majority.[27] What he saw as the danger of unchecked democracy and believing that the people can do no wrong, we would call populism. He argued that the difference between Europe and the US was that, in hierarchical Europe, the majority have relatively little power and the intermediary institutions and interest groups of civil society push back against majoritarian power and keep it in check. American society didn't have all these structures and therefore the dominant group – white Americans – supported slavery and treated Black and indigenous minorities poorly. While the Church, aristocracy, professions and other institutions Tocqueville wrote about have less power than before, the internet has not delivered on its promise of helping minorities fight back against the state.

Professional and occupational associations (or trades unions) and uniformed organizations have to a certain extent been replaced in civil society and political power by corporates, interest groups, single-issue campaigners, lobbying firms and social media influencers. Large fandoms outside politics like K-pop or football can inform their members about issues and marshal enough numbers to enact social and political change, with footballer Marcus Rashford and his fans working with food charity FareShare to feed children. Perhaps politics fandoms could be part of the new mix of Tocquevillian intermediary groups, where their focus is a cause or movement and not an individual. The fandom sits between the state and the people, providing a point of engagement with politics that meets fans where they are. This recognizes the social and individual need for being part of a fandom or similar community without the limitations of being tied to electoral politics (lots of party bureaucracy and a focus on election cycles), uncritical worship of an idol (yikes) or single points of failure (your heroes can only let you down).

Personal relationships within the fandom and the value of the community as a whole can help its members empathize with minorities to which they don't belong, encourage resistance against oppression and perhaps fulfil the role that Tocqueville so admired of keeping despotism in check. In other words, make being part of civil society fun and fulfilling via fandom and maybe society could become more participatory and egalitarian.

4

GRASSROOTS FANDOM

The adults in soft-shell jackets and polar fleece are playing at being spies, or the Secret Seven. Instead of the walkie-talkies of children's secret agent sets, they converse in boomer parent style – slowly typed text messages, WhatsApp photos and quick panicked phone calls. The enemy has been spotted up the hill and the other half of the group will be following him and his handlers down to the meeting point. Action stations.

'Quick, berets on.' It's October 2019, and the mood is feverish. The group outside the Crown Hotel in Harrogate all don their pro-EU/stop Brexit costumes: a European flag as a cape and a blue beret topped with twelve gold stars, implemented as a mixture of intarsia knits and crochets for those who had the wherewithal to make or buy a Remainer hat, and yellow felt and hot glue for the more slapdash members. They start to chant and slow handclap as David Cameron, former UK Prime Minister, walks towards the hotel for his book festival appearance. He speeds past their noisy demonstration, not even taking in the scene.

I get into trouble inside for standing with and talking to the protesters, who are the opposite of dangerous and radical to everyone other than security. Journalism is no defence, we must all put away phones and recording devices to listen to the great man fudge answers to questions about Brexit and austerity, claim to be happy to speak after the event and then be spirited away via the side door and a waiting car to avoid being mobbed. Free speech or protest at a minor promotional event? How impolite.

The Harrogate pro-EU group know they didn't get their message through to Cameron, but it doesn't matter – everyone who attended the event saw and heard them and knew what they stood for. And anyway, they mostly knew that their demands were unlikely to be met. They couldn't stop or reverse Brexit and that kind of protest was too quiet, too civil, too silly, too twee. Feeling like they were doing something while knowing they had no power to change things was part of the point. But also, and more importantly, they had a lovely time.

In June 2019, Chester for Europe, an EU fan group similar to Harrogate's, posted the following on Twitter: 'Do you want to make some new friends and share your pro EU passion? Why not volunteer for your local #PeoplesVote Campaign group. More info here #FBPE https://peoples-vote.uk/volunteer'.[1] Some members of the Harrogate group were very gregarious, organizing the others and starting the chants, and others who were less confident had clearly gained a lot socially through the pro-EU fandom and encouragement from the local fan group – very like Sarah in Finland who found being a Spice Girls fan when she was younger 'made communication with other people easier, as you could do it through that'.[2]

The Remain fandom spilled over from intense online activity into big marches and a major movement for political and social change, from the grassroots up. They had the ear of many in politics and the media and the networks they created are still alive in various forms. This was not a group accustomed to losing: variants of their politics had been at or near the top for a long time. Brexit was a big shock for them.

The movement was able to build swiftly on and beyond the internet for a number of reasons. The simplest one is that there were a lot of well-funded and well-connected establishment figures involved, and that was certainly the case for the bigger organized campaigns like the People's Vote (and its spinoff youth sections) and Best For Britain, a campaign to stop Brexit and continue the UK's membership of the European Union. However, there was a gear shift in both political engagement and social media use at that time, strongly linked to fandom mechanics (the way fandom works) and algorithmic exploitation (exploiting knowledge of how algorithms sort and present content on social media and in search engine results), and the Remainers were well placed to capitalize on that. Climate protesters and Corbynism benefitted from the same changes, as did reactionary 'anti-woke' movements on both sides of the Atlantic. Looking at the structure of the Remain movement helps us to understand how and why all these new networked fandoms grew so quickly and became so influential. This structure combines traditional media, partisan media (their own news websites and print publications), new types of social media platforms and practices, political celebrity and influencer culture. For all these groups, politics fandom became their identity, their social life and more, and affected the wider world of politics.

The Remain fandom were well represented by traditional media, with individual journalists and multiple publications and TV shows on their side, despite the overall pro-Brexit right-wing bias of UK newspapers. The *Independent* were official media partners of the People's Vote marches, the *Guardian* regularly ran pro-Remain pieces, and radio DJs like James O'Brien made even more of a name for themselves by advancing the pro-Remain viewpoint at a time when fans were seeking that kind of content. As with other fandoms like Corbynism and pro-Leave campaigns, popular blogs and vlogs sprang up as new partisan media outlets and the *New European* was set up as a pro-Remain newspaper with a Third Way tinge to its journalism.

Several key changes to social media around 2015–16 also had a big impact on politics and political engagement online, both social and technical. The first is a change in how people used social media platforms and who was using them. Previously, many older people (45+) did not have smartphones and only used social media to keep up with friends and family.[3] From 2015 onwards, over 80 per cent of 45–54-year-olds and 56 per cent of 54–64-year-olds owned smartphones and that number has kept on growing.[4] Having the internet in the palm of their hands made people more likely to use it to engage with their interests, including politics, and to follow and talk to people who shared those interests. Many discovered their political voice with Brexit, Trump, Corbyn and the climate crisis and those people began socializing and discussing politics online with new people. They could find each other via hashtags like #FBPE (follow back pro-Europe – Twitter accounts would follow back anyone who followed them who used this hashtag in their profile or posts). People of all ages learned how to interact with strangers online from what were essentially fandom spaces, which had well-established norms by this point. The more aggressive cut and thrust of fandom disagreements, combined with the ability of grassroots fans to gain status by sharing new information with the community, became increasingly visible on political Twitter and Facebook groups. These had previously been quite 'wonkish' and elite spaces dominated by people who worked in politics, academia and the media.

That's changing again now, with another shift in social media platforms and habits, leaving what tech journalist David Pierce calls an 'everybody-sized hole in the internet' – as people return to a time where they mostly talk online to people they already know[5] – and author Cory Doctorow calls 'the enshittification' of the internet. As Doctorow says: 'Here is how platforms die: first, they are good to their users; then they abuse their users to make things better for their business customers; finally, they abuse those business customers to claw back all the value for themselves. Then, they die.'[6] Changes to X, Instagram and TikTok have made those platforms worse places to be. The previous social networking era that put everyone together in one place and made it easy to find people and content that interested you (alongside acknowledging all the downsides of a more public social media, like harassment and data harvesting for advertising) created unique conditions for politics and fandom. We don't know how moving to private group chats, messaging and forums will impact on democracy, public trust and political engagement.

The other changes to social media in that period are sticking around for now and are still relevant. Crowdfunding has enabled grassroots activists, former politicians and scammers alike to raise money to pay essential bills, fund legal costs and carry out their work, for good or ill. Easier livestreaming and phones capable of taking good quality photographs and videos have changed political journalism, how protests and rallies are documented and who can be part of and even shape political events. Algorithmic social media feeds show us more of what we want to see, and the way that worked at Facebook for a few years was well exploited by political bloggers and influencers (particularly on the left[7]) to gain greater reach for their articles and memes and grow their audiences until the algorithm was changed again in early 2018 to deprioritize political content.

As with other interest groups, Remain social media influencers emerged from the massed noise of grassroots fans, existing politicos and outspoken celebrities. Some of these influencers were already well known – actors, comedians, journalists, MPs – and others made their name or vastly increased their platform as the Remain fans looked for leadership and reliable sources of information, community and excitement. They became fans of influencers. Alastair Campbell was no longer the media bruiser for New Labour and the man who seemed like he would forever be associated with the 'sexed up' Iraq War dossier. Instead, he was on telly and radio and social media as the voice of those who wanted to stop Brexit and his following grew exponentially. He became Editor-at-Large of the *New European* and then a podcaster beloved of the sensibles (a type of centrist who voted Remain and longs for a return to the Third Way politics of Blair and Clinton).

Some influencers were not previously prominent in public life, and quickly picked up their own fandoms. Steve Bray, or the shouty Stop Brexit man as he's known to many, started off posting online and then decided 'to move offline because I wasn't achieving anything. It was just arguments and trolls. It took up so much time and it achieved very little.'[8] Realistically, he combined his physical presence outside Westminster with online activity, as did other single-issue activists like musician and artist Madeleina Kay (crowdfunding stunts and travel as #EUsupergirl) and Femi Oluwole, co-founder of the pro-European Union advocacy group Our Future Our Choice. Bray is still raising money and raising hell, opposing Brexit and falling foul of new protest laws. In January 2023, he confronted controversial Ashfield MP Lee Anderson, who told him, 'It's a new year, but you've not got a new job yet have you? The same old job, you're still a parasite, you're still a scrounger, you're still a malingerer.'[9] Anderson then removed Bray's top hat and a scuffle ensued as Bray tried to retrieve it.

While these new influencers had minimal impact on UK politics, more established politicians and activists did have the ear of leaders and traditional media and made the demand for a second EU referendum seem like a thing everyone was talking about for a while, as opposed to a fairly niche concern, as polling suggested.[10] As if they were a liberation group fighting for the rights of an oppressed minority, as time went on, Remainers began to reclaim insults hurled at them by pro-Brexit newspapers and their political opponents. Their social media profiles bore legends such as 'Remoaner and proud' and 'Member of the liberal metropolitan elite'. Of course, it was usually tongue-in-cheek, but the importance of Remain and Leave to many voters' identities was clear in the polling before the 2019 General Election, when this sort of behaviour intensified. The Liberal Democrats took on the grassroots sticker bellow of 'Bollocks To Brexit', making it part of their official campaign. The same slogans made their way onto the t-shirts, badges, placards and giant flags I saw in the big 'Together for the Final Say' event in October 2019; a last-ditch attempt to make Remainer voices heard. That was probably peak Remain fandom, their Jeremy Corbyn at Glastonbury 2017 moment, where the newspapers repeated organizers' assertions that a million people had marched in support of a second EU referendum. Nobody got kettled in the protest, MPs and celebrities spoke on giant screens and sound systems cycled around playing disco music. It was very much an event for the fans to get together and enjoy themselves, shortly before their hopes were crushed by a significant Tory majority to 'Get Brexit Done' and a new Brexit deal signed by Boris Johnson. The fandom's legacy can be seen in the plethora of podcasts featuring big Remain names, the continued publication of the *New European* and the protest antics, and responses to the same, of climate activists Just Stop Oil, who can be both thrilling and embarrassing.

The songs of the Remain Voice Choir were so bad they were almost good. Anti-Brexit lyrics to popular tunes. I saw them outside Parliament several times, with song sheets and a brass band. Later they changed their name to the Reunion Choir.[11] Songs included 'Your Brexit Deal's Half Baked' (to the tune of 'On Ilkley Moor Baht 'At'), 'I'm Forever European' ('I'm Forever Blowing Bubbles') and 'Holy Tory What a Hell of a Mess We're In' ('Glory, Glory').

It's easy to look at the more outlandish outfits and antics of high-profile Remainers and wonder how many of them started out laughing at the community they ended up joining. Some fandoms start out as semi-ironic appreciation and then sincere warmth and attachment develop.[12] My love of Ed Balls, a recurrent theme in this book, is a bit like that, much as I take flak for it. I started making animated GIFs of his appearances on *Strictly Come Dancing*, because the tension between his image as an aggressive and serious politician and the reality of his giddy, full-throated commitment to terrible dancing made me howl with laughter and sharing those GIFs surprised political friends not watching the show. Along with many others, I supported him through the competition as an underdog. However, declaring my love for him weekly involved a certain amount of exaggeration for effect. I received messages from MPs, Westminster journalists and friends from other areas of my life, who were both entertained by my output and puzzled by my enthusiastic persistence. Eventually Ed's popularity meant that other people began making GIFs of his dances. My competitive nature meant I chased up behind the scenes footage from the show and interview clips to turn into further GIFs, captioning them and adding wry comment, and deepening my knowledge of his politics and background. The performance of fandom had become real: I knew a lot about him, I liked him, I knew other people with a soft spot for him and it was enjoyable to chat to Ed and his fans long after the programme finished its run. Sometimes people would shout at me about things he had done that they didn't like, as if I didn't know or I approved of everything Balls, and would tell me I was pathetic or a New Labour shill. On balance, it was and still is more fun than annoying to publicly be part of the Ed Balls fandom. Well, apart from when he started a podcast with George Osborne. Not everyone from the 2010s can be reclaimed as a national treasure, but it's okay to have fun with politics without necessarily approving of everything a politician says or does.

Some people are embarrassed by 'ludic' or playful politics, theatrical antics and political humour that isn't cutting satire. It's seen as the wrong sort of political engagement, despite being key to keeping a lot of activists and others interested. Playful politics lets power get away with it (if you too wish to protest) and disrespects it on the other (if you think protest is ridiculous and futile). How dare this group act like a bunch of boyband fans waiting for their idols to arrive at a TV appearance or regional radio station? How dare they dress up like they're going to a comics convention? How dare they throw orange confetti at George Osborne? Serious commentators enjoy policing how people choose to do politics. What's wrong with those who want to make some of it fun rather than *weltschmerz*, clowning as much as comradeship? To some in political parties, these fans were less bother when they were writing the odd letter to the local papers and shoving leaflets through letterboxes come election time.

Not all fannish fun is in service of progress or harmless disagreement. However, what comes across in much of the criticism of enjoyable political activity – whether fans are enjoying a campaign heavy on theatrics, a meme t-shirt or a rally for a favourite politician – is social embarrassment. Cringe. And yet, when else do adults get to play? Playfulness is key to a good life. Games have been shown to help people of all ages to manage uncertainty in their lives. Uncertainty is a positive in games, as it is a necessary element in keeping players motivated from moment to moment and makes their achievements meaningful.[13] There is no grassroots fandom without playfulness and sometimes cringey behaviour, the things that make social activity –

which politics needs – fun. Otherwise, it's just endless predictable meetings that don't give anything back to the activists unless they pull off a big election win – and not all politics is about elections.

Deborah Wilde, a retired teacher from London, was carrying a boxed jigsaw of Centre Court when she took action at Wimbledon as part of climate group Just Stop Oil in July 2023.[14] Pieces of the puzzle were tossed onto the grass along with orange confetti. Protest isn't just a game to her, but she made it more fun and interesting by adding that element to it. During wars and famines and political campaigns taking place during crises (such as the ACT UP kiss-in protests at the height of the AIDS pandemic), games and theatricality helped participants cope with the intensity of the struggle, and bond with the group.[15] Visible playfulness gave new ACT UP activists an entry point to the community of resistance. They became fans of what the group seemed to represent, and their antics offered an accessible way of joining in, finding others who shared their interest and releasing the energy campaigners often build up from anger and frustration. Some commentators found the performances and humour distracting and detrimental to the cause, but they seemed to forget that activists and politicians are sometimes trying to grow their community rather than appeal to the wider public. Building up a fandom around enjoyment of artistic expression as well as ideas is important for a lot of political musicians, artists, actors and writers who then use their platforms to further their cause. They prefer not to play to audiences who only like them for their politics. Michael Sheen has probably done more good with his social projects and promotion of campaigns as a 'not-for-profit actor' with a mainstream career and large fanbase than many agitprop creators.[16]

In my defence of 'cringe' and embarrassing political activity, I recognize that there are two types of cringeworthiness in politics: good and bad. Only the good is genuinely defensible, because it's politicians and fans having collective fun and that is necessary to keep politics broad and interesting. Good cringe versus bad cringe can be separated by motivation and intent. If someone is doing something harmless just for the joy of it, like wearing a 'Sparkle With Starmer' t-shirt, I'd say that's good cringe – even if it's not your kind of thing. If someone is trying to make or score a point by doing something cringe, like an acoustic cover version of a pop song as commentary on the government, I'd say that's bad. Anything cringe someone does as part of campaigning to promote a brand or further their own career, including desperately trying to go viral on social media, is not good. Some cases are easy to judge because they're so negative. The I Heart JK Rowling billboards that appeared in Edinburgh[17] and Vancouver[18] were inscrutable to outsiders and cringeworthy to many of those in the know, but were erected in approval of Rowling's stance on trans rights.

'Fandom isn't inherently morally good,' says podcaster and fandom expert Elizabeth Minkel. 'I often stress that, with its extreme highs and lows, it just is what it is, and trying to pin those kinds of values to it is a dangerous gambit. But these are undeniably rough times, and while I still haven't mastered "fandom as pure escapism" – someone help me turn off my brain please – I'm much better at taking pleasure and joy when it's offered to me.'[19]

When things are bad, people go into fandom, but why is it fun? What is fun? It's important to know what we're talking about when I'm advocating for it in politics. Sociologist Walter Podilchak kindly investigated and I'll summarize here.[20] Being in an audience doesn't count as fun unless there is audience interaction (heckling counts!). You have to be actively taking part. Fun is completely absorbing, like a flow state. People having fun together feel positive about each other and like they're co-conspirators in the fun. It's not fun if beginners aren't shown what to do or there's no system to make a fun thing fair for everyone. Equality is important to fun! And, crucially, it's not fun unless you freely choose to take part. Coercion and compulsion are NOT FUN.

Fandom meets these criteria! It's an active pursuit, where people do things and don't just passively consume news. It's absorbing. The community collaborate to make the fandom what it is and develop feelings for each other. Fandoms aren't often hierarchical, unlike most political organizations, and fans help each other out because shared knowledge and skills are valued. Fandom is also democratic – politics isn't something that should happen to people, rather it should be done with their participation, and fun fandom makes people more active participants. Their emotions and contributions to the group – other than standard political volunteering activities – are valued. That matters. Treat people like people and democracy thrives.

No wonder people become stans (hardcore fans, after the Eminem song 'Stan' where a fan goes to extremes while writing a letter to his idol). Equality and free choice are important in politics, fandom and fun. Domestic fans of leaders like Putin, Stalin, Mao and Xi Jinping don't meaningfully have a choice in joining the fandom. The cult of personality is baked into the regime, and citizens are indoctrinated via propaganda and fake history. National identity is nationalist identity and linked to the leader. Citizens are under constant surveillance. Dissidents are punished. This is not in any way free or 'fun'. International fans of dictators, conversely, are often in love with the leadership style and the regime and not the personalities involved.

Leader cults rely on propaganda and ritual, and they are not the same as fandoms in democratic politics – in either intent or appearance. Their rituals are designed to manipulate people into a quasi-religious state, not inspire political action or collective enjoyment. Xavier Márquez is an Associate Professor of Political Theory and Political Science at the Victoria University of Wellington. He says that 'loyalty signaling, emotional amplification, and direct production mechanisms can combine, under specific circumstances, to transform ordinary flattery into full-blown practices of ruler worship'.[21]

It can seem like fans are in awe of power. People with low social status (low income, young people, stigmatized minority groups) are right to believe that governments don't tackle the issues that are most salient to them and policymaking doesn't reflect their preferences, according to the evidence of who is prioritized in political thinking. Policymaking is deeply unequal because the people who have the most influence on policy represent the interests of organizations and groups with money, power and high social status.[22] [23] Pensions are important, policies for young renters are not. Fandoms let marginalized people show their enthusiasm for opposition politicians who care about their concerns, but they can also use the connections of the network to gain higher status and more influence. Fans share information and resources, which makes it easier to meet and talk to politicians and leaders of movements and address some of the inequalities.

'It's a perfectly nice and legitimate thing to be a member of a fan club and they may get a great deal of satisfaction from it but that doesn't mean you belong to the Labour Party,' said Margaret Beckett, former Labour Cabinet minister and deputy leader, in 2016. She continued: 'I'll be sorry to think that vast numbers of those people in fact do not really want to be in the Labour Party, they just want to support Jeremy [Corbyn].'[24]

Margaret Beckett underestimated the Corbyn fandom, incisive though her comment was, but also forgot that the leader who made her a minister, Tony Blair, relied on the party as a fan club. The mass movement plan of the Blair Revolution – as detailed in the 1996 book of the same name by Peter Mandelson and Roger Liddle – was all about recruiting fans, making them feel involved in New Labour and getting Blair elected. Hundreds of thousands joined, just as with Corbyn, and his voters required a lot of support from a fandom who had no interest in the Labour Party before or after his tenure. We know because they left the party when his time was done.[25]

Why do people join parties and groups? How easy is it to get involved in politics and campaigns? It certainly doesn't look exciting or engaging to most people when they get their membership pack in the post, which is why most political parties, political groups and campaigning organization members are passive supporters. Their involvement beyond membership fees or a regular donation via direct debit is rare, and when they do go to meetings it's boring and requires more from members in the vein of volunteer time and factional support for internal roles than enthusiasm. Fans, unsurprisingly, want more of a say, more social experiences than campaign meetings and to do things that aren't just grunt work (perhaps using their creative skills). Even New Labour recognized that. Otherwise, all they've got access to is posting on the internet and beating their rivals.

What happens to fans when it all goes wrong? Leadership contests generate short-term fandoms and intense feelings. When Hillary Clinton lost the presidential nomination to Barack Obama in 2008, some of her fans really struggled with what to do next. Diane Mantouvalos co-founded Hillary fansite HireHeels and a pro-Clinton coalition of fan groups called JustSayNoDeal in 2008. HireHeels began as a brash feminine site awash with images of lipstick and nail varnish, a 'shoetube' channel and an animated pink 'groovin' on hillpod' Hillary iPod.

One early post read:

> We're a bunch of savvy chics [*sic*] who know what it feels like to get the proverbial pat on the ass or be pushed out of the way. And people wonder why we're bitches! We also got sick of the media telling us that Hillary's prototypical female supporters were kid-toting, tip-collecting waitresses – thank you Mr. Matthews! Women across this nation and beyond are feeling Hillary's pain. Yes, we want Hillary, not because she's a woman – but because she's a B-I-T-C-H.[26]

HireHeels evolved into a more professional pro-women website and Diane kept blogging at the site until a while after Trump's inauguration. Her tweets in 2021 told the sad tale of a Covid truther who hated Biden.

New Yorker Harriet Christian was furious at the Democratic Rules and Byelaws Committee decision to give Florida and Michigan delegates half votes as punishment for moving their state primaries ahead of the dates set by the Democratic National Committee. This cost Hillary the presidential nomination and Obama became the candidate. Christian became a viral sensation for her racist rant on video against Obama and vowing to vote for Republican candidate John McCain. 'I am proud to be an older American woman. The Democrats are throwing the election away. For what? An inadequate Black male?. . . And I'm not going to shut my mouth anymore. . . I can be called white, but you can't be called Black? That's not my America. It's equality for all of us! I'm no second-class citizen.' When a reporter asked for her name, she responded, 'Why would you like my name? Maybe you're the CIA, the FBI? I was a second-class citizen before, and now I'm nothing!' Harriet Christian became a star of the reactionary right, invited on to Fox News and to hang out with McCain. She died in 2013.

The Hillary devotees were not all as openly racist as Harriet Christian or as giddily 'girlboss feminist' as Diane and her ultra-femme fansite, but many of those prominent 2008 'fans' of Clinton and Democrat donors struggled with the idea that Obama was legitimately the candidate and then the president for his entire presidency and became Obama anti-fans and McCain fans. Darragh Murphy ran the PUMA (Party Unity My Ass and then People United Means Action) group, which at one point had a large angry network of bloggers trading Obama insults and pro-McCain comments,[27] and she kept blogging for a while. Will Bower became a Hillary BNF (Big Name Fan) off the back of running a 24,000-member Facebook group, which made him well known in the fandom, and then a blog post about Christian that made him popular with the scorned fans.[28] [29] [30] [31] Bower told *Newsweek* on the week of Obama's 2009 inauguration: 'A lot of what scares me is Obama mania and all. I feel like I'm living in *American Idol*, a four-year episode of *American Idol*. . . It feels like mass hysteria – the pictures, the jargon. . . If this were all going on for Hillary I'd like to think I'd take a step back and say, "This is crazy." It is a little unsettling, the fanaticism.'[32] Bower briefly flirted with the Republicans, turned back to the Dems and went on to become an electoral reform campaigner and publicist.

In 1993, a grumpy *Washington Post* journalist mocked US aides for their youth and enthusiasm:

> The Clinton White House, with its star-struck young staffers (the deputy chief of staff keeps a video camera in his desk to catch Hollywood stars passing through the West Wing) pulling their celebrated all-nighters, complete with pizza delivery and bull sessions, gives the impression of a college dorm: energetic, youthful, lightweight. The kind of gang you'd want tinkering tirelessly with stimulus packages and forestry plans. But do you really want them ordering bombing runs on Serbia?

The role of youth can be overplayed in fandom – there are plenty of grownups – and in politics. The popular wisdom, as widely shared in the book *Cultural Backlash* by veteran political scientists Ronald Inglehart and Pippa Norris, tells us that the main split in politics is caused by age. Young people are more progressive, older people are more conservative and more likely to vote against liberalism. But evidence doesn't fully support this claim. Armin Schäfer, Professor of Political Science at the University of Mainz, painstakingly replicated the analyses in the book.[33] He found that there is no polarization of attitudes between younger and older people and voting pattern data shows that, surprisingly, younger cohorts are more likely to vote for authoritarian-populist parties than the inter-war generation. Using z-scores (measured in standard deviations from the mean) exaggerates differences of opinion and gives a misleading impression of polarization, whereas the analysis showed different age groups have broadly similar cultural attitudes.

Several movements started by young people took uncool politicians and brought them into the world of online fandom. The Milifandom was started by teenager Abby Tomlinson in 2015.[34] She was big on social media because of her status within fandoms for Tom Hiddleston and other enthusiasms. Abby didn't fancy Ed Miliband, it was never about that. What she did notice is that the then Labour leader seemed to be a decent person, like her other faves, but unlike them he wasn't treated fairly by the media.[35] 'He was shy, quite endearing, more awkward than other politicians,' she said. 'And he knew how to make fun of himself.'

Abby and her army of teens photoshopped flower crowns onto Miliband, made memes and otherwise perked up his image. Sure, many fans weren't old enough to vote, and sure, he lost the 2015 election. But Abby went on to work in political journalism and social media, using her invaluable skills learned from fandoms, and 'Milibae' eventually showed the rest of the world his personality. Ed Miliband's podcast, occasionally sassy tweets and commitment to environmental issues have been well received and he embraces his geeky reputation by dropping references into parliamentary speeches for his extremely online followers, like the 'galaxy brain' meme.

The Markeyverse took a similar approach with Ed Markey in the US, based on his support for the Green New Deal.[36] That group of teens helped the senator fend off a primary challenge from Joe Kennedy III and turned him into a left-wing icon. It didn't end so well for Markey fans politically, as he made decisions that disappointed them, but some of the group went on to campaign as the Wuniverse and secured the election of Mayor Michelle Wu in Boston.[37] Unlike the Markeyverse, they focused on in-person campaigning and voter outreach. The model was much more like grassroots campaigning, but their fannish organizing chops got together the signatures to get their candidate on their ballot and then got out the vote.[38]

Gabriel Boric's vote share in the 2021 Chilean presidential election increased significantly between the first and final round of voting, and it was in part because so many more voters were moved to cast a ballot. The media were telling them both candidates were unengaging, but fans had a different idea. And it wasn't just standard Boric fans, although there were plenty of those. Many groups worked their connections on social media to get out the vote, turning his messages into viral memes and videos. The slogan 'we continue' took over social networks, together with the tree emoji – an icon of the campaign. A feeling of camaraderie and support was created among animal lovers, environmentalists, feminists, union members from different institutions and a multitude of fandoms.

Chileans compared the result of the first round with *The Empire Strikes Back*, where the triumph of the right-wing candidate José Antonio Kast would represent the advance of Darth Sidious and Darth Vader over Boric's Rebel Alliance.[39] They decided that the second round could be an opportunity similar to *Return of the Jedi*, in which the group led by Luke Skywalker and Leia Organa defeat the emperor's tyranny. In other words, a winning opportunity for Boric and the left. Kast won the first round but the light side of the force had the K-pop fans including ARMY (BTS fans), the Otaku (fans of anime), the dogs and cats of Instagram and Swifties (Taylor Swift fans).

Nancy Alejandra is a Chilean influencer, with more than 20,000 followers on Instagram and 402,000 followers on TikTok. She was also a member of ARMY, the BTS fandom, and told Chilean digital newspaper *Interferencia* that she joined the Boric fandom because of his positive message. 'The boys' speech is the same, and they talk about having hope and not getting carried away. That's why many BTS fans are supporting Boric, because it would be contradictory not to,' she said. As a highly organized group, Chilean ARMY believed that their campaign would be effective. 'ARMY is a group of fans who are super aware of social issues,' claimed Alejandra. 'BTS calls for a lot of awareness and that is something super political.'[40]

Fans of other K-pop groups like Blackpink and SHINee joined K-popersXBoric (the X usually denotes a collaboration between two entities; K-popers is the local term for K-pop fans), uploading videos and memes featuring information about the election and their idols. Otaku Antifascista (antifascist anime fans) shared memes and serious reflections about the importance of voting in the second round and the threat Kast presented to LGBTQ+ rights. Groups also met in person at rallies. A marketing account manager noticed that criticisms of Boric's campaign were focused on the fact that his message appealed to professionals and graduates but their parents and grandparents didn't feel close to any candidates. He decided to reach that audience using the aesthetics of the messages that older women share on social networks, making memes featuring Tweety Pie or popular Latin American performer Chayanne. He picked up thousands of extra followers.

The cheerful Geordie lass on the Brexit Party merch stand at the QEII conference centre told me that the biggest ever spend she'd seen was £84. I saw someone splurge £78. Umbrellas were £24.99, air fresheners £1. I saw a lot of pint glasses (£6), reusable coffee mugs (£4.50) and t-shirted teddy bears (£5.99) shifting, but the biggest sellers were socks (£4.50) and scarves (£7.50). I found myself thinking of the family members who were given them for Christmas 2019.

We have never been particularly big on official merchandise in UK politics. Leadership candidates rarely get it together beyond printing t-shirts for their campaign volunteers. Even Jeremy Corbyn's first leadership campaign only managed one very basic design of shirt and matching badge, sold via the mailing list and a PayPal link. No badges or stickers at hustings or rallies. Party websites flog cagoules, rosettes and clipboards to canvassers and the odd t-shirt and calendar. You can still buy a print copy of the manifesto and some lapel badges. Video footage of 1990s and 2000s conferences don't offer much more – the top item on sale in Blair's day was a paper copy of the leader's speech. Not even signed. The Brexit Party at least worked out they could profit from their fans. Most political movements and campaigns don't tend to do much better, with no dedicated merchandise design or salespeople working on products to advertise the movement and raise income. Activists raise more via crowdfunders and subscriptions. Unofficial merch via bookshops and online marketplaces is the only way to get colouring books, dolls and t-shirts.

In the US, it's a different story. However, not only do the campaigners want the money; at every level of politics, they have recognized that fans can give you more than just the cash. They bring data. According to Federal Election Commission regulations, candidates are not allowed to sell items for personal profit, so the product is what you get in return for your donation. This has upset Obama, Bernie and Hillary fans of my acquaintance – it's illegal to buy that merch from outside the US unless you can prove you are an eligible voter. And this is about more than just selling stuff. They get all the information you have to give to make a donation – name, address, phone number, email address, employer, occupation and whether or not you are retired – plus knowledge about you as a fan from your choice of product.

That's why there's so much choice. Your demographic can be ascertained from the niche items you prefer. For example, the Chillary koozie existed in 2015: a foam sleeve to keep your drink cool, emblazoned with 'More like Chillary Clinton, amirite?' and advertised via an online clip featuring Hillary herself.[41] Customers are segmented into specific fundraising buckets and targeted emails, using the same methods as retail giants like ASOS. More products, more browsing, more clicking, more data. Fans buy more stuff, of course, because it's not just a donation to us. Sanders sells less of a range, Clinton sold more. Even Senator Ron DeSantis sold holiday and pandemic merch.

In 2014 you could buy a Rand Paul mask from a store run by fan Trey Stinnett. Not a cardboard mask like you can buy of UK politicians, or a rubber fancy dress mask. A 3D mask of the conservative Republican senator's actual face, commissioned from a sculptor: 'they're all hand-painted with airbrush and stuff like that. It was a little bit of a process,' said Stinnett. 'Beginning to end, we probably spent two to three months, just back and forth with the sculptor and the manufacturer.'[42] It is unknown how many masks Stinnett sold, but the lengths he went to in creating them go beyond a quick cash-in on a trend.

'It's all about learning who your supporter base is,' said Marshal Cohen, chief industry analyst of the NPD Group and the author of *Why Customers Do What They Do*. 'How do they live? What are their trigger points? What words resonate with them? It's worth its weight in gold, in the political arena just like the consumer arena. We call it demographic profiling, because voter profiling sounds like a dirty word, but that's what it is.'[43]

Fandoms often find and recognize each other on social media via hashtags in their posts and profiles, and politics fandoms are no different. More subtle signals are also used in the form of coded emojis in profile names and even phrases that act as both a shibboleth for the fandom and a warning to opponents. The symbols used for activist fandoms outside electoral politics constantly evolve, as they are often topical references and fandom in-jokes. You might not always be able to work out why a symbol has been chosen but once you spot a pattern across several accounts then you can see who they're aligned with and work out if they're your people or someone to avoid. Some symbols have different meanings in other countries and so you can only work out how they are being used from triangulating the symbols with other signifiers in their profile and tweets. Politicians themselves will sometimes use these references to signal to their fans that they are still listening and share their concerns.

You can't just ignore your fans when you get into power. Trump was always throwing red meat to his base, Johnson and Corbyn (as Labour leader) too. Biden and Starmer struggle to be anyone's favourite, even when they win against weak opponents, because they don't have that ability to stoke people up ('Bernie would have won a landslide!'). They might offer something to the floating voter and the sensibles, but without those fiery fans there's nobody out there to keep the flame burning. That puts a politician in danger of a coup, as much as being hated. Rivals and their fans think they can do it better. Passion is a requirement.

When supporters are passionate, their imaginations start to soar. No focus group could come up with ideas as interesting or bizarre as those of fans. It's time to dig into fan creativity.

5

FAN CREATIVITY

It's May 2017 and I keep being trolled by my friends sending me the same link – usually disguised – and getting both irritated and amused every time. An old man dancing forwards and backwards (reversing the video) in front of a wall, surrounded by banners, and amping up a crowd to join in with the vibes. Obnoxious pop music blasts from my speakers and I rush to mute my laptop for the *n*th time. The Cans4Corbyn website has got me again. It's ridiculous, just a simple website hosting a GIF of Corbyn set to a Robbie Williams track, but it's funny and kind of heartwarming. Somehow it reflects the spirit of that summer.

Site creator Niall Cunningham explained himself to *Vice*:

> To an outsider, Jeremy Corbyn, Rock DJ and Cans™ should have nothing in common. Corbyn's teetotal and seems more into grime and the graps [a reference to Corbyn's Twitter appreciation of pro wrestler Zack Sabre Jr], and Robbie strikes me as the sort of guy who'd love to have a beer with you and would share his crisps and all. . . But stripped to their bare elements, they've both stuck to their core values

> over time: Corbyn won't be defeated by this election, Robbie will always be the only ample member of Take That and on 8 June we're all going to vote and head to green spaces with a big bag of cans.[1]

Cunningham did something creative as a fan for the fans and captured the zeitgeist. It wasn't a clever bit of officially sanctioned marketing or cutting satire; it was a moment of grassroots fun during the hard work of an election campaign that aimed to boost morale and remind people who were already generally supportive to vote for Labour. Party HQ would and could never have come up with it, nor the Corbyn and a big bag of cans with the lads meme that was everywhere that year, including a flag at Glastonbury Festival. The specific acts of creativity this chapter looks at are not those of careerist wannabe politicos trying to get hired by the party or selected for a safe seat. There are people who knock up websites, memes and campaigns for these purposes, and they're not that novel or interesting. I've chosen people doing things more absurd, exciting and orthogonal to the simple purposes of getting a candidate or party elected. I have focused mostly on people enacting their passion for politics via passionate creativity, in ways unlikely to be compensated (financially or otherwise).

In fandom, there is something known as the 'gift economy'.[2] It came about in part because of intellectual property concerns. Fans writing fanfiction or making fanart didn't own the rights to the characters they were using and didn't want to be shut down in publishing their creativity for legal reasons. Not monetizing their work helped avoid that sort of issue. However, the gift economy is about more than copyright and keeping out of trouble – there's a culture of sharing freely and openly with the fan community, rather than trying to exploit it for gain. Fans write stories, make videos or design avatars or create memes as gifts to the community and also for each other as individuals, based on prompts or requests or desires. It is an economy based on giving, receiving and reciprocating in which fans' skills and generosity are valued. Something of that spirit has crept into fan creativity in politics, further enabled by the internet and digital creative tools, and everyone has something to contribute. The days of Saatchi + Saatchi ads for the Conservative Party (remember the one, 'Labour Isn't Working') being the most enduring political images are over. People are more likely to remember memes or watch videos made by political YouTubers or listen to podcasts than recall party political broadcasts and official posters. The media landscape is fragmenting and people are getting their news and views from social media. A lot of what they see has come from fans, either made by them or shared by them with insightful or contradictory commentary, and some of those fans have a lot more trust and authentic support from their audiences than traditional authorities like political journalists or teachers and academics.

Fan creativity has a rich heritage. I have always been a fan of historical politicians as well as avidly following the current goings-on, especially those who clearly loved politics themselves. While I have read a lot of political biographies, autobiographies and political histories, I have a soft spot for overlooked characters. Leo Abse is a particular favourite of mine. Abse was a Jewish Labour MP in the mid-twentieth century who campaigned for the decriminalization of homosexuality and the liberalization of divorce laws, and he was also a Welsh dandy who stole the media limelight on Budget Day every year by walking into Parliament in a new flamboyant suit. Bespoke menswear with a strong eighteenth-century influence, incorporating Welsh textiles, always dashing accessories. I was smitten as soon as I first read about him. Abse was also a keen student of Freudian psychoanalysis and supporter of the European Community and combined these interests in his writing, which was as extra as his dress sense.

Abse wrote psychobiographies (mixing non-fiction and psychological theory) of Tony Blair[3] and Margaret Thatcher,[4] both of whom he disliked, and he accused Peter Mandelson of killing the party that he loved. However, he was a politics fan and knew fandom when he saw it. Of Hugh Gaitskell, the one-time Labour leader who snubbed him, he wrote that 'I found him physically antipathetic, but there were men who were extravagantly in love with him. Frank Soskice once told me, months after the event, that Gaitskell's death had extinguished all his joy in politics, and there were obviously many in Parliament who felt similarly devastated. . . In particular, his caressing voice was extraordinarily seductive.'[5]

One of Leo's books was called *Fellatio, Masochism, Politics and Love*[6] ('to overthrow the god and become the goddess, the penis must be depreciated,' he wrote), in which he analysed a range of political figures, and gave his thoughts on Bill Clinton's affair with Monica Lewinsky. The book includes the heartfelt line 'our laws relating to divorce, suicide, illegitimacy, adoption and homosexuality were unbecoming to any society claiming to be civilized', as befits a political reformer. However, his Freudian schtick was quite full on. In a chapter called 'Sex, Enoch Powell and the Asylum Seekers' – 'My quip about eunuchs and Enochs had pierced his carapace' – Abse finds that Enoch Powell's 'guilt-ridden sexuality' and Nazi Germany's rejection of homosexuals caused Powell to project sexual prowess onto the Black men he so feared and hated. Abse complained that on his ninetieth birthday he never had one word of thanks from any gay activist; he tried to get the Home Secretary to ban an Alice Cooper tour and he campaigned for more restrictions on abortion. Despite all this, I have no choice but to stan.

Leo Abse's older brother was eminent psychiatrist D. Wilfred Abse, who specialized in group-analytic psychotherapy and hysteria. His younger brother was the poet (and doctor) Dannie Abse. The boys' grandmother was German and Jewish and they were brought up in a household where German was often spoken. German socialist literature informed Leo's thinking. He wrote a book in 1994 with the wonderfully baroque title *Wotan, My Enemy: Can Britain Live with the Germans in the European Union? An Autobiographical Response*. In this book, he provocatively argued that Germany was a bully and needed to change its national character if it was to be trusted. Oh, and that Germans should give up any claim to a state of their own. One to animate any Brexit discussion.

In an interview from 2008 – the year of his death – Abse explained how he saw his background: 'I had two great advantages: I was born a Jew in Wales in the benign climate of Welsh nonconformity; we believed we had a covenant with God and God would look after us. . . Being in a minority within a minority, I had the benefit of being an outsider without feeling inferior. And I never went to university, which meant I wasn't groomed to conform.'[7]

Leo Abse's writing is poetic, heartfelt, insightful and often filthy. His take on Gordon Brown is exquisite and belongs in any fan's library, to deepen their understanding of the man: 'Brown indeed sentences himself to a cruel strangulation of affect; we are witnessing a courageous and able politician – and no-one can gainsay that he earns such compliments – prepared to meet and confront anyone but himself. . . He is attempting the impossible; a total dichotomy between the public and private man.'

Abse prefigured the complex analyses of politics and fascinating stories shared by fans today. One of the joyous things about fandom is what fans can do creatively with futures, potential and innuendo. Potential and innuendo are the most exciting phase, as fans build something out of nothing before it's contradicted. They can project their predictions, hopes and dreams onto the characters – including sports fans, if you think of the transfer season in football and the NFL draft, and politics fans, when leadership contests and elections and reshuffles are happening.

In 2017, it seemed for a summer like the UK left could not only meme but also succeed against the odds. They had their own insular argot, and homemade graphics, memes, videos, slogans and events sprang up like dandelions. It hadn't been like this in UK politics for a long time. Fun. Hopeful. Joyous. The Conservative majority was shattered, and you could almost convince yourself that one last heave would put an alternative into contention.

The absolute boy and a big bag of cans with the lads had beaten the melts and slugs into submission (and the Tories). It was all downhill from there, but Labour won the digital war and a bigger vote share. This was the mass movement many had been waiting for. Momentum's app helped people find their nearest marginal constituency and organize lifts. While activists had been using

WhatsApp for a while, the groups run by party officials were used for broadcasting information and whipping internal votes. Self-organizing fans shared more jokes and confessions, bonding people as human beings instead of volunteers. It might have all turned sour, but for a while Corbynism was the spark for all kinds of excitement, mutual aid, art and fun.

More people follow politics closely at times when it is particularly volatile. The Hansard Society asked the UK public how certain they feel that they are going to vote, how they rate their level of interest in politics and how much they think they know about politics itself and Parliament specifically.[8] The past decade or so has been, as the young people say, A Lot, with wild and unpredictable politics on top of world events. As a result, political engagement in the UK – according to those metrics – is higher than it has ever been. However, the same surveys found that the public are increasingly dissatisfied with politicians, parties and the political system. That combination of high political interest and low satisfaction with the usual way of doing things led people to want something different. That translated into protests, campaigns, new political movements and parties, unexpected success for outsider candidates, fandoms springing up around all of these. . . and, thanks to the growth of social media, somewhere for fans of politics and politicians to express themselves. As with other fandoms, politics fans and anti-fans use their creative and professional skills to make content for each other and the world. They promote their faves, attack their enemies, explain issues and make us laugh. The content they make can be endlessly shared, copied, responded to and remixed. Some become political influencers with fans of their own.

Pressure group Led By Donkeys successfully raised money for billboards, projections and other interventions in aid of the Remain fandom. Much of their creative work seeks to highlight the hypocrisy of Conservative politicians and Brexiteers, though its actual effect may be more to shore up the security of the fans who believe in their messaging and fund its transmission than to change public or political opinions. The most successful example in creative terms was when the group contacted *Line of Duty* creator Jed Mercurio and secured the participation of cast members in recording new dialogue in 2022, which was edited together with footage of (then Prime Minister) Boris Johnson and (former Metropolitan Police chief) Cressida Dick and existing clips from the show to make viral videos in the style of the popular TV crime drama. Lead actor Adrian Dunbar said, 'Jed told us, "These guys are really good. Would you record this and that? So we did and I think they treated it a bit so it kind of sounds like us, but might not be. It was very good. It didn't quite get rid of Johnson then but it got rid of Cressida Dick."'[9]

When President Donald Trump visited the UK in 2018, activists crowdfunded a giant helium-filled balloon of Trump as a nappy-wearing orange baby, holding a mobile phone, which is now owned and preserved by the Museum of London. This follows in the same tradition as the Pixuleco balloon in Brazil, installed by anti-fans of Lula da Silva and portraying the politician as a caricature in a prison jumpsuit. Like football fans, politics fans in recent years have generated a wealth of creative chants, songs, banners and memes – which often reference other memes and pastiche popular culture. The Iain Duncan Smiths regularly go viral on social media and YouTube for their satirical songs. They started as a Smiths parody band, having (hence the death of the Blair Revolution, when New Labour no longer needed their mass movement). This leaves space for someone like Nigel Farage to pop up, as he did during 2010–19, and tell a more exciting story.

I spoke to three fans from the UK Lolitics community of different ages, backgrounds and approaches to the fandom: Nat Guest, then a twenty-something blogger with a variety of graduate jobs, 'Cones', then a teenager at school, and 'Tofu', then early thirties and working in London. All three used LiveJournal as a platform for blogging and fan communities in 2010, which was where the UK Lolitics fandom began. The changing nature of the internet has had a big impact on politics and fandom.

The 2010 General Election featured the first TV debate between he three major party leaders: Labour, Conservative and Liberal Democrat. David Cameron was expected to win the debates, as a omfortable public speaker and former PR man. Gordon Brown as always awkward in front of the camera, whereas Nick Clegg as a relative unknown who played to the audience who were sick 'politics as usual'. The Lib Dems soared up the campaign polls 34 per cent and there was chat of them overtaking Labour as the ain Opposition party.

Brown's looping response of 'I agree with Nick' in the first debate came a meme. Overcooked Obama and Churchill comparisons and grant fanboying by the sensibles was quickly dubbed 'Cleggmania', t it never converted into extra votes.[11] [12] The Lib Dems' vote share nt up by a measly 1 per cent and they won just fifty-seven seats, ss of five from the low turnout election of 2005. Shirley from an ction study focus group said:

realized that 'almost all of The Smiths' well-known hits could easily be tweaked to be about Iain Duncan Smith, so really it was a love of music and puns finding itself infused with contempt for IDS'.[10] They have since turned their parodic musical talents to criticizing Boris Johnson, Keir Starmer, Matt Hancock and Dominic Cummings via the medium of comic song, with music videos subtitled for social media sharing. Collage artist and satirist Christopher Spencer has developed a popular and lauded career as the X account @coldwarsteve, publishing books and featuring in documentaries and exhibitions. Without a clear love for and knowledge of politics, none of these people could have made their work – most of which was made for free or paid for by their fans.

The UK has always had a sarcastic, cheeky and flippant side to its political culture when it comes to traditional media and comedy and so the British public taking advantage of social media to create and share their own irreverent takes and those of fellow politics fans is perhaps to be expected. Particularly while politics is more ridiculous than soap storylines or reality TV or sport – the sorts of things that often pepper our small talk with neighbours and colleagues. Even non-fans of politics can appear well informed if the group chats have been popping off with political memes; they can enjoy the back and forth the same way a non-football fan can follow the World Cup for a bit and then go back to not caring.

Videos, podcasts and many other forms of content contain or become memes, memes themselves reference other memes and meme formats, and many are rich in connections to other events and ideas. Historically, satire has always been important to public understanding of politics as well as a way to hold politicians to account. One of the key differences between the heyday of political sketches and cartoons and the age of the meme is who gets to make that satire and where it is published. To really get the joke, you don't need a classical education from a prestigious school or university. You need to pay attention to the national conversation, political history, pop culture, other online cultures and the evolution of meme formats. It's much less about putting forward the position of a newspaper, making a reader feel clever or generating subscriber income. Some people are also wildly creative, with creators using the agency they *do* have to create whole fictional worlds.

'Canon' is what fans in most fandoms outside of politics call the agreed version of events: what actually happened or which sources 'count'. As more 'canonical events' happen and become part of the history of the object of fandom, whether it's a political party or a TV series or a football team, then more possible avenues for the story in the real world are shut off. Fanfiction, fanart and fantasy play can get around those barriers via alternative timelines and alternative universes, imagining what would happen if different choices had been made or if the main players had been around in a different period in history. Much of the content fans make, even if it appears trivial on the surface, is based on a lot of research, synthesis and serious analysis. Memes and parodies can draw people in to fan communities and drive a deeper understanding of politics – all out of a desire to get the references in the jokes.

I can't talk about fan creativity without talking about UK Lolitics and the fanworks that sprang up after the 2010 General Election and the Coalition government. Not least the RPF ('real person fic' – fanfiction about real people). It was a time of much excitement and

possibility. Not because people thought the Conservative a
Democrat parties were brilliant but because a hung parl
something new and different and it took a while after the
sort out what would happen. My online spaces (mostly I
Tumblr and Twitter and some music forums at that
buzzing with news updates, wry commentary and snarl

To me, UK Lolitics is part of a lineage I see from Leo
passionate people engaging with several passions conc
Abse, it was psychoanalysis, biography, the EU and
the Lolitícians, popular culture, explicitly fan-oriented
internet culture, replaced the more highbrow aspects.
which was more of a media phenomenon than a p
Nick Clegg, and 'elite' interest in fandom from tho
media and politics predicted the way fandom has in
media. 2010 was the first year of televised debates bet
leaders, which meant the old practice of electoral h
beyond hardened party members, Westminster an
way, for modern politics fans 2010 was our 1960
JFK exploded onto our screens. The establishment's
Lolitics, mocking it while coming up with their own
timelines, is also something that has returned with a
fandom. UK Lolitics was a source of passion and
politics when we were told not to care because th
aged white men with brown hair and the same p
content from gaps. The combination of chaos and
narrative means people used the space to write t
created similar gaps (and possibilities) in canon
down imaginaries completely by controlling the

> Yeah, I was going to go with the Lib Dems actually. My family have always been Tory and I've always gone with what they were, and I thought I'd go for the Lib Dems, give them a chance sort of thing. . . but on the day I thought – they're never going to get in. So I waited for my husband to get home, we both went and I still wasn't sure, and we got there and the Tory guys were outside, so I walked up and put my cross straight away, and – Tories. In the end, yeah I thought I don't think they're going to do it so I'll just vote Tory.[13]

As it happened, far fewer people voted Lib Dem in 2010 than said they had but many of them were, or became, political activists or journalists. Aaron Bastani of Novara Media and the journalists Sunny Hundal and Laurie Penny all endorsed the Lib Dems in 2010. Tofu was no different: 'I voted Lib Dem in 2010 for what I thought at the time were pragmatic reasons. After nine years of racist war-mongering I could not bear to vote Labour and I very vehemently did not want another Tory government; I thought it likely there would be a hung Parliament and that coalition (which was already touted) would probably lead to better brakes on the Tories than a minority government.'

Nat also hoped for a hung parliament, as she blogged two days before the election:

> I'm for it. I think it would be interesting. And chaotic. At best, it could be fairer; at worst, it would be an awful disaster that would hopefully lead to the political reform that we do desperately need. Now, I have no idea whether the Lib Dems

could actually run the country, should they get into power, and I hope that they would be able to, but most importantly the increased significance of the third party shows a movement away from the two-party politics that we've been stuck with. Any movement towards people voting for what they actually believe in rather than as a protest or a tactical vote is a good thing as far as I can see.[14]

Nat and Tofu were both involved in cult fandoms when they were younger. Their interest in politics fandom came via the 'Clameron' RPS (real person slash) pairing: David Cameron/Nick Clegg. 'Slash' is a fanwork involving two or more characters of the same sex or gender (originally male/male) in a romantic or sexual situation, the name deriving from the slash symbol used to separate the characters' names.

'A lot of it was driven by the language of the media landscape at the time: Clegg jilting Brown for Cameron, the idea of them announcing a partnership in the Rose Garden,' said Nat. 'There was an obvious romantic narrative being painted, together with romantic tropes, and I think that was the starting place for a lot of people who got involved in writing fic about it. I loved the drama of the political theatre (I think the New Labour years would have been great for that too, if I'd been interested or old enough), but to a certain extent I was disconnected from the politics itself. Now, after over a decade of Tory rule, and seeing the ways in which that has damaged the country and particularly the poorest and most vulnerable in society, I don't think I could be involved in the same sort of thing – it would feel crass. Things felt more innocent and less toxic at the time.'

She was aware of ethical concerns but was consciously writing these politicians as fictional characters: 'Prior to that I had been very lairy about "RPF"; there's a large part of the fandom community that sees it as distinctly unethical to write about real people. I both agree and don't agree with that, as you're definitely writing about fictionalized versions of the real people, but yes, they do also have the faces of those people. To a certain extent it always feels quite meta and tongue-in-cheek.'

Politics proper and ironic humour were baked in from the start, as Tofu says, having found the original Clameron fic and 'thought it extremely funny, a well-observed gentle interpolation of existing romantic and particularly fic-romantic tropes into the dull Westminster world. I also can't now quite get across to people quite how fucking WILD the news coverage was, like broadsheets really were printing all this nudge-nudge wink-wink rose garden stuff ['The bride and groom came down the steps into the garden together. The sun shone and the roses bloomed. It was just like a society wedding', wrote former television executive Peter McHugh for Channel 4 News] and all us queers were a little open-mouthed, because it felt like a gay in-joke but not quite in the homophobic way we expected.'

'I was quite young and naïve, and had a bit of a starry-eyed view of things,' says Cones, who was much younger than Nat and Tofu. 'I legitimately thought Labour was going to surge to victory in 2015 and was crushed when it didn't.' She wasn't interested in Clameron, instead taking a more historical approach to alternative political realities.

> I come from a pretty politically active family, but I can really trace it back to being in my mid-teens during the twilight years of the New Labour government, seeing it as a bit crap but scared of the alternative, and dealing with that by drawing awful cartoons of Tony Blair, Gordon Brown et al. for my schoolmates. From there I got into weird Internet communities that took their interest in politics a little beyond, say, your average *Guardian* liveblog. We're talking deadblogging [blogging long ago events as if live] elections from the 1980s and making Blingees [naff sparkling animated GIFs] of David Owen. We're talking buying a stack of *Private Eyes* from 1975 just for one scurrilous bit where Jeremy Thorpe declares his preference for circumcised men.

'A lot of the Lolitics group felt like people using the easy accessibility of political news for stylistic experiments and fun in-jokes, which I broadly approved of,' said Tofu. 'But I didn't like how quickly it moved to "this isn't the place for Real political discussions" stuff – which, while obviously an RPF problem in itself, felt like a really bad idea given the ostensible subject matter.'

Cones agrees: 'That was actually the mantra drummed into you in these spaces: have your fun, but keep it separate from "reality".'

The depoliticization really got to Tofu: 'That's where the fandom went downhill for me, it devolved into an unthreatening walled playground, less than a space for play AND critical thinking.' The internet has changed and so have the fans: 'Whereas before people in Lolitics were very, very, very careful to hide their horny trash, now you have people shitposting [posting something online that is deliberately absurd, provocative or offensive] on Twitter who jump for joy because an MP followed them,' Cones says. 'There was never the same sort of interest during the Corbyn years (and the overwhelming presence of Brexit), and that was sometimes because people were enthused in a happy and hopeful way, sometimes in a despairing way, depending on your politics.'

Every so often, dirtypoliticsconfessions goes viral on X and people are shocked anew.[15] The Tumblr blog posted fantasies about politicians, anonymously submitted by readers. The glory days of the blog also mirrored the Coalition. According to another UK Lolitician, Maarten, 'the 2010 outbreak of horny was a perfect storm of people who had spent their teens in fandom getting older and thus able to vote and really taking notice of politics for the first time, both actually politics-wise with the potential of things being shaken up, and horny-wise with the influx of hotter politicians'.[16] Later governments didn't have the same potential and Putin ice-bath fantasies were enough to finish it off.

Thirst for politicians didn't completely leave us. Every new election sees furtive shared rankings of new MPs and members of Congress. Anonymous author Chuck Tingle writes gay monster erotica, involving all kinds of inanimate and conceptual characters, and he regularly publishes novellas with witty titles and covers in response to topical events. Brexit and Trump inspired him to new heights, with titles like *Pounded by the Pound: Turned Gay by the Socioeconomic Implications of Britain Leaving the European Union* and *Domald Tromp Pounded In The Butt By The Handsome Russian T-Rex Who Also Peed On His Butt And Then Blackmailed Him With The Videos Of His Butt Getting Peed On*. The latter has fifty-six ratings on Amazon.co.uk, with an average of 4 out of 5.

I also have to put in a quick word for the perverts of the X politics fan community. Tyron Wilson memorably posted a cropped photograph of Jeremy Corbyn pulling a face while grasped around the biceps from behind by former Unite union boss Len McCluskey. His caption? 'When he goes in dry'. The joy this meme produced at a time of trauma and division, albeit possibly not for those depicted, is a solid reason for filthy fans to stick around in politics forever.

Fandom has evolved in parallel with the internet and social media. While filth can be found in most online spaces, the same is true of politics. I had a chat with Martin Belam, who ran the experimental Ampp3d and UsVsTh3m platforms for the *Mirror* and accidentally ended up producing content by and for politics fans. UsVsTh3m was all about shareable digital humour and politics, from quick and funny versions of news stories to interactive 'toys' like a Doctor Who Plot Generator and the Ed Balls Teaches Typing game.[17] 'Was there a coherent plan to do politics stuff?' he said. 'Not really. Once you've done something that's funny and viral and successfully once, I think you're always looking for the next thing, but one of the other things about it was it was hard. You couldn't just say "right and then on Wednesday we'll make a politics game".'

The team of writers and techies in the office would discuss moments from the news as they happened and turn an idea into a game by lunchtime. 'Everybody would share it if it was fun and playable. And I sort of miss that. I just wish someone was still kind of doing that sort of stuff, but it only seems to come out of having a bunch of really always online people together and there just aren't enough always online people in media organizations to get people to understand that.'

MrKennethClarke, a parody X account, has been posting since 2018 and still manages to deceive people into tagging him in their earnest pleas and loving or outraged replies. Parody Trump, Priti Patel and Boris Johnson accounts still regularly catch people out too. While these accounts are a basic form of roleplaying on social media, unconvincingly cosplaying as celebrities, parafiction accounts engage in politics online with more creative and meaningful disruptions. These posters attract attention and build fandoms for characters and interventions of their own creation. Parafiction, says Professor of Architecture Michael Young, adopts 'the aesthetics of the factual and works to produce spaces for people to consider alternate possibilities for how the world could be'.[18]

In parafiction, as defined by art historian and Harvard professor Carrie Lambert-Beatty, fictional or fictionalized characters and stories interact with the real world and are presented as true. Lambert-Beatty was first drawn to parafiction when she was caught out by Michael Blum's artwork, *A Tribute to Safiye Behar*. The mixed-media installation recreates Safiye Behar's Istanbul apartment and a display of documents, but Behar is a fictional woman Blum inserted into real history and presented as real. Blum told Lambert-Beatty that people like Safiye did exist, but he had to make her up because women like her aren't represented in official histories. Lambert-Beatty changed her mind about Blum and the artistic and political possibilities of what she called parafiction.[19]

Probably the best-known parafiction artists in politics are Andy Bichlbaum and Mike Bonanno (whose real names are Jacques Servin and Igor Vamos respectively), aka the Yes Men. Their first big prank was GWBush.com. While George W. Bush's political strategist Karl

Rove had registered all the obviously insulting domain names, he missed variations of Bush's name that could be passed off as real. The Yes Men mirrored Bush's official website and language and tweaked the text to expose the truth behind his policies, highlighting facts like Texas becoming the most polluted state in the United States during his tenure as governor. They wouldn't use the same tactics now because the internet is a different place. 'Talk about learning as you go,' says Bichlbaum. 'Websites were new. There weren't a lot of corporate sabotage websites, and you could publish it on the web and journalists would find it. Even if they kind of only half believed it, they would write about it.'

Bonanno explains that the Yes Men weren't intending to fool people forever.

> With the G. W. Bush website, the idea was to always reveal our real position in an interview with the press, as we do with all of the stuff we've done. There is a phase in which you reveal it, and then we get more attention and get to tell the whole story – you get to get the facts and information in that you want to. What we're doing is not really "fake news", although it uses trickery to get there. It fits in better with traditions of satire, where the goal of the satire is not to make people believe something that is false, but rather to get them interested in discovering the truth. Jonathan Swift didn't write *A Modest Proposal* so that more people would think that the Irish should eat their own babies. He wrote it to provoke a reaction and, through that reaction, reveal that the English were starving the Irish.[20]

Carrie Lambert-Beatty originally felt parafiction was deceptive, but she eventually changed her mind: 'what if we thought about play instead of strictness? What if we thought about curiosity as what drives us to find out more, rather than discipline being how we are moved to find out things?'[21]

Streatham Rovers FC (SRFC) is a parafictional South London non-league football team with a real following that trolls politicians, right-wingers and credulous journalists. SRFC are part of the Trevor Bastard Extended Universe (TBEU), an inspired bit of world-building that evolved from a single Twitter account and some comedy football shirt sales into a network of characters with their own linked storylines and a Patreon account bringing in hundreds of pounds a month. The cast includes manager Taff Goose, rival teams like Dynamo Catford, and divorce solicitor and SRFC lawyer Oliver Laughdugry (a full-time anti-Brexit activist and Corbyn anti who now has to tweet via his wife's account since his was banned).

In this parafictional universe, Laughdugry is friends with Simon Hedges, a sensible journalist and #BeKindOnline activist[22] – another parafiction account that interacts with the TBEU but is also operated outside of it by an office worker, Greg. Hedges pokes gentle fun at the predictability of centrist dads and prominent UK journalists, sometimes making his point via the act of 'liking' tweets with niche appeal to his targets. For example, a 2015 tweet by former Lib Dem MP and figure of fun Lembit Öpik (best known for dating one of reality pop stars the Cheeky Girls): 'Specsavers Employee of the month for me: rebecca [*sic*]. With Mark on right – these guys shine'.[23]

'Simon is a middle-aged newspaper journalist who still lives with his mum and hates the fact that there are left-wing people in the

Labour Party,' says Greg. 'In fact, he hates the fact that lefties exist at all. He thinks that they're all just pretending.' Hedges' fans are 'under 40, on the left, have at least critical support of Corbyn and the Labour Party and, most crucially, they know the types of Twitter personas Simon is meant to be satirising'. Greg describes the sensibles he targets as 'people with no ideas, no analyses, no real policies. It's a shallow-minded Aaron Sorkinesque [*West Wing* creator] view of the world, where the smart sassy people turn up and make everything OK.'[24]

Trevor Bastard is the alias of Belfast-based Robert Vaughan, who was born in South London and lived there when he started the TBEU. The social media accounts that make up the TBEU are suffused with the fannish joy of early Corbynism. 'I never created it to trick people,' Vaughan says. 'I created it to give people a moment of foolery, so they'd get that nice little shudder: "This ridiculous thing might be real. Ah, no, it's not." If I really wanted to trick people I would have made it more realistic.'[25] TBEU employs the absurdist humour of both 'Weird Twitter', as epitomized by dril (an absurdist social media account that somehow captures the zeitgeist with its gnomic pronouncements), and Peter Cook and Dudley Moore's drunken alter-egos Derek and Clive. The Greyhound ultras – Streatham Rovers superfans – and Enya Fans 4 Communism – a parafictional protest group – are based on Vaughan's own experiences as a non-league football fan and left-wing activist. Former Tory minister, leadership hopeful and London mayoral candidate Rory Stewart drew mirth from TBEU fans by interacting first sincerely with the Streatham Rovers account[26] [27] and then going along with the joke: 'Unfortunately my staff member defected to Venezuela last night – apparently his extradition vehicle was not mobile friendly – but he assures me is sending another team member with a pooper scooper to @Streatham Rovers tonight. Thanks again'.[28]

During the 2019 UK General Election campaign, TBEU had more political interactions with the 'shitpost left', an online group that emerged from Corbyn fandom and has some similarities to the US-based 'dirtbag left'. 'Shitposting,' explains Robert Evans from Bellingcat, 'is the act of throwing out huge amounts of content, most of it ironic, low-quality trolling, for the purpose of provoking an emotional reaction in less Internet-savvy viewers.' The shitpost left mixed shitposts and humour with calling out political hypocrisy and promoting Corbyn's policies. The persistence and callousness of some leading members often amounted to harassment of their opponents, which is why their Twitter accounts kept being suspended. Others, like Loki Nash from Cumbria, were able to use their vigilante tendencies for good; conducting rigorous background and funding checks avoided by political parties and helping to expose sexual harassment, racism and antisemitism across the political spectrum. Two Lib Dem parliamentary candidates were deselected as a result of Nash's work.[29]

The shitposters' forays into parafiction involved writing satirical articles about centrist and right-wing politicians and using Google Chrome's inspect element tool on UK news sites to present the stories as convincing screenshots. Their articles were posted on Twitter to amuse their friends and troll the public, using obvious tells for the journalist names, and were promoted/reacted to by characters within the TBEU like Blairite politics professor Dr Robert 'Rob' Zands. The screenshots fooled a lot of people, circulated beyond their original tweets and upset political and media elites. One story reported 'harrowing' footage of then Lib Dem leader Jo Swinson killing squirrels with a slingshot. This tale, under the guise of a real *Mirror* article, went viral and led to awkward media questions. 'They're quite sophisticated and people do believe them,' Swinson told LBC. 'This isn't the only one of the very fake news stories. There was one using the byline of an established journalist. There was one that used Peter Walker's name from the *Guardian* and he had to go online to debunk it and say he never wrote it.'[30]

To people outside the UK, right-wingers and Corbyn anti-fans, left shitposter parafiction accounts were just irresponsible in-joke merchants spreading fake news. Occasionally they did push it too far. Sometimes their pastiches were too close to reality and went for the wrong targets, provoking moral outrage at the merely annoying, and they hadn't considered what would happen when their stories were circulated as cropped screenshots without the satirical 'tells' as context (for example, the use of consistent obviously fictional journalist names on a fake newspaper page). What the posters were trying to do was make people question what they were seeing so they would consider if the media were telling the whole story or had decided to favour particular narratives. As Daniel Hallin wrote in *The 'Uncensored War'*, his book about the media and Vietnam reporting: 'journalism. . . plays the role of exposing, condemning, or excluding from the public agenda those who violate or challenge the political consensus.'[31] Shitposting and satire give those without mainstream media power a chance to do the same.

During the 2020 Labour leadership contest *Observer* journalist Catherine Bennett wrote a column that accidentally mirrored a post by the TBEU. Bennett's headline was 'Why should Keir Starmer step aside? His rivals have few feminist credentials'. Trevor Bastard replied to the newspaper's tweet about her article in character as Dr Robert Zands. He accused her of plagiarism and attached a screenshot of his parafiction from twenty-four days earlier: a column by Zands entitled 'Forget Rebecca Long-Bailey, Keir Starmer is the woman we need'. Bennett deleted her Twitter account.

The spirit of UsVsTh3m and UK Lolitics has not been lost as the internet has become angrier and more fragmented. This book opened with the little lettuce that could: the salad vegetable that outlasted Liz Truss. Journalist Ed Keeble was making viral content for his employers at Reach (owners of the *Daily Star*), sure, but the attention to detail in the lettuce livestream proved that this was a politics fan making niche jokes for fellow politics fans and insiders. 'Letty's' popularity shows that there is still room for playfulness in politics and experiments from mainstream newspaper brands. When I spoke to Keeble he explained that the community – fandom – that grew up around the stream is what made it so successful.

While most newspapers wouldn't do something like the lettuce because it is too frivolous for a news brand, there was a reluctance to make the *Daily Star* political because politics wasn't 'fun'. Yet the lettuce managed to combine political comment and fun without trivializing either. 'The front pages during Covid changed that, I think,' said Keeble, 'and got the ball rolling to what happened with the lettuce.' The paper had used the pandemic as an opportunity to broaden their reach and change their image, using the increased profile of Tomorrow's Papers Today (a social media account where a small group of journalists post the next day's newspaper covers) and the front-page roundups on the news while there was no live sport or socializing to keep the public entertained. The *Star* ran sharply funny covers that resembled online memes while reflecting the public mood. A Dominic Cummings 'free do whatever you like and sod everybody else mask' was a particular highlight, showing what was possible when everyone was a kind of politics fan for a while.

Editor Jon Clark, who also suggested the lettuce livestream, told *Press Gazette*: 'The mask sprang to mind as I sat there thinking about the ruling elite and how they thought they had got away with murder. That night it went viral. The success of a page like that is not necessarily in sales but in redefining people's old fashioned perceptions about what the *Daily Star* stands for. There are some terrible snobs in the government and media and this gave them something to think about.'[32]

I asked Keeble what Clark asked him to do: 'The brief was just livestream a lettuce. I thought it was going to be easy, leave the cam on, flick the light on at night. That changed immediately when thousands of people started tuning in and making suggestions for the stream. A chap called Andrew Gilpin asked if it could be tampered with. Then suggested a clock. And off we went from there.' Keeble was supposed to be on holiday and had complete freedom with the stream. The ideas coming in suggested that, like him, many of the regulars watching the stream were fans of politics with the knowledge to mix in political references with absurd additions. Keeble did have to tell the commenters to keep it 'good vibes only' to avoid mean-spirited or misogynist jokes.

Public anger at being presented with two unelected Prime Ministers in a row reflects a wider dissatisfaction with UK politics.

Many people didn't feel like they had a say in politics before big, rupturing events like the Brexit referendum and the anti-lockdown protests. The silly stuff gives us a bit of Wizard of Oz: the public can see behind the curtain for a while. The lettuce wasn't a static image, it was ever-evolving – reflecting the instability of the political situation. 'She' started as a plain lettuce, then had googly eyes, a wig, arm and other props superglued to the leaves. A framed portrait of Truss herself appeared, thanks to Ed's helpful neighbours. There was a lettuce rave, with music and disco lights. As time went on, the lettuce was served various food and drinks. Fans kept coming back because they would see their suggestions for additions make it to the screen. 'A lot of people suggested the wig for example,' said Keeble. 'That's theirs now, in some way.'

The lettuce livestream was a genuinely participatory experience, rather than Keeble or the newspaper dictating what should happen. In a way, traditional satire is saying to the reader 'we are better at jokes and clever references than you'. It invites them to think and laugh but not to respond or improve the joke. Not to over-egg it, but embracing the spirit of the lettuce community points to a way for newspapers like the *Star* to regain public trust in the media. Valuing the contribution that fans have to make is key. 'I think the country is crying out for an election but they [the government] won't do it, as they'll be destroyed by it,' explained Keeble. 'So the system becomes more and more absurd to hold it back. Hence the lettuce.' It makes sense.

He made a comment during our chat that I think about most days: 'I almost see politics and optics as the same thing. I think once something is *perceived* to be, it *is* that – regardless of the politics or intention.' Images and stories contribute to a politician or situation's vibe – and that's what voters are really reacting to, not necessarily the truth per se. Fan creativity disrupts the optics those at the top are so careful to preserve and creates their own, where they can dream of bringing a different politics into being.

All of this fan creativity comes from love, and passionate commitment to the hope offered by new ideas. Even when times are very dark. The fans telling stories, whether it's to help someone they support to get elected or undermine someone they see doing harm, are doing it because they care. There is no cool detachment from politics or from the world. They are passionately engaged with both. While nearly half of the UK population think they have no influence at all in national decision-making, creative fans give me hope. If sometimes it feels like the much-venerated grownups of moderate politics can only offer more of the same – 'better things aren't possible' – the joy, imagination and absurdity of fans suggest that visions of the future need not be so constrained.

Many creative fans are interested in politics and current affairs as well as their favourite politicians and movements. Both aspects of their fandom are evident in the richness of their creations, which requires engagement with the substance beyond partisan lines. Without passionate and consistent support for a particular viewpoint, they would not feel driven to create and communicate their stories.

Among those who study sport, a debate has been raging for over twenty years about what type of spectator is the good or ideal fan – and if such a fan exists at all. The 'partisan' loves and supports their team no matter what, and the 'purist' approaches each game as a neutral and only continues to support their team (if they have one) if this is justified by their performance. All the talk of people feeling 'politically homeless' over the past few years makes me think of this debate, as the purist approach to politics is sold as sensible and rational in contrast to the partisan fans. Paul Davis, a lecturer in the sociology of sport at the University of Sunderland, makes the point that deep partisans have a real appreciation of excellence in their sport as well as loyalty to their team.[33] The two are interconnected. It's human to enjoy sport (and culture, science, current affairs and more) through following interesting stories and people. Only 19 per cent of voters in the UK don't see themselves as supporters of any political party, according to the Policy Institute at King's College London in July 2021.[34] That makes 81 per cent of UK voters partisans, of a sort. The purists are in the minority, and may not be sensible or rational at all.

6

THE SENSIBLES ARE NOT SENSIBLE

'I'd been fairly apolitical throughout my life, just letting them get on with it as long as the country was run in a reasonably sensible manner,' Finbarr O'Halloran told the *Guardian*, on his way to a People's Vote march in 2019. 'And it's only the craziness of Brexit that's made me mad.'[1] O'Halloran's conversion to enthusiastic participation is not unusual. Politics was patently not 'reasonably sensible', and events over the past decade or so stirred the emotions of many.

Whig politician and philosopher Edmund Burke asked (in a 1775 letter to Charles O'Hara), 'What think you of that political Enthusiasm, which is able to overpower so much religious Fanaticism?' Burke claimed to despise enthusiasm of any kind, which was seen in the eighteenth century as a disturbance of the imagination, even though his political opponents saw him as over-emotional and destructively passionate about politics. In some ways, this prefigured the response to fandom and 'ideology' and signs of partisan commitment to the left or right now. To (crudely) satirize: 'I am sensible and reflective about politics; you are uncritical and ideological.'

There are some fans who don't think they're fans at all, nor vulnerable to manipulation. They're moderate and well informed, not partisan or emotional about politics or current affairs. The 'sensibles', who self-define as liberal and fair-minded and somewhere in the middle. Not all sensible people are sensibles and not all sensibles identify as sensible. What characterizes a sensible is the belief that all elections are won from the centre – sensibles were shocked when suddenly they weren't. Sensibles described themselves as politically homeless from 2015 to 2020. They don't mind the label on the bottle, as long as the politics are sensible. Ed Miliband was too left-wing. Bernie Sanders was too left-wing. Jeremy Corbyn was unthinkable. They opposed Scottish independence in 2014 but would take it now if it meant they could stay in the EU. They loved New Zealand's former Prime Minister Jacinda Ardern and liked Alexandria Ocasio-Cortez until she seemed a bit too extreme.

The psychology of sensiblism is interesting, being as it is full of contradictions. It is reassuring and appealing to be situated at the centre of politics, far from the disturbing extremes, just wanting things to work. The sensible fondness for bipartisan podcasts is understandable: they're in love with politics but embarrassed by emotion and allegiance. Tuning in to podcast *The Rest Is Politics* means they can be knowledgeable and into current affairs but above the fray. Ideas that seem straightforward and inarguable can't possibly be too ideological, as politicians argue when they present them as 'perfectly sensible' in Hansard. This was a common retort for sensible favourite Kenneth Clarke, when his views were challenged.[2] Clarke's *Telegraph* article in July 2023 praising the government's Rwanda immigration plan played on the idea that everyone should agree with him.[3] But if the sensible view is so. . . commonsensical, why is it not as common as they think it should be?

Political commentator Ian Dunt perhaps most perfectly captured the sensible frustration and insensible outbursts of the time in 2022: 'But what we really need in the British political system, and what we sorely lack, is deliberation, evidence-assessment, cautious policy formulation and effective delivery systems. Not a bunch of stick-thin politics nerds shouting: FUCK YOU LOOK AT THE SIZE OF MY DEATH COCK'.[4]

Following the demise of Liz Truss, centrist policy guru Ben Judah posted a statement on Twitter that crystallized the position of many in the Westminster bubble and beyond: 'With Rishi Sunak's elevation to Prime Minister a long period of populist chaos in British politics – defined by Brexit, Boris and Corbyn – draws to a close. The next chapter belongs to Sunak, Starmer and their "sensibles".'[5] Broadcaster Emily Maitlis tweeted in a similar vein, ignoring both Sunak's positions on various issues and his documented role in Johnson's government: 'Sunak tone spot on – talked about "compassion" in his decisions – we haven't heard that word for a long, long time. And bold enough to say he was there to clean up Truss mistakes. No hiding from that.'[6] Later the same day, those sharing the sentiments of Judah and Maitlis were gasping in shock at the appointments Sunak made to his Cabinet. The 'grownups' are repeatedly claimed to have returned, based on little more than a politician's vibes, and yet the chaos continues.

Perhaps the centre is more vibe than truth. The middle has eroded in everything: state, income, housing, employment, health, class, politics, education. It's been happening for a lot longer than most people think, not just since 2016 or 2008 or any other recent Year Zero. Politics professor Rod Rhodes was talking about the hollowing out of the state in a famous academic paper in 1994, where he showed that governments were shifting their responsibilities upwards to supranational bodies like the EU, downwards to local authorities and charities and sideways to the private sector.[7] The (centrist) New Labour commitment to public-private partnerships has come home to roost in recent years, hollowing out the NHS as struggling hospital trusts have to pay millions of pounds[8] in interest charges from companies for private finance initiative contracts.

Did anyone actually govern from the centre, or just run from there? Clinton and Obama weren't consistent centrist politicians, nor were Blair and Cameron – all moved to the right. To return to the incoherence of sensiblism, Obama criticized the US's Covid response in a virtual commencement address in May 2020: 'You know, all those adults that you used to think were in charge and knew what they were doing, turns out they don't have all the answers. A lot of them aren't even asking the right questions.' In 2016, he had been so sure that Trump would lose that he stated voters would 'make a sensible choice in the end'. That there may be no grownups to save us nor sensible choices to be made is a thought never considered.

When did fandom explode? After 2015. Why did fandom explode? Not just because Donald Trump and Nigel Farage and Jeremy Corbyn turned up – sensiblism had already died. Why is misinformation part of the sensible story? Not just because of foreign state actors weaponizing information online.

If left and right are too extreme, then the centre is a reasonable place to be and where most of the public are most of the time. But do sensibles have the same views as the majority of the public? No, because the people and ideas they like aren't winning elections. They want to go back to when Tony Blair was still in power and they have used the campaign to remain in, or rejoin, the European Union as a proxy for returning to how things used to be. The good old days, when they were on top and nobody complained. This might sound mean, and it's not meant to be. Most people would like things to be less fraught and for the march of reactionary forces to stop winning. But we can't look back to the past, a time with very different economic and social conditions, to move forwards. If the chaos now is a reaction to the politics of the 1990s and 2000s, which weren't good for everyone, it is not a good idea to try to recreate that time.

'In our time,' wrote tech billionaire and Trump supporter Peter Thiel, 'the great task for libertarians is to find an escape from politics in all its forms – from the totalitarian and fundamentalist catastrophes to the unthinking demos that guides so-called "social democracy."'[9] The only difference between Thiel's vision and that of the sensibles is the latter group often really like elections. They are huge fans of them as events. 'I love elections. I love the massive, mad, manic effort of it all for just a few short weeks,' wrote former political commentator and current policy adviser Alice Miles.[10] 'I love seeing politicians go "talking to ordinary people", pursued only by five television cameras and 35 reporters.'

The sensibles had enjoyed politics in a depoliticized form, following election cycles as though they were the Olympics or a World Cup in a different time zone – choosing favourites to follow, keeping odd hours for a few weeks and then going back to their regular lives because, like O'Halloran at the start of this chapter, they were happy to let the politicians get on with it until Brexit upset them. Ah, the thrills of the post-Thatcher/Reagan consensus period. . . the sensibles' glory days. Arguments about whether or not neoliberalism and neoconservativism were real. Cool Britannia. Statues of Tony and Bill. Baby boys in Kosovo being named Tonibler and Klinton.[11] The Coalition and 'Call Me Dave'. Obama and hope. Hug a hoodie. London 2012. Nobody mention the wars. This is the period the sensibles hark back to, even those who were barely alive in 1997.

Fandom is largely a response to status threat and uncertainty so it's fair that fans of the Third Way/Blairism/centrism felt threatened by the end of the politics they loved. The drama of 2015–20 makes the uncertainty even harder for everyone to bear. What makes the sensibles different from other fans? Centralized government, technocracy, minimal social unrest and politics without conflict means little room for disagreement or emotion. Sensible policy preferences are what set us up for fandom culture, by keeping lots of people out of politics.

When I wrote about hardcore Remainers and Leavers acting like pop fans for *The Times*, I was predictably attacked by both sides. The most committed Leavers made ad hominem comments about my appearance. A segment of Remainers, often using the #FBPE hashtag on Twitter, objected to the idea that they could be fans at all. They told me they held the only sensible views and it was only silly and weird to be a Brexiteer.

The fact that I wasn't saying either side were fannish for their political beliefs but instead for how they behaved passed them by. I wrote about the online skirmishes defending their respective positions, using hashtags to find community, vociferous praise for their favourite politicians and activists and unusual activities such as crowdfunding in support of a singer of pro-EU songs and creating giant fibreglass effigies of Theresa May for protests. All of that matches our understanding of fandom: identity (they strongly identified as sensible centrists and pro-Remain); community (they found others like them and drew strength and enjoyment from that); and intention (they joined in with these others by choice, rather than being put into a category by other people).

New fandoms popped up that solely appealed to the sensibles' end of the Remainer contingent. EU Supergirl (Madeleina Kay) was a viral social media star of the pro-EU movement, and a vehicle for the hopes of those who put their faith in youth. She managed to crowdfund thousands of pounds for her anti-Brexit art, Remainer songs and travels around Europe. Led By Donkeys also crowdfunded thousands for billboards and stunts featuring Brexiteer tweets. Justen Hyde crowdfunded thousands to send every MP a copy of Ian Dunt's book *Brexit: What the Hell Happens Now?* Femi Oluwole crowdfunded thousands for his campaigning work and Our Future Our Choice youth Remain group. I'm sure you can spot a theme.

The king for the sensibles, the don, the best politician of all time, is Tony Blair. Things were never the same for the sensibles with Gordon Brown, but they liked a lot of the Cabinet and loved the early days of the Coalition and David Cameron. Their warmth for Bill Clinton has mostly been transferred to Hillary, post-Lewinsky, and they adore the whole Obama family. Like many people, even I have residual warmth for some New Labour politicians. I grew up with them. They're like distant family members. Sensibles, however, will defend Blair furiously in response to criticism, whatever he's done.

'Steering a course of stability in an uncertain world, that is the right strategy for the long-term and we will pursue it. So stability

– that is my message tonight,' said Tony Blair, speaking at the Lord Mayor's Banquet in 1998. 'It may not be sexy enough for the headline writers but in my view, stability is a sexy thing.' Sensibles agreed. They were excited by the idea of Theresa May as Prime Minister because she wanted a 'strong and stable' government. Her lack of sexy stability and the bad management of Brexit eventually let them down. They had to keep chasing the dream of going back to normal, whether it was marching for a People's Vote, starting new centrist parties or shouting 'come back Tony!'

In fairness to Sir Tony, he had a great run in his first term as Prime Minister and there were a lot of factors driving fandom in that period. The UK was so tired of the Tories and the Tories so tired of life that Labour leader John Smith would likely have been the next Labour Prime Minister, had he not died suddenly in 1994. There was a big swell of good will behind the party when Blair replaced Smith. As political commentator Steve Richards puts it, 'In the space of a few hours Tony Blair moved from being a young Shadow Cabinet member with no experience of government to being a Prime Minister in waiting.'[12] Blair himself has a line he likes to use about starting government at your most popular and least capable and leaving at your most capable but least popular. He was signing autographs for fans outside supermarkets and cheering while being cheered at the football during Euro '96.

Britain was riding high on 'Cool Britannia' confidence when New Labour were elected in 1997 and the Gen Xers and old millennials that make up most of the sensibles today were voting for the first or second time. Blair was portrayed as cool and young, the sun was hot, and it was all very intoxicating. There was chat of the Lib Dems going into coalition with Labour, and Roy Jenkins was dispatched to look at electoral reform. Many voters for smaller parties lent Labour their vote in that election and it made the landslide victory look like a personal endorsement. Getting the Tories out was euphoric. Something new was afoot.

Reflecting in his autobiography, Blair justified his continuation of many of Thatcher's reforms, in the face of anger from those who wanted a complete break from Conservatism:

> Because political power is the outcome of a political fight – 'our' ideas, platform policies against 'theirs' – the inclination is to treat the business of government as the closing of the door on the old home and moving to somewhere new. . . Unfortunately that education [learning how to govern] is inconsistent with the way politics is conducted. In an age in which objectives are often shared and it is policy that is crucial, where the issue is often not right or left but, as I have said earlier, right or wrong, this is a significant democratic disadvantage.[13]

What some sensibles took from Blair's philosophy is that only Tony Blair or a copy of Tony Blair can win elections for Labour and that it's only worth beating a specific kind of Conservative Party – one that is as worn out as the end of Major's government, or one that is pro-Brexit. They are fans of New Labour but not Labour or the left, and many of the younger sensibles were Conservatives from the start. Will, an anonymous political aide during the Cameron era who was profiled in the *Guardian*, typifies the sensible attitude from the right. In 2019, he expressed his horror at the 'ideological project' of Boris Johnson's Tories but still couldn't back Labour: 'Even if it was soft left, if they were the grownups in the room I'd vote for them. But this is what's happening because of Corbyn; this crisis is only a crisis because there isn't an opposition that could take over. I'd vote for anything that was broadly sensible.'[14]

Emily Robinson, a lecturer in politics at the University of Sussex, says that the 'progressive' label embraced by so many of the sensibles presents change as inevitable – just keeping up to date – rather than something we fight for. Perhaps that's why those who self-describe as moderate and progressive find fans of other politics so distasteful. Citizens don't get to thrash through what we need and want from changes to society because 'social and political reform is therefore imagined as simply appropriate to a particular time and place'.[15] One of the hallmarks of New Labour and the Coalition was handing over large chunks of policymaking to the 'experts', whether they were Tony Blair's sofa government or George Osborne's bankers.[16] Those governments steered clear of discussing anything with the public or even in the House of Commons, where possible – never mind giving their members and fans a say. It sounds an awful lot like Plato's idea of politics – leave the politicking to experts and philosopher kings and let change happen to people. Taking that feeling of a voice in policy away from voters can lead people to some strange places. The sensibles only wanted to kick back against the system in 2015, when they stopped being the people in control. Jeremy Corbyn was elected as leader of the Labour Party, instead of sensible favourite Yvette Cooper, and that was followed by Brexit and Trump and other decisions that didn't go their way.

While Jeremy Corbyn was beyond the pale for the sensibles, a complete break with the era to which they were devoted, they hadn't been keen on Ed Miliband either. Former Labour MP Chris Mullin spoke for all of them when he criticized Miliband's Shadow Cabinet in 2013 for featuring too few of their Blairite faves: 'Personally, I would bring back some of the grownups.'[17] Relief that the 'grownups' or 'adults' were back was common from sensible commentators when Keir Starmer was selected as Labour leader and Joe Biden won the US presidential election in 2020, and then when Rishi Sunak became Prime Minister.

Sensible grandee Michael Heseltine told the *Financial Times* that he could see Sunak was 'getting down to the hard nitty-gritty of trying to work out solutions'. He added: 'The adults are back in charge.'[18] Perhaps this language is so popular around Westminster because people are desperate for relief from the uncertainty and chaos, and they want it to be true. Trade minister Kemi Badenoch claimed that 'Scottish businesses are happy with what we are doing, and in particular they are happy that the grown-ups in Westminster have stopped them making the catastrophic decisions that are destroying the internal market.'[19]

Sensible and grownup and centrist and moderate contrasts with radical and ridiculous and partisan and extreme. The not-sensibles. You can see how a problem might start to brew. Will and co.'s satisfaction with any politics within a particular range, regardless of the vast differences in the way the country is run and experienced under different governments, validates the view that all mainstream politicians are broadly the same. This view was held by both those who thought all the politicians were okay and those who thought they were all bastards.

'We have cleared out the deadwood of outdated ideology, policy and organisation,' wrote Tony Blair in 1996, meaning the left and many in the old trade unionist right of the party, 'and made the party relevant again to many thoughtful people who want to vote for a credible alternative to the Conservative party.'[20] The people Blair didn't think were thoughtful eventually got fed up of being told they were wrong. When the thoughtful people – Blairites – lost control of the Labour Party to the left, they started to sound a lot less thoughtful.

Blair wrote this in an article called 'Ideological Blurring'. He went on to say, 'The totalizing ideologies of left and right no longer hold much purchase.' It led Leo Abse to dub him 'Tony Blur', pre-dating all the Tony B-Liar anti-fandom monikers that came out of the Iraq War.[21] Blair asserted that 'the task is to combat apathy and disillusionment with politics without sacrificing realism and credibility'. It is possible that the limits of 'realism' can't help but lead to apathy for those who don't support your programme. But apathy isn't sensible; Blair was clearly saying so. All those feelings after the sensibles stopped winning needed somewhere to go.

At a Liberal Democrat leadership hustings after Vince Cable resigned in 2019, I was unsurprised to find that the new Lib Dem member influx also included a lot of people who had previously been members of other parties. Party members are serial joiners. Many were pro-EU sensibles, who revealed themselves in their questions to hopefuls Jo Swinson and Ed Davey. In many cases, these new members attacked left-wingers and blamed them for political discord and for Brexit. The long-time members asked questions about liberalism, party democracy and climate change instead, or joined me in admiring a beautiful golden-coated assistance dog at the front of the room.

One former Conservative Party member had more of a comment than a question: that the world had gone mad and we just needed a proper centrist party to unite the country and sort everything out. He had joined the Lib Dems instead of one of the new parties, because he felt that wouldn't work in the First Past the Post voting system, solely to stop Brexit. A woman who had left the Labour Party under Corbyn agreed vociferously and asked what the candidates would do to stop Russian automated social media accounts, or bots, from stealing elections and misleading the public. The belief that foreign interference was the real reason for the wins of Brexit and Donald Trump was just one of many reassuring fantasies I heard over and over at pro-EU events. An attendee at a Fabians conference, frantically taking notes in a leather-bound book, wanted to know why Labour weren't telling Leavers loudly enough that they had been lied to and brainwashed by social media. MP Kate Green explained that her constituents in Greater Manchester had mostly voted Leave and that many of them had good reasons to do so, so patronizing them wasn't helpful. 'I'm not,' said the attendee. 'It's just obvious that no sane person would have backed Brexit.'

A man on the front row was upset that it was against the rules of Labour to back another party: 'I would vote for any party that promised to keep us in the EU and get rid of all this poisonous hard left ideology.' He meant Change UK – The Independent Group – a newly formed centrist party comprising MPs who'd left other parties in February 2019. I went to a rally in Sheffield, which was held in a wine bar in Kelham Island, and the speeches mostly called for sensible politics, remaining in the EU and an end to left and right extremism. Former Labour MP Chris Leslie attacked ideology. It wasn't very busy, but we were all given free t-shirts with an abstract logo of black stripes on a white background. Former Conservative MP Anna Soubry got the biggest cheers, via a pre-recorded video, and the former Labour and Conservative councillors and MPs in the room clearly just wanted their old political lives back pre-Corbyn and Brexit. Change it was not, and the public weren't with them either as they failed to win either seats or a significant percentage of the vote anywhere they stood for election. The party later collapsed acrimoniously, with several former MPs standing for the Liberal Democrats, before being readmitted to the Labour Party.

Actor Eddie Marsan, a leading advocate for sensible politics, tweeted at the height of Brexit fervour in August 2018: 'If I was running a GE campaign for a new centrist party, the Party political broadcast would just be a re run of the 2012 Olympic opening ceremony, with the words "Make Britain Great Again" at the end.'[22]

I call the London 2012 Olympics the end of the Long '90s. The opening ceremony holds a special place in the hearts of sensibles. It has its own fandom that regularly resurfaces on social media and in conversation, uniting the base in love for a time when we were better than this. Nostalgia for 2012 says something about how sensibles view the country: a place where, as the character Ian Fletcher would say in Olympic mockumentary *Twenty Twelve*, 'Everything is fine'. A sensible country that then was broken by Corbyn, Brexit, Johnson and Trump. Ceremony producer Tracey Seaward told the *Guardian* in 2022 that 'there was this moment that we were holding in our hand like a treasure, and that has been over the 10 years, picked apart'.[23]

Many right-wingers were furious during the original broadcast of the ceremony. Aidan Burley, then a Conservative MP best known for dressing up as a Nazi, went viral on Twitter for hating it. 'The most leftie opening ceremony I have ever seen – more than Beijing, the capital of a communist state! Welfare tribute next?' A minute later Burley tweeted: 'Thank God the athletes have arrived! Now we can move on from leftie multicultural crap. Bring back red arrows, Shakespeare and the Stones!'[24]

There is nothing wrong with the feelgood story of *Isle of Wonder*, as it was known, written by screenwriter and novelist Frank Cottrell-Boyce and directed by film director Danny Boyle. The ceremony did its job perfectly and annoyed all the right people by choosing to represent parts of history that are normally left out of civic celebrations. However, that 'moment' contrasted with the cost and controversy of hosting the event, the austerity measures of the Coalition government and the social unrest that was more characteristic of the time, such as the riots in English cities in August 2011 and anti-cuts marches in London and elsewhere the same year. Disabled people even protested at the Paralympics just weeks after the ceremony. 2012 as a better time is a comforting myth, but it requires not remembering what it was really like.

Fantasies are alluring. The RS Archer Twitter account at its peak had over 113,000 followers, and has still retained over two thirds of his fans – mostly sensible-identifying Remainers. He built up a base from tweeting stories mocking the antics of Brexiteers in France, where the details rarely added up and the dialogue failed to ring true. Archer lovers overlook the offensiveness of some of the posts because they don't like Leavers. Fans said in 2020 that if the tweets were made into a book, they'd buy it. The author claims he won't share his real name out of fear of 'Brexit extremists', but little about his account is real.

Creators of viral narratives, whether on X or Facebook, usually do so for the attention and the boost in self-esteem they experience when they get high engagement numbers. They and those who share their content want to feel that they are part of something and in on the truth. Sometimes, perhaps, they believe what they are saying, or can convince themselves they do. Readers often say that they never believed the stories, just enjoyed them, and that no harm was done. However, stories that are openly fictional do not get anywhere near as much traction – even when written by famous authors experimenting with online formats. Large amounts of engagement have been won by 'true' stories – often in the form of long social media threads (multiple linked posts) – that are later revealed to be made up. What makes them addictive is that you believe that they are true and log in for the next instalment as the story unfolds in real time. It's like a friend telling you gossip or listening to your neighbours having a row. In 2019, anonymous account @sixthformpoet shared a detailed account of laying flowers on the neglected grave of a man who he later found out had killed his wife and her parents. @sixthformpoet claimed that he met his now wife – purportedly the niece and granddaughter of the deceased – when instead placing flowers on the graves of the victims. His story could not be corroborated,[25] but those who shared it mostly believed his lengthy and emotive tale.

It's a short hop from romanticizing the past and enjoying stories that feel true but aren't to sharing damaging misinformation and conspiracy theories. Australian MP Daniel Andrews picked up a lot of sensible fans as Premier (head of government) of Victoria, not least as a result of his response to the Covid-19 pandemic.

'Dan Stans' are well known for having a go at journalists and commentators, mostly female, who criticize their man. Even his wife Catherine got very into the #IStandWithDan fandom – she was spotted having liked hundreds of tweets on the hashtag, including ones that attacked individuals by name. Anti-fans of Andrews and the government also tried to make #DictatorDan and #ChairmanDan happen but were drowned out by the stans. A study into the various hashtags found that only a small number of people were actually tweeting #IStandWithDan, but they were very active in responding to any criticism to reshape and control the story of his handling of the pandemic.[26]

The numbers of Twitter accounts tweeting for and against Andrews were almost on par, but the researchers found that the negative hashtags had lots of sockpuppet accounts – accounts set up to distort and manipulate public opinion. Sockpuppet accounts are anonymous or have made-up identities. They use fake images for profile photos, or pictures of pets or historical/fictional characters, and often are dedicated to a single topic. This use of 'fake' accounts operated by real people to artificially boost the visibility of hashtags is distinct from automated accounts (i.e. bots).

The researchers defined an authentic account as 'an account with sufficient evidence of being a real person or entity, including a profile photo that is not a stock image or stolen from the web (i.e. reverse image search engines show zero results aside from the account itself); tweets that explicitly or implicitly include personal details and post original photos that do not appear elsewhere on the web; and a tweet history that covers a range of topics, even if there are periods of sustained interest in one or two particular topics for a given time period'.

#DictatorDan was started by an Australian opposition MP and used as a nickname for Andrews by Sky News. This gave the hashtag more reach and explains why it picked up partisan media attention beyond genuine anti-fans. After the initial MP and Sky News flurries of tweets, it was mostly tweeted by the right-wing media provocateur Avi Yemini. Yemini co-ordinated his fans to retweet it often, alongside Sinophobic memes and hashtags. A tweet campaigning to keep the #DictatorDan hashtag trending went viral, which made the co-ordinated activity obvious – often the planning of brigading (organized aggressive replies or comments online) activity like this takes place in group chats so that the result looks vaguely authentic.

'The #IStandWithDan supporters probably do have some valid criticism in terms of the level of scrutiny being applied to the premier, compared to, say, the prime minister during this pandemic,' said Jill Stark, a writer who criticized Dan Andrews on Twitter. 'But it seems like it's gone beyond the usual ideological or political tribalism and it has a much more emotional, almost anxious energy to it. Which I think is understandable given that in Melbourne we've been going through a collective trauma in the last few months.'[27]

The #IStandWithDan tweets were mostly from accounts that could be identified as authentic and without signs of co-ordinated activity, just very active defensive fans. In contrast, most of the #IStandWith. . . hashtags that have trended in the UK in recent years have been characterized by co-ordinated campaigns and sockpuppet accounts, plus self-retweeting. The same people also tweet other hashtags opposing LGBTQ+ rights, which researchers proved have been manipulated by a small group of accounts. Graphic designer and activist Alex Gwynne demonstrated that a typical method of manipulation is to quote every tweet on the hashtag, beginning with one or two authentic (albeit often anonymous) accounts tweeting the hashtag. They add the hashtags to their quote tweets but no substantive content. On the occasion showcased by Gwynne, the small group did this eighty-two times in two and a half hours.[28]

Software engineer David Allsopp tracks and reports on all these hashtags and found that a single account tweeted one of the #IStandWith. . . hashtags sixty times in one day in September 2021 and another account retweeted tweets using the hashtag over 220 times the same day.[29] [30] The number of accounts tweeting these hashtags was low and few were authentic, some even new or stolen accounts used for a single brigading campaign and then deleted or suspended, but they were able to game the algorithm to make their defensive fandom visible via Twitter trends. All without affecting their real-world (or even regular anonymous online) identity or reputation.

Well, mostly. Scottish MP Joanna Cherry thanked her fans, believing the group to be large in number, when #IStandWithJoannaCherry trended in November 2021.[31] This came after she appeared to call for conversion therapy to be allowed to remain legal in the case of trans people.[32] As Allsopp said, 'People may be interested to know that 1,000 of the tweets on that hashtag are actually retweets from just 8 accounts, some retweeting over 200 times each. Not quite the grassroots support that it might appear.'[33]

Despite the split in authentic and inauthentic social media activity, there are similarities between the defensive Daniel Andrews fans and the defensive fans of Joanna Cherry. Social media expert and academic Diana Bossio pointed out that there was only a 'very small group of people' who were generating the #IStandWithDan hashtag, which was then retweeted by a larger group. 'For me it is kind of reminiscent of the kind of Trump-like conspiracy theorist, it has echoes of that,' she said. 'Because it's not necessarily the politics or the message, it's actually the political identity and sense of community that plays into that factionalism. Social media is a tool for creating engagement and intimate connection, and sometimes that happens in really uncivil ways.'[34]

Around the time of Brexit, many sensibles fantasized about a new Prime Minister, just as they had fantasized about new political parties. They got their chance when Theresa May was finally toppled by the Tories and resigned, triggering a leadership contest. As is common in the Conservative process, the initial line-up was broad and drew from across the party. Among the rabid Brexiteers and no-hopers, there lay a man to stan. A new lead character for their stories. Rory the Manic Pixie Dream Tory: a riff on the stock movie character of the 'Manic Pixie Dream Girl', who exists solely to inspire and guide sensitive men.

I went walking in Derby with Rory Stewart during his short-lived bid for the crown. The rain poured and the fans were mostly from out of town. We chatted about my PhD and his sadness at losing access to the academic database JSTOR – since restored via his academic affiliation with Harvard University. People pointed out what was wrong with Derby and he nodded sympathetically. He was happy to travel anywhere in Britain where there was interest, to go walking and chatting with the people.

I spoke to two very enthusiastic self-identified Stewart fans – both had just finished their A-level exams and were members of the Liberal Democrats. 'He's competitive, soft, attractive,' said one. 'Truly sincere as well,' said the other. 'A lot of the candidates have very tactical campaigns, whereas Rory just wants to speak to the members.' Not many politicians do let the public speak to them outside of Q&A sessions at hustings, formal events and constituency surgeries, and rarely visit smaller cities and towns outside of election campaigns. Nigel Farage is an exception, and so is Stewart.

Oddness and camp are usually requirements for politics fandom. People say their favourite talks like a normal person – but it is rarely true. Stewart's Blairish habit of speaking slowly with lots of pauses and a posh voice, and his willingness to perform on stage and screen, attracted the sensibles early on. Obviously he had no chance in a party dominated by right-wing populism. Sensible interest resurged when he put his name in the hat for London Mayor and then, after he withdrew from the contest, a video he made early in the coronavirus pandemic made them love him again. It went viral again before the vaccine programme had rolled out. Their very own fantasy Prime Minister. Every now and then he pops up again with a snippet of wisdom to make them sigh, and people who would never vote Tory look at him wistfully once more.

Once Boris Johnson won the contest and became Conservative leader, the howls of the sensibles who hated him (but not as much as they feared Jeremy Corbyn) were hard to ignore. The nail in the coffin for all of their hopes was the collapse of the People's Vote campaign in late 2019, just months before Johnson won the General Election with a large majority. The campaign fought for a second referendum on leaving the European Union. It featured 1990s fan favourites like Peter Mandelson and Alastair Campbell, sought advice from Blair and completely fell apart after a period of glowing media coverage and well-attended marches.

Chair Roland Rudd was nearly couped by Mandelson and Campbell, fired senior campaigners, upset all the staff and had to change the locks on the campaign offices. New director Patrick Heneghan was removed for allegations of sexual harassment. Aside from all that, the primary goal of the People's Vote, and indeed the sensibles, failed – long before Johnson ensured that Britain got a hard Brexit, the referendum campaign had been haemorrhaging support from soft Leavers in favour of a small but fervent group of internationalists who could not accept the original referendum result. The campaign's internal chaos mirrored the incoherent approach of the sensibles themselves: anti-emotion but wildly passionate, convinced they knew what the public really wanted but unable to convince them, desperate to take back control for themselves and their friends.

Henry Mance put it best in the *Financial Times*: 'It showed how to create a noisy minority, or even a narrow majority – but how that's not the same as taking charge. It showed how passion can be poisonous. "I've done oil deals in Russia, and I've never seen anything like it", is how Geeta Sidhu-Robb, a former lawyer and one of Rudd's appointees to the Open Britain board, describes the infighting.'[35]

And so we move to the end of the story. Jeremy Corbyn resigned after the 2019 election and Keir Starmer took the Labour leadership. What could sensibles do once Brexit was done and Corbyn was gone? For a while Covid was a distraction, with its own fandoms for experts and campaigners.

Sensibles ended up caught between shielding Starmer from criticism related to his lack of support for trade union strikes and being upset that he said he wouldn't rejoin the EU or any part of it. When he said 'There's no case to go back to the Single Market, to go back to the Customs Union,' their disappointment was palpable. Joe Biden also let them down by not being enough of a 'grownup' in handling crises as the war in Ukraine raged and Roe vs Wade was reversed in the US. Both failed to do as well in polls as some sensibles thought would have been inevitable after their predecessors departed.

Baroness Hale made a Supreme Court judgment against Boris Johnson for proroguing Parliament and a horde of sensibles immediately added a spider emoji to their Twitter name in tribute to the arachnid brooch she was wearing in court. A star was temporarily born. A t-shirt designed in her honour, featuring a spider, sold over 6,500 units and raised a large sum for charity. I feel a bit sad for American sensibles – and a few Brits – who declared themselves to be 'Cuomosexuals' in early 2020 at the start of the Covid pandemic.[36] Anyone who seemed like they were a proper grownup had sensible appeal and the Democrat New York governor Andrew Cuomo was broadcasting daily in a reassuring voice. 'There's something nice about having someone in government whom you can actually trust,' wrote American writer and political commentator Molly Jong-Fast. 'Yes, Andrew Cuomo may be imperfect, but he's still the closest thing we have to an FDR for our time.'[37] As with Hale, fans bought a lot of merchandise. 'He really made us think that we were going to be OK,' filmmaker Kely Nascimento-DeLuca told the *New York Times*. 'In spite of having very mixed feelings about him and his family, I definitely was a "Cuomosexual" in that moment. . . I wouldn't do that today, obviously. But I feel like it represented a moment in time.'[38]

Fandoms represent moments in time that anchor our lives and our politics. Fandom can't be forced by a party or the media – it has to come from real enthusiasm, and it has to go somewhere and achieve something. In the 2019 General Election campaign, the Liberal Democrats seemed sure that their anti-Brexit stance and young people's love of social media would translate into support for their new leader, Jo Swinson, and usurp Jeremy Corbyn. They built their whole campaign around her and even set up a 'Swinzone selfie zone' at an Edinburgh rally. A photograph of the deserted zone went viral online. Swinson lost her seat. Never enter the Swinzone.

Social psychologist John Jost says not only are humans not rational when we look at the world and make decisions about it, we're irrational in the same sorts of ways.[39] Most of us overrate the established (or sensible) way of doing things and would rather keep what we have than end up with something worse or nothing at all. Our existing beliefs, social networks and ideologies distort our thinking when it comes to political, economic and social systems and make us gullible to justifying inequality to keep things the same. Even minorities under attack can justify the system as it is and blame themselves for not working hard enough or asking for too much when times are hard. It is normal to be anxious about making the wrong decisions in our own lives, but applying that caution to other people's lives affects politics negatively – for example, the Labour Party refusing to drop the Conservative government's two-child policy for child benefit (no benefit is paid out for further children). The cost of repealing the policy is low, and the benefit is to the most vulnerable people in society – children who live in poverty. If the best aspects of fandom fuel positive movements based on hope and progress, the people who think those fans are going too far are at risk of becoming reactionaries. People who are resistant to what they see as too much, too quick or the wrong sort of change in society are attracted to negative movements. Those who scored highest in polling for Right-Wing Authoritarianism (this kind of attitude) in 2016 overwhelmingly voted for Trump.[40]

Journalist and moral panic researcher Michael Hobbes tweeted: 'Reactionary centrism consists of exactly one principle, to wit: The leftists made us do it.'[41] I'll hand over to former House Select Committee communications director Aaron Huertas, who came up with the term in the first place:

> Opinion columnists, influential academics, and think tankers feel a need to occupy a middle ground, even if it's one that is increasingly a product of their own imaginations. As a result, they wind up giving the right wing a free pass or accepting its worst impulses as a reality we have to live with, while reserving their criticism and armchair quarterbacking for anyone to their left. I've come to call these pundits 'reactionary centrists.' *Reactionary centrist (n) – Someone who says they're politically neutral, but who usually punches left while sympathizing with the right.*[42]

In order to still position themselves as reasonable and sensible, reactionary centrists claim that the campaign priorities of marginalized groups are unreasonable demands. The implication is that the campaigners are either fringe extremists or naïve to who is really pushing these ideas – like the popular theory that Brexiteers were duped into voting Leave by Russian bot accounts on social media. The reactionaries pushing this line in liberal media both pick up fans who have been on the same radicalizing journey and influence people who follow them for 'sensible' politics into believing both sides are at fault. Those fighting for and against progress on civil rights are both let down by their extreme fringes and it could all be sorted out with a nice sensible sit down and a chat.

A century ago, the same arguments were made about Black activists and trades unionists in America, fighting for workers' rights and against racism. The establishment claimed they were extremists and a front for a communist revolution, with *New York Times* headlines such as 'REDS TRY TO STIR NEGROES TO REVOLT; Widespread Propaganda on Foot Urging Them to Join I.W.W. [Industrial Workers of the World] and "Left Wing" Socialists'[43] and 'REDS ARE WORKING AMONG NEGROES; Widespread Propaganda by Radical Leaders Known to the Government. TAKES BOLSHEVIST FORM Two of the Negro Propagandists Said to be Harvard Graduates'.[44] It still works now in the US, where antifascist resistance to the far-right is sold as an extremist communist plot (headlines like 'Yes, antifa is the moral equivalent of neo-Nazis'[45]), and in the UK, where Black Lives Matter activists are portrayed as Marxist extremists.

So what? Sensibles are just a fandom, a subset of a group supporting politics that used to be very popular – why do they matter? Sensibles have a lot of institutional power, even if their sway over public views is fading. Leading sensibles come in all shapes and sizes: actors, writers, current and former politicians, senior journalists, heads of institutions and industry commentators.

Many sensibles are fans of American data scientist David Shor and his theory of popularism: progressive/left-wing parties should focus on issues that are electorally popular, instead of social and cultural issues that can be seen as divisive or irrelevant. But their caution, supported by this theory, is holding back Labour and the Democrats from making policy that would change lives and opposing powerful movements attacking civil and workers' rights. Technocracy can't help itself, sometimes, and neither calling your dad (even if he's Tony Blair) to get him to come back or suggesting that technology is the solution will fix all the problems. Sensibles can't see that delegitimizing bolder positions made politicians seem indistinguishable and made those fandoms they despise most – Farage, Trump, Corbyn – happen. The drop in support for centre-ground politics revealed that it was folding in on itself.

Now what? The cycle seemed to start again with the fall of Johnson, with sensibles plumping early for Tom Tugendhat as their new Manic Pixie Dream Tory. But he was unable to get past the first round of MP votes in summer 2022's leadership election, and the affections of some shifted to Rishi Sunak. Others put their heart and soul into defending Keir Starmer from any criticism.

If the sensibles accept that they can't have Tony Blair – despite his regular 'Tonterventions' commenting on policy – or Obama back or replicate them, that would be a productive start. Where can their fandom energy go? All of that giddiness about watching Brexit votes on BBC Parliament and marching for a People's Vote and excitedly sharing information has some value. What positive things can be done with sensiblism? It is possible that they could embrace their internationalism and desire for fair play to strengthen and defend institutions and civil society organizations that are currently under attack. That's both sensible and grownup and they have the tools (including resources, they mobilize well) and the relationships – thanks to fandom and the community of sensible enthusiasts – to achieve those goals.

One of the sadder things about the decline of the sensibles has been watching well-known people break character and become radicalized in real time. There's been a slide into sharing misinformation, conspiracy theories and culture war nonsense. Big names from culture, sport and academia. It used to be mostly harmless: conference appearances, Downing Street receptions, an article for a newspaper, a big donation or a role in party political broadcasts. Mirroring the rest of society, some struggled with the political turmoil of the past few years and became drawn to harmful fandoms, conspiracy theories and moral panics. These big names have lots of followers online, due to their fame, and they use the power and reach of that network to promote ideas. Former footballers, novelty pop stars and influential thinkers who you'd expect to be genuinely sensible have spread misinformation about Covid, Brexit, Ukraine and social justice issues to a huge audience. However, positive uses of social media still emerge from sometimes surprising places. TV property expert Kirstie Allsopp has gone all out defending trans rights, and celebrity mathematician Carol Vorderman recently discovered her political voice and has been holding both the government and conspiracy theorists to account.

7

WHEN FANS GO BAD

I feel my stomach lurch like I'm going down a big rollercoaster drop whenever a group of fans comes for me online. I write about topics that can divide opinion and sometimes people object to the things that I say, but my aim is never to wind people up. Unfortunately, there are people who get a kick out of aggressive social media interactions, particularly when they involve politics. They act like posting and 'pwning' (slang for owning, or beating, your opponent) is a useful form of activism, likely because it makes them feel like they are attacking the 'enemy'.

Writer Sunny Moraine captures some of the appeal of fighting on social media: 'I honestly wonder if part of the reason why we're so eager to do pile-ons is that we are STARVED for any sort of consequences for bad behavior on the elite level so we're inclined to go for what we feel is attainable'.[1] If dishonest government ministers will not resign and former presidents aren't jailed, an everyday citizen might feel that the only way to make the world feel less unfair is to make a stranger pay for upsetting them online. Social media's reputation for holding power to account can give the 'little people' back some agency, whether by trying to resolve customer service issues or calling out a sexual predator.

Internet-cultures expert Alice Marwick researched victims of online harassment. She found that there is a specific impulse behind harassment by a group connected via social media – she calls it 'morally motivated networked harassment'.[2] It begins when a member of the social network or group (or fandom) accuses a specific target (person, brand or organization) of going against the network's norms. This accusation triggers moral outrage, which motivates the network to send harassing messages to the target to enforce the norm. As Marwick says: 'Members of the amplifiers' *networked audience*, who share an ideological or moral framework, individually send ad hominem attacks, insults, slurs, and in the worst cases, threats of death, rape, and violence to the accused'.

If the network can't send hate via replies directly to the target – if they are all blocked on social media, for example – they will be angry and they won't stop. They often set up multiple alternative accounts solely for harassment, try to access the target on other platforms, harass the target's friends and family and professional network, and make frequent posts about the target instead. The 'crime' of going against the group doesn't just motivate the harassment but also justifies anything the group does to the target. Research shows that online social networks learn from each other what to be angry about and what's an acceptable way to react. In networks where people express moral outrage more often, individual members learn to ignore people outside the group, telling them that they are bullies or going too far because they have internalized what is normal for their network.[3]

I have experienced this type of harassment. An article I wrote about hate memes on pro-Brexit social media led to me receiving a lengthy email saying I deserved to 'go the same way as Jo Cox' (the MP murdered by a far-right extremist in 2016). I had to ask my university to remove my email address from their website as a result. In this case, Brexit fans used their shared worldview ('We want Brexit'), object of fandom (Brexit itself), and defensive identity (they believed their perspective was being unfairly treated or silenced by the majority) to morally justify their behaviour and to scare and dehumanize me.

Without knowing how fandom in politics works, it would be hard to understand why someone would join in co-ordinated activity and go that far to defend their views unless they were paid or brainwashed. Furthermore, it seems contradictory to try to have someone sacked or their work destroyed in the name of free speech – yet it happens often. Criticism in the eyes of these fans is an attack on free speech that must be silenced. However, having a common enemy helps the group reinforce their views and their sense of security within the network, and being part of the network can be actively enjoyable – affirming, even. So the behaviour continues.

Any individual or group of fans can become toxic, but some fandoms are more prone to overall toxicity than others because of a dominant demographic or the behaviour modelled by their idols. Gamergate was an online harassment campaign in 2014 and 2015 that targeted women in the video game industry as a right-wing backlash against feminism, political correctness, diversity, inclusion and more in video game culture. It was co-ordinated via anonymous message boards and had real-world consequences for the women at the centre of the attacks.

Sports journalist Kyle Wagner predicted this would be how the culture wars would play out in an article about Gamergate, which he described as 'all the rhetorical weaponry and siegecraft of an internet comment section brought to bear on our culture, not just at the fringes but at the center. What we're seeing now is a rehearsal, where the mechanisms of a toxic and inhumane politics are being tested and improved. . . all of them working feverishly in service of the old idea that nothing should ever really change.'[4]

The Gamergate boycotters contacted companies who advertised on video-game-focused websites that had published articles with a social justice or pro-feminist take on gaming, in some cases successfully persuading them to remove their financial support.[5] Some of the boycott instruction manuals are still online at Google Docs and Pastebin.

The tactics of the fans involved in Gamergate are now commonplace: '"Daily boycotters", for example, are instructed not just to email targeted companies to express their grievances, but to spam these targets on Sundays and Wednesdays to maximize congestion – shit up the Monday-morning rush and dogpile in the middle of the week so the mess has to be addressed before the weekend. They're told never to use the actual term "Gamergate", as that will allow the message to be filtered.'[6]

Groups like Stop Funding Hate target advertisers to achieve more positive goals, such as persuading advertisers that their brands shouldn't appear alongside negative articles about immigrants or LGBTQ+ people, or in publications that 'stoke hate and division'.[7] However, a more common use of the targeting tactic is for boycotters to bombard organizations who use racially diverse and LGBTQ+ inclusive language and imagery, or who feature transgender and gender non-conforming people in their advertising or content.

In 2023, there was a flashpoint around a partnership between transgender influencer Dylan Mulvaney and the beer brand Bud Light.[8] While the partnership did not extend beyond Mulvaney being sent a personalized beer can to celebrate her first transition anniversary, which she displayed in a sponsored Instagram video, the brewer behind Bud Light (Anheuser-Busch) revealed that sales fell as a result of a boycott led by right-wing celebrities and influencers.[9] Other brands were mocked and threatened with the 'Bud Light' treatment in social media comments and on conservative TV broadcasts if they made socially progressive posts on social media or used inclusive language in communications.

In November 2021, a Milton Keynes chicken restaurant was bombarded with phone calls and social media posts calling their staff 'racist'. This was because the restaurant's racially diverse staff refused to serve the far-right activist Tommy Robinson. Within twenty-four hours, Wing Kingz were hit with over a thousand bad reviews from customers who had never been there, dropping their star rating from five stars to two.[10] Robinson repeatedly posted on the social media site Telegram complaining about the support Wing Kingz received from local press and anti-racist groups. However, he minimized his actions while urging fans to keep up the harassment after the restaurant released a statement about the incident. He tweeted: 'So "wing kingz" refused to serve me food for my children, a few bad reviews were given online by people who seen and heard about it, and THEY call the police in and play the "victim", couldn't make it up, let them know how you feel about this ludicrous statement they just put out'.[11]

Robinson is widely perceived as an extreme figure with extreme views. Other politicians and activists may be closer to the mainstream, but they too have divisive views and either consciously direct their fans to act in particular ways or make unguarded statements without thinking about how their fans might respond. If a leading campaigner on a contentious issue complains about a business, journalist or even an individual social media account, they can send the most toxic of their fans on a hunt for revenge without even trying to. Making a 'don't harass them' comment in the wake of their complaint is not likely to hold many back.

Much less controversial figures have fans who act just as badly with no provocation.[12] My go-to example of this category of toxic fandom comes from outside politics, in the popular cartoon *Rick and Morty*. A McDonald's limited-edition sauce, available briefly in 1998 to promote Disney's film *Mulan*, was featured in the first episode of the third season of *Rick and Morty*, 'The Rickshank Rickdemption', which premiered in April 2017. McDonald's decided to bring the Szechuan sauce back for one day as a PR stunt in October 2017 but didn't produce enough to meet demand. Thousands of *Rick and Morty* fans queued up at stores to get the sauce and were disappointed. Most just went home sad and maybe posted about it online. At multiple stores, however, the fans were intimidating McDonald's workers by chanting about the sauce and reacting angrily.[13] One vlogger claimed that a group of fans jumped on the counter and snatched the remaining sauce supplies.[14]

This was not the worst toxic fandom incident for *Rick and Morty* that year. Fans disappointed in the third series of the show harassed and doxed (the act of distributing someone's personal information against that person's will as a form of retribution) two of the show's female writers who wrote episodes of the show they didn't like.

Co-creator Dan Harmon was horrified and in an interview for *Entertainment Weekly* he had strong words for these fans:

> These knobs that want to protect the content they think they own – and somehow combine that with their need to be proud of something they have, which is often only their race or gender. It's offensive to me as someone who was born male and white, and still works way harder than them, that there's some white male [fan out there] trying to further some creepy agenda by 'protecting' my work. I've made no bones about the fact that I loathe these people. It f—ing sucks. And the only thing I can say is if you're lucky enough to make a show that is really good that people like, that means some bad people are going to like it too. You can't just insist that everybody who watches your show get their head on straight. . . And I'm speaking for myself – I don't want the show to have a political stance. But at the same time, individually, these [harassers] aren't politicians and don't represent politics. They represent some shit that I probably believed when I was 15.[15]

Harmon points out the toxic combination of a sense of ownership over something they didn't make, an entitlement to control over its direction, and the desire to protect both the object of their fandom and the aspects of their (dominant group) identity they feel are under threat. This is common in politics too. Toxic fans will not just share and discuss their views, but attack and harass individuals and organizations. They do it to defend the honour of things they view as sacred or to emphasize their objection to policy changes, political decisions, media coverage, and outreach to groups they don't like. Sometimes these toxic fans are themselves politically powerful: they are journalists, commentators, backbench politicians, elected officials, representatives of influential think tanks, celebrities and academics.

Here is one such example from Trump loyalist Republican Senator Ron Johnson. 'Do I expect Democrats to follow the rules?' said Johnson, who called in November 2021 for Wisconsin lawmakers to ignore the findings of the bipartisan Federal Election Commission. 'Unfortunately, I probably don't expect them to follow the rules. And other people don't either, and that's the problem.'[16] [17] Here, Johnson neatly discredits Trump's opponents as untrustworthy rulebreakers.

Have you ever looked up something online and found it hard to get an answer you can trust? Michael Golebiewski, a senior manager at Microsoft, coined the term 'data void' in May 2018 to describe search engine queries that turn up few or no results, especially when the query is for something new or obscure. In the early days of the Covid-19 pandemic, there wasn't much reliable information to be found and the public were desperate for answers to their questions. A data void had been created. Lots of people and organizations tried to fill the information gap by writing news articles and social media posts and adding commentary – sometimes helpfully, sometimes less so. Some deliberately published biased or factually incorrect content either to further a viewpoint or because they got lots of engagement online. These opportunists used the data void and disagreements between scientists to undermine confidence in expertise and acceptance of vaccines.

When an issue becomes a hot topic, data voids can be weaponized to confuse the public into thinking that 'both sides are extreme' by presenting the most partisan and emotive examples. They can also be used to manipulate audiences when a story breaks to create further confusion. For example, in October 2022 a man broke into the home of US House of Representatives Speaker Nancy Pelosi and attacked her husband, Paul.[18] It took some time to establish the full facts and initial reports were sparse. Conservative websites and right-wing social media accounts fed the public's thirst for information by publishing conspiracy theories and speculation about Pelosi's alleged attacker and his motivations. Search results for the attacker or victim's name were flooded with misinformation. The outcome was that within a few days, many Republican Party supporters came to believe in a conspiracy theory claiming that Paul Pelosi was attacked by his left-wing gay lover. Elon Musk tweeted a link to a dodgy website repeating this conspiracy theory, and many people shared his tweet before it was deleted. The alleged attacker had actually been posting extreme right-wing content for years and claimed to have been radicalized by Gamergate in 2014.

Toxic fans will find and use the content made by their leaders and others in their fandom to fill data voids by replying to people who ask questions on social media and boosting misinformation. If there are few highly visible (mainstream media, top-of-search-engine results) sources on a topic that outsiders will readily trust, this helps toxic fans to undermine narratives they don't like (and so boost their own viewpoint).

As with any organization or relationship, fandoms are strengthened by shared values and resources. An individual's status in a fandom, their sense of community belonging and their fannish feelings get more intense through sharing information, analysis, language and culture. Fans can also feel more purposeful and intelligent and as if they are doing right by their politics when they create and share information and memes that are seen as credible to defend their position and attack others. Data voids are not just useful to terrorists and state-backed interference, but to anyone who wants to manipulate others and influence politics. Misinformation is a powerful weapon in the wrong hands, and data voids are part of a range of techniques used by both politicians and fans.

'These vicious claims about me of inappropriate conduct with women are totally and absolutely false,' said Donald Trump in 2016, *denying* accusations of sexual assault.[19] He continued with an *attack* on the Clintons, who published the claims: 'These claims are all fabricated. They're pure fiction and they're outright lies. These events never, ever happened and the people who said them meekly fully understand.' Trump *reversed* the story, to explain that he was the *victim* of a smear campaign: 'These false attacks are absolutely hurtful. To be lied about, to be slandered, to be smeared so publicly, and before your family that you love, is very painful.' Trump turned his fire back on Hillary Clinton, reminding everyone that she was the real *offender*: 'Hillary Clinton is guilty of all the things that Director Comey stated at his press conference and Congressional hearings and far more.' Finally, he reminded his fans that the pain is worthwhile: 'Nevertheless, I take all of these slings and arrows gladly for you. I take them for our movement so that we can have our country back.'

Trump's strategy in this Florida speech is a classic example of DARVO, which stands for Deny, Attack, and Reverse Victim and Offender.[20] DARVO was first identified by psychologist Jennifer Freyd in 1997 as a way of explaining how perpetrators of wrongdoing react when held accountable for their behaviour. Trump was accused of wrongdoing, denied anything happened, attacked the person confronting him and reversed the victim and the offender roles in his story. A bully often portrays their victim as a liar – as Trump did with the women making the claims and the Clintons for sharing them. His fans mirrored his reaction in his defence. TV personality and self-confessed 'Trumpette' Rhonda Shear told ABC News: 'I was mortified that the tape came out. At that time I felt like, "Wow, you know, if Pence perhaps was the presidential candidate, then maybe all of this would calm down." No, no, I mean it did calm down for me very quickly. It wasn't a shock what he said. It was a shock it came out. I don't doubt the Hillary campaign put that out'.[21]

It's easier for perpetrators to control the story if they are popular, powerful or from dominant groups, as they have more power in the situation than their accusers. Victims in politics fandoms are often from marginalized groups and are easy to delegitimize. More sophisticated manipulators use the language of advocacy and allyship, like gaslighting and DARVO, as weapons for their own accusations.

Safeguarding is another weapon used by fans to justify their bad behaviour. These fans often accuse their targets of being paedophiles, and their critics of opposing safeguarding for women and children.

According to a 2022 joint report by the Center for Countering Digital Hate and Human Rights Campaign, a small number of social media accounts with high numbers of followers (including Libs of TikTok, Gays Against Groomers, Chris Rufo, Tim Pool and James Lindsay) have become notorious for amplifying 'dangerous lies' about LGBTQ+ people and their allies, which have resulted in both online and offline harassment and abuse.[22] One slur, 'groomer' (suggesting that the recipient is grooming children for sexual activity or medical transition or both), has been widely popularized by these accounts. In the month following the passage of the 'Don't Say Gay' law (a bill limiting teaching of gender identity and sexual orientation in primary schools in Florida) in March 2022, the volume of 'grooming' related content on social media increased by 406 per cent. The most powerful of the accounts identified in this report is Libs of TikTok, which operates across multiple platforms but had 2.4 million followers on X and 409,000 followers on Instagram at the time of writing. Libs of TikTok promote a narrative that children and young people are being 'groomed' into homosexuality and what they call 'transgenderism'. Posts created or boosted by this account, run by former real estate agent Chaya Raichik (who is visible in videos of the Capitol Riot), reach huge audiences and often go viral. In August 2021, feminist journalist Julie Bindel said, 'Libs of TikTok is the Millie Tant of the modern day and therefore very funny. Except Millie Tant was a parody' (Millie Tant was a comic character in *Viz* magazine, caricaturing militant feminists). Since 2021, the content of the account has not changed (reposting videos and screenshots to mock or 'expose' anti-racist and LGBTQ+-inclusive social media users, brands, schools, libraries and hospitals), but its reach and influence have grown exponentially.

This influence has led to real-world repercussions. Christina Pushaw, press secretary for Florida governor Ron DeSantis, claimed Libs of TikTok opened her eyes to issues[23] and Raichik has been credited with inspiring the 'Don't Say Gay' law. LGBTQ+ teachers, including non-binary teacher Skye Tooley, have received abuse from Libs of TikTok fans after being targeted and their employers bombarded with calls to remove them from their posts. Tooley says they first received messages from people telling them to 'leave kids alone' after their video was highlighted by the account, which quickly escalated to them 'calling me a "groomer" and using words like "paedophile". . . And then I started getting death threats, whether in my emails, DMs, or in the comments section.'[24]

Most worryingly, Libs of TikTok fans – who are not just individuals following an account but a highly networked and visible community – have made bomb threats to hospitals in Boston, Omaha, Pittsburgh and Washington, DC in 2022[25] and an Oregon medical clinic in 2023. The account highlighted that these facilities were providing healthcare for transgender people, and in the Oregon case they claimed that a cancer patient had been dropped by the clinic for her anti-trans statements, in which she alleged 'as a gender critical woman, who believes gender to be a nonsense, and sexed bodies to be a reality, I do not feel comfortable coming into Richmond with that enormous transgenderism banner hanging like a Nazi flag behind the reception desk'.[26] [27] Libs of TikTok fans were incensed on her behalf, commenting furiously and many taking the opportunity to tag in the clinic and call for it to be shut down.

It might seem like a one-way relationship, with the fans being motivated by their favourites or taking direct instruction to act in harmful ways. However, some political figures are influenced by their fans. Fans regularly make suggestions and develop ideas via social media and their heroes take them on board. This can be a democratic and positive move for politics, if politicians and activists can moderate and critically evaluate the input fans give them. However, it's more often the case that ego and the signal-to-noise ratio get in the way, and bizarre and extreme messages from enthusiasts cut through. A good example of reciprocal influence between fans and favourites is in entrepreneur Elon Musk and his fans.

Musk's wealth and power – and control over the Starlink satellites,[28] key to the war in Ukraine – make him a political figure rather than a harmless eccentric. Musk's fans – the self-styled 'Musketeers' – engage in the usual hardcore fan behaviour of praising him regularly and defending him from attack, to the point of harassing his critics.[29] What is interesting is how responsive Musk can be to their comments. He has implemented feature requests for X and Tesla vehicles[30] and claimed to learn about controversial topics from his fans.

Musk has multiple draws for his fandom: wealth, innovation, memes, free speech, 'anti-woke' views, space travel. . . However, at the heart of it all is a group of people looking for somewhere to belong. The SpaceX (Musk's spacecraft and satellite company) fans who gather at the Rocket Ranch in Texas haven't just found somewhere to watch spaceship launches or talk tech. Fans have found their people. Executive coach and Musk fan Rand Harper 'opened the door and everybody was talking SpaceX and Tesla and the future and immediately I'm like, I'm home'.[31]

'Belonging is stronger than facts,' says the sociologist Zeynep Tufekci. 'The problem is that when we encounter opposing views in the age and context of social media, it's not like reading them in a newspaper while sitting alone. It's like hearing them from the opposing team while sitting with our fellow fans in a football stadium. Online, we're connected with our communities, and we seek approval from our like-minded peers. We bond with our team by yelling at the fans of the other one.'[32]

The combination of rolling TV news and social media means that fans are exposed to extreme views and bad behaviour from politicians, activists and fringe supporters on their side. Their dislike for the other side, who they also see acting up, and feeling of being marginalized can persuade them towards justifying more and more extreme views and actions in a constantly reinforcing feedback loop. As a group of Canadian researchers found in 2020:

> Many partisans may privately struggle with the transgressions and extreme policies of their party elites (from accusations of sexual assault to inhumane border detention conditions), but when faced with the alternatives of rationalizing their party or rejecting it, the latter may be unthinkable to the extent that they believe their opponents to be even more monstrous. This dissonance could push people to double down, excusing even the more egregious policies and scandals that would have seemed unthinkable in the recent past.[33]

Rationalizing the toxic stuff your fandom does, even when it doesn't help you get ahead, beats changing team or giving up the game. That's why we saw such polarization around Kyle Rittenhouse, a teenager who shot protesters in August 2020 following the shooting of African-American Jacob Blake by police in Wisconsin. Many on the right decided that Rittenhouse was not only innocent on self-defence grounds, but also that the protesters should have been shot for protesting against police brutality. He started being offered internships and received calls from supportive major figures who said he could be president one day.[34] [35] [36] Some on the left, meanwhile, spread misinformation that his victims were Black (they were in fact white) to make the story around his guilt and immorality sound even worse. Their posts were fact-checked with corrections, but most people who consume misinformation never see the debunking.[37] [38] [39] Each side felt justified to defend their actions, and Rittenhouse ended up both as a star with his own fans and a villain with antis. The glow of feeling morally right once a side has been taken overrides the rights and wrongs of the specific actions at play.

Some say that many of these conversations wouldn't have happened without social media and that it's easy to opt out from fan wars by not engaging or being less online. But that seems unlikely. Politics fans were publicly arguing with each other, spreading malicious gossip and calling out people who had wronged them in pamphlets and broadside ballads from the moment the printing press was invented until the dawn of radio and television. Fans still send letters and make telephone calls and use media coverage to help fight their wars. As fans took their conflicts onto social media, the main changes were participation level and scale. The impact on those involved remains the same, there's just more of it.

Ultimately if you get caught up in a fan war, it's a conflict involving human beings who feel hurt – and an unpleasant minority who get their thrills from stoking anger. They're doing it in a place where everyone can see it, but also where they find information, happiness and support networks. Staying off social media to avoid being targeted means losing the good as well as the bad. It's like running away from home.

I'm often asked how I cope after fans have come for me. How do I still believe in the goodness of fandoms and not just wish it would disappear? Well, I try to think about how the supporters of harmful movements ended up in that place, as well as remembering the enjoyment and friendships that have come from my own fandoms. We know how the negative fans were won, and I have empathy for those fans – their worries were real, though I don't support their choices.

Moral panics and radicalization are negative fandoms at their most extreme. When negative movements have real money and power behind them, their fans come out from the fringes and impact politics. Political influencers and provocateurs – modelled by Tommy Robinson – will keep emerging. Some will become elected politicians. Many more will influence policy direction (like Nigel Farage).

8

MORAL PANICS AND RADICALIZATION

Misinformation, moral panics and smear campaigns all form part of the business of politics. They're powerful rhetorical weapons – as powerful as networked harassment – and can reach large numbers of people. Fans have cottoned on to this, especially those with access to media and political power, and use these techniques to promote their favourites and delegitimize opponents. In a moral panic, something or someone becomes defined as a threat to society and its values. Those who fear the (exaggerated) threat are seen as worthy of social and political support, and those who don't are portrayed as deviants. In the UK, we often see signs of moral panic in newspapers and political speeches, like the rhetoric around asylum seekers crossing the Channel in small boats.

The moral panic about trans people, stoked by the media and by leaders of the anti-trans movement, works by scaring people into believing that transsexuality is something to be feared and that trans people are dangerous. Moral panics surrounding transness include believing that children are being coerced into sterilization, unhappy teenagers are being given irreversible medical treatments, young gay and lesbian people are being converted into straight people by homophobic parents, and women are being erased by trans inclusion in spaces and sports. These panics play on existing fears of LGBTQ+ people, modern medicine going too far, prevalence of paedophiles and predators, and societal change. Fans of the movement push moral panic rhetoric beyond the newspapers and current affairs broadcasting and out to their friends, family and the internet.

An example of moral panic in action can be seen in the co-opting of Erin Reed's Anti-Trans Legislative Risk map. Independent journalist and activist Reed wanted to help trans people evaluate the risk of laws that could restrict their rights to medical care, accessing toilets and other services, and more. In December 2022, she created a map to track bills moving through state houses across the US. However, social media users who wanted to spread misinformation and scare people into opposing trans rights seized on and misrepresented the map. They recaptioned it to claim that it showed which states were the hardest and which were the easiest to obtain gender affirming surgery for very young children. 'The dark red states are where it's hardest to get your 3-year-old a sex change operation,' the text above the map claimed in one widely shared graphic.[1] Gender-affirming surgery is not available in America for under-fifteens or in the UK for under-eighteens. People all over the world shared the wrongly captioned graphic, and it fed into the baseless moral panic around trans rights.

The politics of fear – scaring people into action or inaction based on something that hasn't yet happened – is perhaps the strongest motivating factor in politics.[2] Many people in modern society are experiencing status threat (when a group feels that their competence or social status is being devalued). Add to this uncertainty about what is happening in the world due to the proliferation of misinformation in politics and confusion, caused by ignorance and toxic fans, and it's easy to scare people into believing moral panics and conspiracy theories. Radicalization methods have changed from the familiar traditional cult or far-right recruitment tactics, which involve targeting and approaching individuals and then isolating, indoctrinating and controlling them. Individuals are now proactively seeking answers, and they are finding extreme solutions.

Joining a fandom begins when someone feels strongly connected to the object of their fandom and then finds a point of connection with another fan. Radicalization is the same. It isn't faceless villains, state brainwashing or online bots that radicalize most people – it's human beings and their connections. The journey always starts with a person finding a point of connection with another. It's a relationship between individuals, whether that's far-right nationalism or Islamic fundamentalism.

The stars of politics, whether they are elected politicians, candidates, prominent activists or online influencers, are a mixed bunch. Some are ideologues: they strongly believe in what they are saying and doing, whether or not their positions are consistent or coherent. Some are opportunists: they pick up support for something they said or did, or spot a gap in the market, and reap the rewards. Careerists sit between the two, in that they hitch their political ambitions to something that is popular but aren't necessarily committed to its principles. All these political stars exist in both positive and negative movements. As in other fandoms, politics fans prove their commitment and authenticity by spending money as well as time on their favourite stars. There are always things to pay for: event tickets, travel, Substack newsletter subscriptions, donations to activists' legal costs, merchandise, memberships and more.

People are hungry for points of connection and these connections can lead, in a minority, to radicalization. When politics and strong views are important to someone's social identity, their friends and followers react positively when they share their views. Online, polarizing posts get more engagement, both positive and negative, and help someone to pick up more followers. A post of this nature could even turn someone from a fan into an influencer, which in turn can encourage them to take more extreme positions going forward in order to get a bigger reaction from their followers (and stop their followers from getting bored).

A crisis, whether based in reality or created by scaremongering, can be exploited by politicians, the media and others for their own gain. Specific social groups can be targeted and stories shared about them until negative opinion and misinformation are widely accepted as common sense. This is how much moral panic is created. But while your average person loses interest as the crisis dies down or bigger news stories rise to the top, a minority of people are radicalized by the misinformation, and they make this target group a longer-term priority issue and obsession. This kind of radicalization can have a huge knock-on effect. For example, moral panic about political corruption and paedophilia made it easy for the conspiracy theory Pizzagate (an untrue story about a paedophile ring connected to high-level Democrats, including Hillary Clinton, operating out of a Washington, DC pizza restaurant called Comet Ping Pong) to be exploited by QAnon (at the time just an online collective) to help gain support for Donald Trump.[3]

By 2020, Pizzagate had gained a following on TikTok, extremist forums and social media channels and beyond, and now implicated a broader and less political range of celebrities, including Justin Bieber and Bill Gates; followers believed these celebrities were part of an international elite group of child abusers. QAnon fans were radicalized into believing that Trump was fighting a secret war against Democratic politicians, government officials and celebrities involved in satanic rituals, child abuse and political corruption, and this led to real-world violence. Eventually, radicalized fans turned up at the Capitol Riot, as well as anti-lockdown and anti-vaccine protests and other violent events across the world.

It's hard to disentangle moral panic, fandom and radicalization when leaders and movements weaponize events and rumours for their own gain. It's not just an American problem. UK politicians regularly make inflammatory comments about migrants and small boats, and their supporters turn up to protest the arrival of refugees. Far-right groups exploit tensions around asylum seekers to gain support, radicalizing a portion of their audience in the process. Patriotic Alternative's Telegram channel[4] regularly shares the far-right groups' activities, 'warning' local residents in various areas about places where refugees are being housed and asking for donations from their fans to help 'motivate' the public into 'pro-White action'. In early 2023, Patriotic Alternative claimed to have delivered hundreds of anti-migrant leaflets to houses in Merseyside in the days before a riot took place outside a hotel in Knowsley that housed asylum seekers. The rioters brought fireworks and hammers.[5] Was this the action they hoped to motivate?

Fans of the individuals and groups that rose in influence during the Covid-19 pandemic often followed this pattern of behaviour, a pattern that can also be seen in the way Brexit fandoms formed. Indeed, some of the bigger pandemic names were initially known as leading Leavers or Remainers. These individuals became popular due to their response to a moral panic or flashpoint issue in a news cycle, especially as the public were scared, confused and looking for information and guidance. Their followers (online and offline) joined the conversation, gradually forming a community around the individual or group.[6] Some of these fans became increasingly conspiratorial and radicalized in their thinking. Examples exist at both 'extremes' of pandemic responses: those whose (Covid-concerned/Zero Covid) advice and behaviour was ultra-cautious and in favour of mitigations, and those whose (Covid-sceptic) position was anti-vaccine and against lockdowns, restrictions and masks.

During the pandemic Eric Feigl-Ding, a US nutrition researcher, regularly posted cherry-picked stats and excerpts of preprints (research published ahead of peer review, which can often be substantially revised through the review and editing process) to grow a large following, whose panic he fed with alarmist comments about each new variant of Covid-19.[7] The post that propelled him to fame began with 'HOLY MOTHER OF GOD!' (He later deleted it, as the preprint it was based on was withdrawn.) At one point, he tweeted about Mexico's national positivity rate being 50 per cent – which was technically true, but at the time the country was not testing many people and most of those tested were already ill. Feigl-Ding's fans defend him vehemently,[8] and he is quoted regularly in newspapers and on television. In the comments of his posts, fans still scared to eat indoors or travel express conspiracy theories about the 'return to normal' in their country, and the use of the virus for social control, just as fans of Covid-sceptic journalist Toby

Young made similar government-control claims against Covid vaccines in replies to his tweets and blog posts, and shared stories of deaths they attributed to lockdowns or vaccine injuries.

While social media is obviously an important factor in these fan journeys, traditional media has platformed many of the individuals and groups involved. Fandoms wouldn't grow so big or become so influential without being able to reach beyond those who spend a lot of time engaged in online debate. Conspiracy theorists and people who stoke moral panics can quickly build up a fandom on social media, but every amplification of their misinformation requires a personal connection. Once an idea takes hold, newspapers and broadcasters can legitimize their claims as well as increase their reach. Former footballer, sports broadcaster and Green Party candidate David Icke, for example, stopped being famous for anything other than conspiracy theories decades ago. He was so entertaining to write about, his brand was boosted for years by mainstream journalists writing previews and reviews of his tours or joking about his celebrity pals.

American journalist Damon Linker wrote that 'politics requires changing minds – and changing minds doesn't happen by presenting a set of ostensibly neutral, indisputable facts. Minds are changed by telling a gripping, cogent story that opens up the possibility of a new reality that voters choose to inhabit.'[9] The Johnny Depp–Amber Heard trial[10] has been described as 'Gamergate for normies' (a galvanizing event, involving misogyny and harassment, but instead involving people not steeped in niche online cultures). Depp's supporters weaponized misinformation, misogyny and social media algorithms to delegitimize Heard and her testimony. The trial briefly became a bigger issue in the US than abortion, and content creators on YouTube and TikTok who pivoted to trashing Amber Heard saw huge boosts in their popularity. People with no previous interest in either celebrity took a side in the fan war, but few were watching the trial live or reading neutral facts. Their positions were based on clips edited with commentary to tell a particular story.

Sharing misinformation, especially if it served the pro-Depp story, was rewarded by massive online engagement from fans and casual viewers alike. This sort of attention can be addictive, as well as lucrative, and that can serve to radicalize those involved. For the amateur sleuth, there was a wealth of potential evidence featuring the two protagonists, including previous videos of the couple in public, their video testimony in court and their and their supporters' accounts and transcripts from the trial. This was mined using a combination of tactics to give misinformation the sheen of legitimacy. For instance, a false story was spread that Amber Heard plagiarized a speech from the movie *The Talented Mr Ripley* on her first day on the witness stand.[11] People knew transcripts existed for this case, so the evidence presented – a fake transcript – was accepted. Fact-checkers reviewed nearly seven hours of footage to disprove the false story, but the debunking was nowhere near as visible as the original claim.

Video-based social media platforms use algorithms to predict what users will be interested in based on previous video views and engagement, and the habits of other users with a similar profile. Content creators saw an opportunity to hack and monetize the attention of those seeking information on the Depp–Heard case. For an increasing number of viewers, it's those creators and not broadcast journalists who are breaking news and defining the online narrative around major events. YouTubers and TikTok creators pivoted to

Depp–Heard videos to increase their income. Alyte Mazeika is a law-focused vlogger or 'lawtuber' who reportedly made $5,000 in one week on her YouTube channel, LawBytes, by deciding to livestream every day of the six-week trial.[12] She had previously improved her financial and social status by streaming about Kyle Rittenhouse for hours at a time. ThatUmbrellaGuy, an anonymous YouTuber who dedicated his whole channel to pro-Depp content, was estimated to have earned over $80,000 in a single month.[13]

My FYP (For You Page) on TikTok was full of anti-Heard videos, and the hashtag #JohnnyDeppIsInnocent had over 1.5 billion views. There was money to be made in supporting Depp, so that's how the narrative went. 'I have made lots of friends in this community,' a member of the #JusticeForJohnnyDepp army told Slate.[14] 'For the most part everyone has been very supportive and loving of one another. Overall, everyone here is very kind.' Heard supporters found the opposite, being hounded off the internet and sent death threats by 'Deppheads'.[15] The hashtags #AmberHeardIsALiar and #AmberHeardIsAnAbuser were used more than 100,000 times on Twitter.

There is a popular marketing concept that has existed for over a century that could help explain how, of all the people who follow a story in the news or become interested in a political movement, some people become fans and a smaller number are radicalized into extreme views and actions. American advertising and sales pioneer E. St. Elmo Lewis usually gets the credit for this idea. It's a model called AIDA, which stands for Attention, Interest, Desire and Action.[16]

The 'customer' moves through stages of learning about something (attention), working out how they feel about it (interest, potentially followed by desire) and then deciding whether or not to buy it (action). Another way of looking at the model is what marketers call the sales funnel. The funnel starts out wide with a large potential market for something. A smaller number of people are interested in finding out about the thing. A subset of the people who look into the thing seriously consider buying it, and only a small number of people become customers. Some of those customers will become loyal repeat customers. Or fans, if you like.

Why do people move to the next stage of one of these models? If you think about elections, one of the most important things for political parties is to 'get out the vote', which is a conversion from interest to action, albeit with no money changing hands. Marketing guru and business professor Badis Khalfallah says that there are only two real stages in a sales funnel: fandom and fulfilling a need.[17] What he means by fandom is a person becoming a fan of a brand – it sounds like their kind of thing – and a possible future client. In politics, this means a person could see themselves voting for a person or party – potentially. The fulfilling-a-need stage is where the client sees something in the brand that they value – perhaps it's a leader they like, perhaps it's an issue that matters to them. The important part of the funnel is between the two – where interest becomes desire – which then converts into sales or taking action. Khalfallah states that brands need to offer something with scarcity value to make that conversion happen, like a limited-edition product or a flash sale (short-term discount). In politics, we see politicians and activists trying to create a sense of urgency all the time, with slogans and emotional appeals like '24 hours to save the NHS!' and 'Get Brexit Done!' The scarcity value of *now* being the moment and tomorrow being too late, amped by the date of an election or campaigning ahead of an event, gets out the vote (or petition signatures, or protesters at a march).

American artist Joshua Citarella researches political movements on social media platforms. Late in 2018 he noticed how something similar to the sales funnel was radicalizing people. It went like this: people struggling with the pressures of modern life and all its uncertainties would go online to find ways to cope, and they would find likeminded people and political solutions to their problems. As they tried to work out what they thought and get answers to their questions, they moved down a version of the funnel from mainstream content at the top, through political organizations in the middle and then down to more radical and extremist content at the bottom. Citarella's initial version of the funnel, reproduced in Figure 1, shows Gen Z's political journey through irony to radicalization.

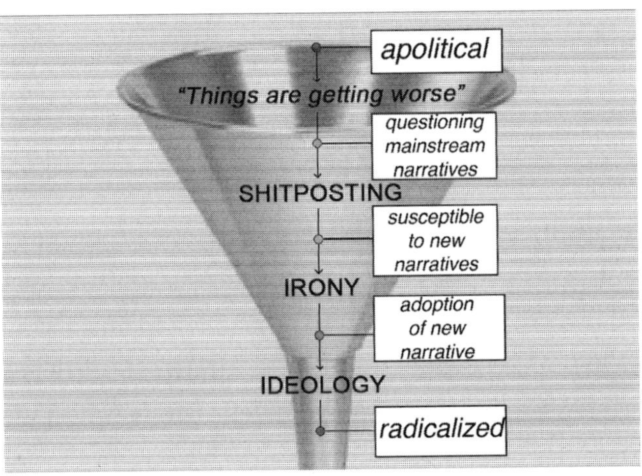

Figure 1: Radicalization of Gen Z by Joshua Citarella and New Models[18]

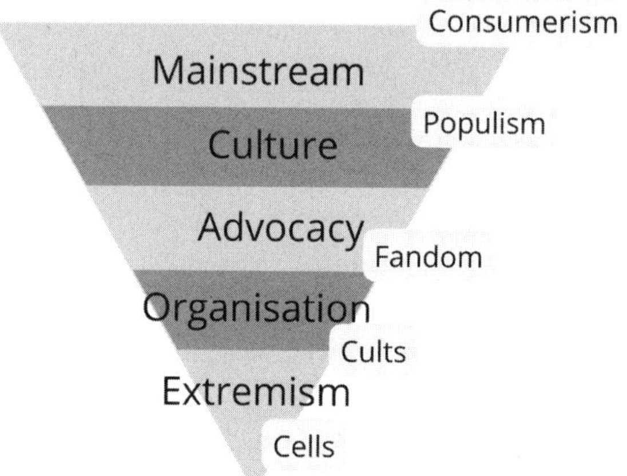

Figure 2: Radicalization funnel (adapted by the author from Joshua Citarella)

By 2021, Citarella had developed the funnel model further[19] to show the different types of politics sought out by all groups on a self-radicalization journey. Figure 2 shows a simplified adaptation of this version. The middle of the funnel is where people might join political parties and fandoms. If they still aren't satisfied or are looking for something deeper, they might move on to more radical organizations or seek out niche influencers. In that level they can encounter alternative histories, conspiracy theories and more extreme content. The bottom tiers are where people are fully radicalized into extremism and even violence. Each tier offers opportunities to resist the persuasive messages of charismatic people and organizations, but they reduce as people move through the funnel. The drivers towards radicalization can be so strong that people can jump from content related to advocacy – like posting online, voting and protesting – straight down to radical extremism. Kicking users off platforms or banning content like QAnon on Facebook means they gather again in smaller groups in different spaces.[20]

'In many cases,' explains Citarella, 'people go down ideological rabbit holes not because they are cynically misled by platforms, but because they cannot find satisfactory answers in mainstream media or discover hypocrisies in the narratives they have been told.'[21] I have seen the same patterns in the UK and Europe, but with older internet users than the teens and twenty-somethings studied by Citarella. These people start with latent prejudices and fears about an issue like immigration or vaccines. These beliefs are activated by mainstream media articles, comments by politicians and celebrities, posts on forums and Facebook, discussions on broadcast media and posts from X accounts with large followings. Those lead to anxieties and questions.

Many become more active on social media and join the fandoms of movement leaders and influencers: activists, journalists, academics, celebrities. Then as they move down the funnel, smaller numbers join pressure groups and dedicate time and money to the cause. They can't stop talking about their topic in person or posting about it online. A smaller subset of these people will get further and further into extremist spaces and activities.

In Citarella's dataset, far-right activists would set up fairly ordinary right-wing meme accounts that reposted popular content from big Republican pages and pick up followers by using those images. They would then make much more extreme posts without warning once or twice a week. 'While regular posts would feature familiar conservative tropes like "having an iPhone means you can't criticize capitalism" and "Venezuela proves that socialism doesn't work",' he says, 'extreme posts would contain racist caricatures and anti-capitalist messaging in favour of white identity.'[22] These posts would get negative feedback, be deleted quickly and then reposted again at a later date.

This technique allowed the accounts to build up big followings and almost subliminally expose them to slow-drip extremist content, eventually ramping it up and getting banned before starting again – having successfully moved the views of some of their 30–40,000 followers to the right. That 'martyring' act of deliberately sacrificing a social media account or aiming to get a temporary ban happens in the UK too, to increase notoriety.

In continental Europe and Latin America, the opposition to trans rights is part of the anti-gender movement. The real threat is 'gender ideology', which is also known as 'gender identity ideology' and 'transgender ideology' – a philosophy that developed in the Catholic Church. The Vatican's opposition to sexual and reproductive rights, protections for sexual orientation and gender identity, liberalizing divorce laws and the move away from traditional families and sex stereotypes comes under the banner of 'gender theory'.

University of Chicago Law School professor Mary Ann Case found that Pope Benedict (Joseph Ratzinger) had been working on 'gender ideology' obsessively since the 1980s, angry at what he saw as 'every role interchangeable between man and woman'.[23] He ranted that 'sex no longer appears to be a determined characteristic, as a radical and pristine orientation of the person', and he saw human beings as an endangered species. The current Pope, Pope Francis, said (in an interview for an Italian book on his social views) that every historical period has 'Herods that destroy, that plot designs of death, that disfigure the face of man and woman, destroying creation'.[24]

'Let's think of the nuclear arms, of the possibility to annihilate in a few instants a very high number of human beings,' he continues. 'Let's think also of genetic manipulation, of the manipulation of life, or of the gender theory, that does not recognize the order of creation.' Francis includes gender theory alongside nuclear weapons, as something that is 'destroying creation'.

Politicians like Brazil's Jair Bolsonaro, Hungary's Viktor Orbán, Poland's Andrzej Duda, Italy's Marco Bussetti and their fans have taken on this language wholesale. The 'anti-gender' or 'pro-family' movement makes attacks on women's liberation, LGBTQ+ people, sexual and reproductive rights, sex and relationships education and (in universities) gender studies. Big anti-gender protests have been held in many countries, including France, Spain, Italy, Brazil, Mexico, Poland, Hungary, Bulgaria and Argentina. Giving a speech in Brzeg, Poland in 2020, Duda compared gender ideology with communism: 'this is not why my parents' generation for 40 years struggled to expel communist ideology from schools, so that it could not be foisted on children, could not brainwash and indoctrinate them. . . They did not fight so that we would now accept that another ideology, even more destructive to man, would come along, an ideology which under the clichés of respect and tolerance hides deep intolerance'.[25] In Duda's estimation, LGBTQ+ people and feminism are the Other – alien and threatening – that can be scapegoated and dehumanized for society's ills, and communism is the ultimate bogeyman.

In the UK, some people use the terms 'gender ideology' and 'gender identity' ideology. However, the majority of these people – who call themselves 'gender critical' – claim to have no association with the far-right or the anti-gender movements. Some gender critical people identify as feminists, some openly say they are not feminists, but all share the core belief that biological sex can't be changed and reject the concept of transgender identities. The shared goal of the gender critical movement is to oppose trans rights and inclusion, and both the movement itself and leading lights within it have picked up a fervent fandom (a strong sense of identity, community and purpose – plus t-shirts and stickers). Here, the movement against trans people is driven by the media and politicians – just like in the US – but they do not always split along the same partisan lines. Journalists and academics have been writing anti-trans pieces since the 2010s in centre and left media like the *Guardian* and the *Observer*, and their ideas are supported by MPs and councillors in the Labour Party and the Scottish National Party, and supporters of the Liberal Democrats, Greens, Conservative Party and smaller parties to their right. The culture wars backed by the Conservative Party and right-leaning media focus heavily on trans rights as a wedge issue.

In January 2023 alone, according to the Dysphorum media-tracking project, the *Mail* published 115 articles on trans issues – all hostile. This reflects a pattern, as in May 2022 they published 163 – more than five articles a day. Research (using this project's data) by pro-trans activist Helen Islan in 2022 found that 13,015 articles were published in the UK news media (excluding LGBT media) on trans topics between 1 July 2015 and 30 June 2022, with an average of 154 articles published per month in that period.[26] I was able to reproduce similar results using the Nexis subscription database, where I found that *MailOnline* had published 1,907 articles on trans issues between 1 January 2023 and 1 August 2023, the majority of which were hostile. The few neutral articles were short stories reproduced from news agencies like Reuters. My May 2022 results produced 287 trans-related stories from *MailOnline*, thirty-five of which were neutral or positive about trans people. The majority of the positive and neutral stories concerned trans celebrities popular in the US or the failure of politicians with anti-trans views in Australian elections.

British culture prioritizes young people, families with school-aged children and pensioners. Diversity initiatives work with the most marginalized throughout their lifespan. That can leave people from more comfortable backgrounds in a position where they feel overlooked as they get older, because as a society we aren't very good at dealing with how people age from their late forties to the end of their working lives. Many of this group are vulnerable to political radicalization in fandoms that don't look like the far-right or populism – gender critical, alternative health and wellness influencers, niche environmental groups – but can lead to a world of conspiracy theories and extremism.

Ethan Zuckerman, media expert and Associate Professor of Public Policy, Communication and Information, said that QAnon is formed of 'people who lost trust in one institution and then found a coherent worldview that says, "Don't just mistrust this one institution – mistrust all the institutions. All of them are in it together."'[27] This is known as anti-system politics[28] – not just rejecting a particular politician/party/government, but the whole political system and the way society is organized.

Because moral panics involve a good deal of conspiracism, it can be difficult for fans who have been deeply involved in one to admit that they were hoodwinked or made a mistake. If they don't leave the fandom, they can end up doubling down in defence of their fandom and even go deeper into the conspiracy – however much it conflicts with their previous values.

Drag queens reading stories to children – at daytime events, suitably dressed and with parents and carers present – are popular at libraries, museums and arts festivals. Often branded as Drag Queen Story Hour or Drag Queen Story Time, the events have become a moral panic on both sides of the Atlantic in the 2020s. Far-right protesters have turned up to protest in the UK, US and Canada as well as circulating leaflets and writing letters to local authorities. The gender critical fandom had begun to take the line that drag queens reading stories was part of a concerted effort to mainstream the sexualization of children and normalize the acceptance of transgender identities.

When political movements take on fandom-like characteristics, mechanics exist that – when connected to a conspiracy theory or a moral panic – accelerate tensions between fans and their communities and increase radicalization. Look no further than Big Name Fans (BNFs) – people who are either celebrities in their own right who have joined the fandom or figures who have become well known within the fandom. They are appreciated for advancing the group's position (via publicity or through the roles they take on politically or socially) and often take on more risk than other fans through the attention this brings. They also have access to powerful people such as political leaders or other important supporters.

Over time, these BNFs act more like social media influencers or celebrities in their own right – particularly in movements without a single individual (such as a specific politician) as a focal point, and not just online. In politics, we've had political 'outriders' for a long time – in the UK, this word is used to refer to people who are close to a leader and share their views, so are willing to defend them in the media and at events. These outriders can be frontbench or backbench MPs or partisan journalists, but increasingly there have been former advisers, single-issue experts, comedians and other prominent figures who can hold their own on TV and have more freedom to say controversial things without reputational damage than leaders or those in official roles. There is crossover between outriders and other types of BNF, as was the case with both Corbyn and Johnson, where it wasn't just MPs who promoted and defended their leaders on broadcast media and online, but others too. These people picked up their own followings due to their visibility, networks and proximity to the inner circle of the movement, and became a kind of BNF themselves.

Outside the fandom, BNFs and outriders are seen as voices of the movement or proxies for leaders' views, and journalists and political wonks follow them for insight and information. If the BNFs are already celebrities, they have a head start in promoting their cause. Inside the fandom, their relationship with other fans becomes more hierarchical and parasocial. Their followers become fans of the BNFs themselves, supporting them financially and defending them when they are criticized by others. That gives the BNFs a platform to influence the views of fellow fans and how the wider world, via the media, perceives the movement. These auxiliary fandoms, or fandom by proxy, can make politics and activism more accessible by being available and willing to explain a news story or policy demand. They can also do a lot of damage.

When a BNF gets caught up in a central conspiracy theory or moral panic, and they become buoyed with affirmation and excitement, it is unsurprising that they can end up promoting more and more extreme positions. They can become addicted to the positive response from the fans and beyond, but they don't have the restraining structure of being an elected leader or official spokesperson. All of this sounds serious, and it is, because BNFs can have a lot of power with very little accountability – but it also means we can end up with very silly actions from supposedly serious people. Some BNFs are so far gone that they can say or do something completely bizarre and their fans still feel compelled to defend them and build on their actions.

This leads us to the story of Tala, the non-binary alien storyteller. Tala the Storyteller is a friendly alien who likes to go on journeys, seeking out stories and rhymes to share with children. Tala was created by Hertfordshire artists Emma Phillips and Eva Povey using funds from an Arts Council National Lottery Project Grant for Hertfordshire County Council.[29] The artists held interactive workshops with families to find out what appeals to young children and develop their design for a new character to promote reading. Tala is an alien with blue-green skin who is neither male nor female, which means children of any race or gender can identify with them. All very charming and with positive local engagement – or at least that was the consensus until prominent gender critical activists found out about it and ranted to their large followings for several days running. Fans felt the need to both amplify this and add to the harassment of library and local authority staff.

Tala's gender caused problems for the gender critical activists. First it was claimed that giving the character a non-binary identity was an attack on gender critical views. Then it was declared that Tala was being used to promote queer theory and the sexualization of children. This is another variant of the conspiracy theory cited in objections to drag queens telling stories to children.

What makes this case interesting is where the story went from there. The gender critical fandom demanded to know how alien Tala reproduces, what kind of genitals they have and more. Yes, we are still talking about a fictional alien. In response, LGBTQ+ people and allies – including gay journalists, lesbian comedians, bisexual poets and trans illustrators, their friends and fans – joined together in an act of creative solidarity: taking the piss, in style, with Tala art, jokes, memes and absurdist flights of fancy about alien reproduction.

So, how do we deradicalize people who have gone too far down the funnel? Joshua Citarella has some ideas. His first suggestion is to intervene when people are in the fandom tier of the funnel, where joining political organizations and fandoms or being involved in advocacy activism is still enough. Once someone has gone beyond that point, they are too invested and talking to them won't help. His second is for the left to market their own content in the same way as the extremists of the right. 'Swapping normie meme accounts into political content is an effective tactic,' he points out.[30] He has seen teenagers get into radical and progressive left politics online because material that appeals to them was there when they were searching for a new political identity. If people are disillusioned with the centre, what they find online will determine whether they turn left or right. Maybe they should find more solidarity, silliness and fun.

If someone has already fallen into radicalization, it can be solidarity and fun – or at least the love of family and friends – that helps to pull them out of a bad situation. Some of those who became isolated and interested in conspiracy theories and reactionary views during lockdowns found that becoming more socially active again and starting new hobbies made their pandemic-era obsessions and online communities seem less attractive. For others, a more active approach was needed, reminding the radicalized where their interests really lay. Will (name changed for anonymity) told Novara Media about how he and his trans brother Arthur (name also changed) went about deradicalizing their transphobic mum. Will told his mother, '[This online community doesn't] really care for you. If you're sad, they're not there to call [. . .] they're not substantially your community. They don't care for your wellbeing, they care for you insofar as you become an ally to them in the fight against trans people. [. . .] Look, I will always love you, but being there for you, and being family with you, is conditional on you recognising my brother.'[31]

We have the means to counteract moral panics and radicalization because we know what triggers them in the first place. People want answers to their questions and ways to manage uncertainty during hard times. It takes work, but that's something we can provide – particularly for people we love. Will and Arthur's mum knew deep down that her relationship with her sons mattered more than the community she found through opposing trans rights. What she needed was to feel seen, just as Arthur did. Bringing things down to the human level, rather than a sense of abstract threat, is what counts.

CONCLUSION

Kirsty Sedgman, an expert in audiences, asks: 'What separates a march from a riot? A concerned citizen from a careless thug? A democratic collective from a mob of yobs? An acceptable level of civic disruption from an intolerable inconvenience?. . . the answer depends both on who is doing the looking and whom they are looking at.'[1] There is no such thing as an objective view of politics or its fans. I have taken you on a journey into fandom through my eyes, looking at the things I have seen. I hope you enjoyed the show.

The Technicolor dreamworld of fan creativity and political history helps me deal with the bleakness of UK politics and world events. My friends and I shitpost through political crises because it's embarrassing to be sincere and hard to express emotions. It's that or outright nihilism, disengagement and depression. Most people have very little say in politics outside general elections and not much then, so this is how we cope. It gives us a point of connection with others who then give us positive feedback for making, sharing or reacting to memes.

The cultural critic Lauren Berlant said in 2012 that 'mainstream politics clogs the consciousness with situations that raise and shape anxiety levels by offering up the consolation of having an image captioned by an opinion'.[2] That's how it has felt to look at most of the media for the past fifteen years, be it online or on the TV: endless anxiety, images and opinions and then opinions and images reacting to those images and opinions. It's not just memes or headlines. It's everything. Rishi Sunak's office churned out images from social media graphic design app Canva promoting Eat Out To Help Out and other policy announcements from the start of his tenure as Chancellor of the Exchequer, each branded with his signature. Labour made weak attempts to respond with poorly imagined graphics of their own. In the 2000s, Sky News printed politician Top Trumps cards for party conferences, truly treating politics as a game, but also creating desirable items for fans to collect on eBay. The proliferation of three-word campaign slogans in the UK and the US over the past few years also feels trite and anxiety-inducing: Get Brexit Done, Take Back Control, Strong And Stable, Yes We Can. Everything is a trading card game, with politicos trying to score points using images and headlines and little nuance. It's human to want to find a way through all that, without just turning off the news and ignoring social media. The most human way is to look to other humans for guidance on what to do and how to feel about it. We find our leaders and our communities who share our interests, our hopes and our fears.

When I started writing this book, people told me that fandom was a thing of the past, because Corbyn and Trump were gone. When Boris Johnson resigned, I was informed that this was definitely the end and things would go back to normal. But Trump, at the time of writing, is a candidate again and losing elections doesn't mean fans disappear – Corbyn supporters are as noisy as ever. Boris fans still exist, including pop stars like Rod Stewart, who told Sky News, 'I was and still am a bit of a fan of Boris because I think he's got wonderful charisma. But you know, you knew what you were getting with Boris, so it's not unusual. He's told a few porkies over the years. So, I'm not surprised. He's in big trouble now, but how's he going to make a comeback? I dunno, maybe he should talk to me. I've been making comebacks for years.'[3]

Politics is where life-or-death issues meet the utterly ridiculous, and both are vital if people are to stay engaged and participating in politics outside of times of crisis. Having fun with politics makes politics feel relevant, and it doesn't mean someone isn't taking issues seriously. Fighting for marginalized identities doesn't mean someone doesn't care about the economy or healthcare. The fandoms and groups who worked together to elect Boric in Chile and Lula in Brazil show that fans can build solidarity networks as a mirror to the reactionary networks who agitate for regressive immigration policies and rolling back civil rights. Capitalizing on networked politics needs politicians and movements to recognize and invest in their own fans and the network of fans from other fandoms, and to keep investing in them after an election or a campaign. This also works for charities and stakeholder groups, who are cast aside between campaign cycles. If you want to do something good with the power of fans, you need to care about what they care about and see it as a reciprocal relationship for the longer term. The fans also need to understand the full context of the politicians or movement leaders they support. They have histories, strongly held views and constraints of their own.

In the US, Ed Markey didn't think the views of the Markeyverse fans were important enough to consider once he was elected, because he wasn't going to go for another term. Their media portrayal went from an exciting group of young people giving him support to a demanding mob once they disagreed with him about Palestine. Calla Walsh from the Markeyverse has since sworn off politics fandom. In her article for political blog Mondoweiss, written with all the zeal of a new atheist, she says, 'Therein lay my naivety: deep down, I thought Markey's newly-garnered youth support and bold progressive imagery had changed him. I was profoundly wrong. Markey never "changed"; his messaging and branding did. And I, and the rest of the stans, had facilitated this change.'[4]

'I don't claim to speak for the entire Markeyverse and I don't want to undercut the empowering nature of our youth organizing work,' she solemnly explained, 'but the experience permanently disenchanted me from electoral politics and made me question whether "accountability" even exists for representatives of a capitalist, settler-colonial empire like the United States. That May, I took my poster of Markey's September 2020 victory speech off my wall, and I don't work on campaigns anymore.'

It wasn't Walsh's fandom that was the problem, nor the idea of 'stanning' for a politician. It was the naïvety about Markey, about politics and about when to use the power of the network for accountability. The Markeyverse could have used their skills as fans to research the positions he already held – his views on Israel were well documented – and used their power before he was elected. He wasn't unaccountable, the fans just didn't take his existing views and other supporters into account. Ed Miliband is still in touch with Abby Tomlinson of the Milifandom. She still supports his politics. The Milifandom didn't assume they could change Miliband's policies or personality, only his image. They liked the policies and personality he already had. Miliband's consistent support for climate action, solidarity with marginalized groups and promotion of new ideas in politics via his podcast showed that his relationship with his young fans wasn't a one-way street but something that strengthened the politics of both parties.

As ideology and emotions ebbed away in favour of technocratic competence and policy, the centre shrank. Voters got heavily into reality TV and culture wars because there was so little meaningful participation left in politics – it was all decided between countries at big international jamborees and consent and consensus were assumed instead of checked. In other words, established political parties and politicians didn't invest in their relationship with the voters or give them a meaningful role in decision-making and reduced their dissent response to 'vote!' The Democrats are still at it. Maybe politicians don't need to cultivate fandoms, but they do need to make voters feel like they are on their side.

Most fans never reach fanatic status – sometimes they aren't even that politically committed to the movement. It's more of a social thing. Fanaticism is rooted in failures of current forms of political representation to reflect reality. Fanatics are trying a new politics and they feel like their cause needs addressing urgently. Whether we call it radicalism or extremism depends on whether we sympathize with the people involved and want the changes they are agitating for, not their passion or desire to disrupt norms. As political theorist Andrew Poe says: 'When fanaticism succeeds, it is easy to forget how radical such a movement was – for in inheriting its cause, we share its radicalism.'[5] Some of the fandoms that excite people today will turn out to be harbingers of fascism and some of those that horrify people at the moment will spark the new ideas that democracy so sorely needs.

We need more politics in politics, we need more humanity in politics, and we need to 'refind hope', as writer and critic John Berger put it.[6] Our societies have fans in them and fandom mechanics have helped me to understand other people in politics, with empathy and frustration, in a way that the good intentions behind slogans such as 'more in common' perhaps never could. Even the most ridiculous interactions in my own worst experiences in politics had a logic within fandom. Following chains of influence that came about through politicians' fannish inclinations meant I could understand not only their rhetoric and appeal to audiences but also aesthetic choices and policy obsessions. Liz Truss cosplaying both Margaret Thatcher (deliberately) and Vivienne Rook from Russell T. Davies's *Years and Years* (accidentally) was just funny, at a time when the news could often be very dark. It appealed to my interest in fashion and my love of politics and popular culture.

To be a fan is to make an active choice to get involved, to find other people who share your politics and give part of yourself to people and ideas even if they let you down. Behind those feelings of hope and enthusiasm is an ability to see the world as what it could be as well as what it is not. Emotion and imagination need to be turned into action to be meaningful. To quote Berger again: 'Hope, however, is an act of faith and has to be sustained by other concrete actions. For example, the action of approach, of measuring distances and walking towards. This will lead to collaborations that deny discontinuity. The act of resistance means not only refusing to accept the absurdity of the world-picture offered us, but denouncing it. And when hell is denounced from within, it ceases to be hell.'[7]

Our passion for things we care about, hope for change and our desire to be part of something bigger will often come out in the shape of fandom. It helps us deal with big problems and ideas and work out how to make things happen. Fandom is a recognizable way of seeing things and a way to tell stories about ourselves that fits with the societies we live in and the culture we consume. We watch telly and films, instead of visiting preachers. We play games together online, rather than perform ceremonies or mummers plays in the street. We read social media, not pamphlets or tracts. Being a fan and engaging with politics through fandom is not significantly different to quoting Pericles in a debating hall or discussing the issues of the day in a coffee house, other than the fact that it includes more people.

More people can see a way to be politically active and involved because they know how being a fan works. Fandom is an accessible route into politics. Some of the people fandom attracts will use their voice and power to act in bad ways, and that's okay – unless your problem with democracy is that there are too many people involved. It's not a holy book, classical education, folklore or Shakespeare, but fandom offers a similar set of shared tools for understanding a complicated world and expressing our place in it. Politics is too important and too full of possibility – there's much more to it than vibes and philosopher kings. It's also often too much fun.

Now, where's that attractive sound engineer with the Downing Street lectern ('hot podium guy' Tobias Gough, who has his own fandom)? Surely it must be time for another appearance. It's been such a curious dream. . .

ACKNOWLEDGEMENTS

This book would have been impossible to write without the support of many people, especially given the conditions of production. Both my life and the wider world of politics have been. . . eventful, to say the least. Two monarchs, three Prime Ministers and Grant Shapps taking every job in British politics while George Osborne collected as many roles in public life as he possibly could and Donald Trump kept getting indicted.

My agent, Jaime Marshall, helped me reshape the massive project I've been working on for years into something that looked like a workable proposal. He also put up with all my angst and panic. My editor, James Pulford, was patient with this first-time author and gave this book space to become its own animal. I also need to thank Chris Cook for commissioning my first long read on this topic and supporting me to attend events and do some of the research that made it into these pages.

Multiple friends and fellow academics lent keen ears and critical eyes to my ideas, drafts and worries. I promise that I wasn't making a cannibalistic soup; just a book. The Trade Writing group chat, Carbonara crew and Drag Them To Hell gang kept me vaguely sane. Louie Stowell and Chris McCrudden provided vital early support and insight. Catherine Fletcher and Caroline Pennock checked my history homework and made valuable suggestions. Lori Topper was there at some of my lowest points, and my pocket friends on social media made this whole thing possible.

I need to talk about my loved ones. Emil Andrews kept me together in body and soul, as he always does, being the stable completer-finisher and most vocal cheerleader while I flap about with mad schemes and messy enthusiasms. Philippa Neville let me howl at her and check whether what I'd written was a) grammatical and b) accessible to people who aren't full-on politics nerds. She also made me very, very happy.

NOTES

Introduction

1 Desilver, Drew (2022) 'The polarization in today's Congress has roots that go back decades'. *Pew Research Center.* [online] Available from: https://www.pewresearch.org/short-reads/2022/03/10/the-polarization-in-todays-congress-has-roots-that-go-back-decades/ (Accessed 31 August 2023)

2 Mellor, Joe (2022) 'Tory MP says church is making Conservatives feel "unwelcome" following Rwanda comments'. *The London Economic.* [online] Available from: https://www.thelondoneconomic.com/news/tory-mp-says-church-is-making-conservatives-feel-unwelcome-following-rwanda-comments-326840/ (Accessed 31 August 2023)

3 Andrews, Phoenix C.S. (2020) 'Receipts, radicalisation, reactionaries, and repentance: the digital dissensus, fandom, and the COVID-19 pandemic'. *Feminist Media Studies*, 20(6), pp. 902–07. [online] Available from: https://doi.org/10.1080/14680777.2020.1796214 (Accessed 20 July 2020)

4 Shulman, David (1996) 'On the Early Use of Fan in Baseball'. *American Speech*, 71(3), pp. 328–31. [online] Available from: https://www.jstor.org/stable/455556 (Accessed 27 December 2021)

5 Stephen, Bijan (2018) 'The gospel of Elon Musk, according to his flock'. *The Verge.* [online] Available from: https://www.theverge.com/2018/6/26/17505744/elon-musk-fans-tesla-spacex-fandom (Accessed 4 June 2022)

6 Andrews, Phoenix C.S. (2019) 'Can I have a selfie, minister?' *Tortoise.* [online] Available from: https://members.tortoisemedia.com/2019/09/10/political-fandom-190910/content.html?sig=1p-GjquwM0-7iHxoVR2EXMOW2eF4j5N-hPiCIhJqQqM (Accessed 20 April 2020)

7 Real, Evan (2017) 'The Internet Is Freaking Out Over Justin Trudeau's Bubble Butt'. *US Weekly.* [online] Available from: https://www.usmagazine.com/celebrity-news/news/the-internet-is-freaking-out-over-justin-trudeaus-bubble-butt-w468781/ (Accessed 24 August 2021)

8 Moore, Thomas (1854) *Life of Lord Byron: with his letters and journals, in six volumes*, London, John Murray.

9 Hallahan, Kirk (2000) 'Inactive publics: the forgotten publics in public relations'. *Public Relations Review*, 26(4), pp. 499–515. [online] Available from: https://linkinghub.elsevier.com/retrieve/pii/S0363811100000618 (Accessed 17 November 2021)

10 Krupnikov, Yanna and Ryan, John Barry (2020) 'The Real Divide in America Is Between Political Junkies and Everyone Else'. *The New York Times*. [online] Available from: https://www.nytimes.com/2020/10/20/opinion/polarization-politics-americans.html (Accessed 27 July 2021)

11 Druckman, James N., Klar, Samara, Krupnikov, Yanna, Levendusky, Matthew and Ryan, John Barry (2021) '(Mis-) Estimating Affective Polarization'. *The Journal of Politics*, p. 715603. [online] Available from: https://www.journals.uchicago.edu/doi/10.1086/715603 (Accessed 30 October 2021)

12 Shaun (2020) 'brigaded by the vile trolls again, simply for deliberately provoking them with lies and insults'. *@shaun_vids*. [online] Available from: https://twitter.com/shaun_vids/status/1221942299732606976 (Accessed 24 December 2021)

13 Coles, Richard (2022) 'Could the King, within his powers of course, FIRMLY ENCOURAGE the calling of a General Election, for the good of the country?' *@RevRichardColes*. [online] Available from: https://twitter.com/RevRichardColes/status/1583113678525583360 (Accessed 25 October 2023)

14 Bailey, Peter (1986) *Music Hall: The Business of Pleasure*, Open University Press. [online] Available from: https://hdl.handle.net/2027/heb00972.0001.001 (Accessed 26 October 2022)

1. History

1 Plutarch (n.d.) 'Plutarch, Pompey, chapter 48'. [online] Available from: http://www.perseus.tufts.edu/hopper/text?doc=Perseus:abo:tlg,0007,045:48 (Accessed 18 August 2023)

2 Keegan, Peter (2014) *Graffiti in antiquity*, London; New York, Routledge.

3 Thucydides (1950) *The History of the Peloponnesian War*, New York, E.P. Dutton & Co.

4 Atkinson, J.E. (1990) 'The Nika riots and "hooliganism"'. *Acta Patristica et Byzantina*, 1(1), pp. 119–33. [online] Available from: https://www.tandfonline.com/doi/full/10.1080/10226486.1990.11745808 (Accessed 5 October 2021)

5 Holstun, James (ed.) (1992) *Pamphlet wars: prose in the English Revolution*, London; Portland, OR, F. Cass.

6 Peacey, Jason (2004) *Politicians and pamphleteers: propaganda during the English civil wars and interregnum*, Aldershot; Burlington, VT, Ashgate.

7 Buchan, Lizzy (2018) 'John McDonnell criticises Labour supporters for perpetuating "antisemitic stereotypes"'. *The Independent*. [online] Available from: https://www.independent.co.uk/news/uk/politics/john-mcdonnell-jeremy-corbyn-antisemitism-labour-nec-christine-shawcroft-momentum-a8281401.html (Accessed 28 August 2023)

8 Rublack, U. (2010) 'Grapho-Relics: Lutheranism and the Materialization of the Word'. *Past & Present*, 206 (Supplement 5), pp. 144–66. [online] Available from: https://academic.oup.com/past/article-lookup/doi/10.1093/pastj/gtq016 (Accessed 12 October 2021)

9 *Economist* (2011) 'How Luther went viral'. *The Economist.* [online] Available from: https://www.economist.com/christmas-specials/2011/12/17/how-luther-went-viral (Accessed 12 October 2021)

10 Dallmann, William, (1918) *Patrick Hamilton : the first Lutheran preacher and martyr of Scotland*, St Louis, MO, Concordia Pub. House.

11 Leatherdale, Duncan (2016) 'Patrick Hamilton: Recreating the trial of the first Scottish martyr'. *BBC News*, 3 May. [online] Available from: https://www.bbc.com/news/uk-england-36037253 (Accessed 14 October 2021)

12 Smylie, James H. (1995) 'Madison and Witherspoon: Theological Roots of American Political Thought'. *American Presbyterians*, 73(3), pp. 155–64. [online] Available from: https://www.jstor.org/stable/23333418 (Accessed 28 August 2023)

13 Bucher, Matt and Chipperfield, Grace (2020) 'How to be a Fan in the Age of Problematic Faves'. *Life Writing*, 0(0), pp. 1–12. [online] Available from: https://doi.org/10.1080/14484528.2021.1864090 (Accessed 2 March 2021)

14 Reyburn, Hugh Young (1914) *John Calvin: His Life, Letters, and Work*, London, Hodder and Stoughton.

15 Scribner, R.W. (1986) 'Incombustible Luther: The Image of the Reformer in Early Modern Germany'. *Past and Present*, 110(1), pp. 38–68. [online] Available from: https://academic.oup.com/past/article-lookup/doi/10.1093/past/110.1.38 (Accessed 20 June 2023)

16 Jenner, Greg (2020) *Dead Famous: an Unexpected History of Celebrity from Bronze Age to Silver Screen*, London, Weidenfeld & Nicolson.

17 Hammond, J.L. (1964) *Gladstone and the Irish Nation*, London, Frank Cass and Co. Ltd.

18 Jerman, Bernard R. (1954) 'Disraeli's Fan Mail: A Curiosity Item'. *Nineteenth-Century Fiction*, 9(1), pp. 61–71.

19 Piette, Onesime L. (1977) 'The Hughenden Papers: Mother Lode of Disraeliana'. *The Courier*, 9(3), pp. 13–24. [online] Available from: https://surface.syr.edu/cgi/viewcontent.cgi?article=1077&context=libassoc (Accessed 28 August 2023)

20 Anon (1916) *PRIMROSE DAY IN LONDON (1916)*, British Pathé. [online] Available from: https://www.britishpathe.com/asset/ (Accessed 28 August 2023)

21 Borthwick, Algernon (1885) 'The Origin and Objects of the Primrose League', a speech by Sir Algernon Borthwick at the opening of the Northumberland Habitation, at Norfolk House, St. James's Square, London, on 27 October 1885. [online] Available from: https://openlibrary.org/books/OL23341507M/The_origin_and_objects_of_the_Primrose_League (Accessed 25 November 2018)

22 Selden, Charles A. (1930) 'BALDWIN IS ASSURED OF TORY LEADERSHIP: Conservative Primrose League Votes Continued Confidence in Spite of Factional Rows'. *The New York Times*, 5 April.

23 Sheets, Diana Elaine (1988) 'BRITISH CONSERVATISM AND THE PRIMROSE LEAGUE: THE CHANGING CHARACTER OF POPULAR POLITICS, 1883-1901'.

Submitted as part of a PhD at Columbia University. [online] Available from: https://core.ac.uk/download/pdf/4818363.pdf (Accessed 14 February 2019)

24 Hendley, Matthew (2001) 'Anti-Alienism and the Primrose League: The Externalization of the Postwar Crisis in Great Britain 1918-32'. *Albion*, 33(2), pp. 243–69. [online] Available from: http://www.jstor.org/stable/4053372?origin=crossref (Accessed 25 November 2018)

25 Hendley, Matthew (1996) 'Constructing the Citizen: The Primrose League and the Definition of Citizenship in the Age of Mass Democracy in Britain, 1918-1928'. *Journal of the Canadian Historical Association*, 7(1), p. 125. [online] Available from: http://id.erudit.org/iderudit/031105ar (Accessed 25 October 2018)

26 Hansard (1928) 'Representation Of The People (Equal Franchise) Bill'. [online] Available from: https://hansard.parliament.uk/Commons/1928-03-29/debates/b9b9566b-fd11-4fe6-a338-b7b0beb26252/RepresentationOfThePeople(EqualFranchise)Bill#contribution-4d78d3f8-781d-433e-8b97-99d83310a75f98-9818-3c94c6c4941b (Accessed 6 December 2021)

27 Montz, Amy L. (2012) '"Now she's all hat and ideas": Fashioning the British Suffrage Movement', 3(1), pp. 55–67. [online] Available from: http://www.ingentaconnect.com/content/10.1386/csfb.3.1-2.55_1 (Accessed 13 November 2021)

28 Mercer, John (2009) 'Shopping for Suffrage: the campaign shops of the Women's Social and Political Union'. *Women's History Review*, 18(2), pp. 293–309. [online] Available from: https://doi.org/10.1080/09612020902771053 (Accessed 11 November 2021)

29 Smith, Angela (2003) 'The Pankhursts and the War: suffrage magazines and First World War propaganda'. *Women's History Review*, 12(1), pp. 103–18. [online] Available from: http://www.tandfonline.com/doi/abs/10.1080/09612020300200349 (Accessed 30 November 2021)

30 Binns, Amy (2018) 'New Heroines for New Causes: how provincial women promoted a revisionist history through post-suffrage pageants'. *Women's History Review*, 27(2), pp. 221–46. [online] Available from: https://www.tandfonline.com/doi/full/10.1080/09612025.2017.1313806 (Accessed 21 November 2021)

31 Mayhall, Laura E. Nym (1995) 'Creating the "suffragette spirit": British feminism and the historical imagination'. *Women's History Review*, 4(3), pp. 319–44. [online] Available from: https://www.tandfonline.com/doi/abs/10.1080/09612029500200088 (Accessed 11 November 2021)

32 Kean, Hilda (2005) 'Public history and popular memory: issues in the commemoration of the British militant suffrage campaign'. *Women's History Review*, 14(3–4), pp. 581–602. [online] Available from: https://www.tandfonline.com/doi/abs/10.1080/09612020500200440 (Accessed 13 November 2021)

33 Gleiberman, Owen (2017) 'The London Underground Scene of "Darkest Hour": So False, So Winning, So Slam-Dunk

Oscar'. *Variety*. [online] Available from: https://variety.com/2017/film/columns/darkest-hour-underground-scene-gary-oldman-1202622763/ (Accessed 31 August 2023)

34 YouGov (2021) 'Winston Churchill popularity & fame'. [online] Available from: https://yougov.co.uk/topics/international/explore/historical_figure/Winston_Churchill?content=all (Accessed 8 November 2021)

35 Stelzer, Cita (2019) *Working with Winston*, London, Pegasus Books.

36 Griffiths, Andrews (2013) 'Winston Churchill, the "Morning Post", and the End of the Imperial Romance'. *Victorian Periodicals Review*, 46(2), pp. 163–83. [online] Available from: https://www.jstor.org/stable/43663687 (Accessed 8 November 2021)

37 Weidhorn, Manfred (1988) 'CHURCHILL AND THE BRITISH LITERARY INTELLIGENTSIA: SKIRMISHES WITH SHAW AND HIS CONTEMPORARIES ON THE FRONTIER OF POLITICS AND LITERATURE'. *Shaw*, 8, pp. 111–30. [online] Available from: https://www.jstor.org/stable/40681237 (Accessed 8 November 2021)

38 Toye, R. (2007) 'H.G. Wells and the New Liberalism'. *Twentieth Century British History*, 19(2), pp. 156–85. [online] Available from: https://academic.oup.com/tcbh/article-lookup/doi/10.1093/tcbh/hwn007 (Accessed 8 November 2021)

39 Toye, Richard (2010) *Churchill's empire: the world that made him and the world he made*, London, Macmillan.

40 Harrison, Ellie (2023) 'Jilly Cooper "thrilled to bits" that Rishi Sunak reads her bonkbusters'. *The Independent*. [online] Available from: https://www.independent.co.uk/arts-entertainment/books/news/rishi-sunak-jilly-cooper-riders-this-morning-b2345655.html (Accessed 30 May 2023)

41 Toye, Richard (2006) 'Churchill borrowed some of his biggest ideas from HG Wells'. *University of Cambridge*. [online] Available from: https://www.cam.ac.uk/research/news/churchill-borrowed-some-of-his-biggest-ideas-from-hg-wells (Accessed 8 November 2021)

42 Valgarðsson, Viktor Orri, Clarke, Nick, Jennings, Will and Stoker, Gerry (2021) 'The Good Politician and Political Trust: An Authenticity Gap in British Politics?' *Political Studies*, 69(4), pp. 858–80. [online] Available from: https://doi.org/10.1177/0032321720928257 (Accessed 14 November 2021)

43 Harris, Hunter (2016) 'The Real Story of the *Life* Magazine "Camelot" Interview in *Jackie*'. *Vulture*. [online] Available from: https://www.vulture.com/2016/12/jackie-life-camelot-interview-theodore-white.html (Accessed 13 December 2021)

44 Vancil, David L. and Pendell, Sue D. (1987) 'The myth of viewer–listener disagreement in the first Kennedy–Nixon debate'. *Central States Speech Journal*, 38(1), pp. 16–27. [online] Available from: http://www.tandfonline.com/doi/abs/10.1080/10510978709368226 (Accessed 28 June 2023)

45 Hornaday, Ann (2021) '"JFK" at 30: Oliver Stone and the lasting impact of America's most dangerous movie'. *Washington Post*. [online] Available from: https://www.washingtonpost.com/arts-

entertainment/2021/12/22/oliver-stone-jfk-anniversary/ (Accessed 6 July 2023)

46 Perlstein, Rick (2014) *The Invisible Bridge: The Fall of Nixon and the Rise of Reagan* First Simon & Schuster hardcover edition, New York, Simon & Schuster.

47 Blow, John (n.d.) 'Margaret Thatcher had disdain for Spitting Image, says Sir Bernard Ingham as show returns'. [online] Available from: https://www.yorkshirepost.co.uk/news/politics/margaret-thatcher-had-disdain-spitting-image-says-sir-bernard-ingham-show-returns-1749157 (Accessed 6 November 2021)

48 Law, Roger (2013) 'Margaret Thatcher and Spitting Image: we had no idea we would be joined at the hip'. *The Guardian*, 17 April. [online] Available from: https://www.theguardian.com/commentisfree/2013/apr/17/margaret-thatcher-spitting-image-joined (Accessed 6 November 2021)

49 Bartley, Jonathan (2009) 'In-depth interview with Michael Portillo'. *High Profiles*. [online] Available from: https://highprofiles.info/interview/michael-portillo/ (Accessed 22 July 2022)

50 Thatcher, Margaret (1968) 'Conservative Political Centre (CPC) Lecture ("What's wrong with politics?")'. [online] Available from: https://www.margaretthatcher.org/document/101632 (Accessed 30 November 2021)

51 Bikard, Florian (2019) 'Vichy – Memories of a Past that is still Present: Re-surging Nationalism and the Limits of the "devoir de mémoire"'. RUB Europadialog. [online] Available from: https://rub-europadialog.eu/vichy-memories-of-a-past-that-is-still-present-re-surging-nationalism-and-the-limits-of-the-devoir-de-memoire (Accessed 26 November 2021)

52 Bancel, Nicolas (2013) 'France, 2005: A postcolonial turning point'. *French Cultural Studies*, 24, pp. 208–18. [online] Available from: https://doi.org/10.1177/0957155813477794 (Accessed 25 October 2023)

53 Barber, Tony (2021) 'France invokes the golden age of de Gaulle'. *Financial Times*, 18 November. [online] Available from: https://www.ft.com/content/5d78158c-1695-4701-a32a-a38978743037 (Accessed 26 November 2021)

54 Lichfield, John (2021) 'Why all French politicians are Gaullists'. *POLITICO*. [online] Available from: https://www.politico.eu/article/france-charles-de-gaulle-gaullists-emmanuel-macron-marine-le-pen/ (Accessed 26 November 2021)

55 Wollen, Peter (2003) 'Fridamania'. *New Left Review*, 22, pp. 119–30. [online] Available from: https://www.proquest.com/docview/1301999099/citation/329189F1BEE549C3PQ/1 (Accessed 28 June 2023)

2. The hows and whys of fandom

1 Harris, Sarah Ann (2017) 'Labour Leader Delights Fan By Joining In With His Own Version Of "Oh, Jeremy Corbyn"'. *HuffPost UK*. [online] Available from: https://www.huffingtonpost.co.uk/entry/jeremy-corbyn-table-tennis_uk_59ca025de4b0cdc773341119 (Accessed 10 July 2023)

2 Pelley, Rich (2022) 'Martin Freeman: "I'm one of few people in my family who would ever unironically go into a church"'. *The Guardian*, 16 July. [online] Available from: https://www.theguardian.com/culture/2022/jul/16/martin-freeman-actor-this-much-i-know (Accessed 17 July 2022)

3 Groene, Samantha L. and Hettinger, Vanessa E. (2016) 'Are you "fan" enough? The role of identity in media fandoms.' *Psychology of Popular Media Culture*, 5(4), pp. 324–39. [online] Available from: http://doi.apa.org/getdoi.cfm?doi=10.1037/ppm0000080 (Accessed 1 September 2023)

4 Rosenbaum, Martin (1997) *From Soapbox to Soundbite*, London, Palgrave Macmillan UK. [online] Available from: http://link.springer.com/10.1007/978-1-349-25311-1 (Accessed 26 October 2023)

5 Billig, Michael and Tajfel, Henri (1973) 'Social categorization and similarity in intergroup behaviour'. *European Journal of Social Psychology*, 3(1), pp. 27–52. [online] Available from: https://onlinelibrary.wiley.com/doi/10.1002/ejsp.2420030103 (Accessed 13 September 2022)

6 Kinnock, Neil (1985) 'Leader's speech, Bournemouth 1985'. [online] Available from: http://www.britishpoliticalspeech.org/speech-archive.htm?speech=191 (Accessed 28 December 2021)

7 Bayliss, Eddie (1986) *Meet the Challenge Make the Change*. [online] Available from: https://www.youtube.com/watch?v=UED3rcZlUPQ (Accessed 28 December 2021)

8 Benn, Tony (1996) *The Benn Diaries*, London, Arrow.

9 Benn, Tony (2007) 'My last real conference?' *The Guardian*, 20 September. [online] Available from: https://www.theguardian.com/commentisfree/2007/sep/20/comment.politics (Accessed 30 November 2020)

10 Hobsbawm, Eric (1980) 'Eric Hobsbawm interviews Tony Benn'. *Marxism Today*, (October), pp. 5–13.

11 Gauja, Anika and Grömping, Max (2020) 'The expanding party universe: Patterns of partisan engagement in Australia and the United Kingdom'. *Party Politics*, 26(6), pp. 822–33. [online] Available from: https://doi.org/10.1177/1354068818822251 (Accessed 27 December 2021)

12 Bale, Tim, Poletti, Monica and Webb, Paul (2018) 'A Man's Game? The Grassroots Gender Gap in Britain's Political Parties'. *Political Insight*, 9(2), pp. 7–10. [online] Available from: http://journals.sagepub.com/doi/10.1177/2041905818779324 (Accessed 13 March 2019)

13 Barnfield, Matthew and Bale, Tim (2020) '"Leaving the red Tories": Ideology, leaders, and why party members quit'. *Party Politics*, p. 1354068820962035.

[online] Available from: https://doi.org/10.1177/1354068820962035 (Accessed 22 November 2021)

14 Burton, Matthew and Tunnicliffe, Richard (2022) *Membership of political parties in Great Britain*, London, Commons Library. [online] Available from: https://researchbriefings.files.parliament.uk/documents/SN05125/SN05125.pdf (Accessed 16 August 2023)

15 Ypi, Lea (2016) 'Political Commitment and the Value of Partisanship'. *American Political Science Review*, 110(3), pp. 601–13. [online] Available from: https://www.cambridge.org/core/journals/american-political-science-review/article/political-commitment-and-the-value-of-partisanship/0F4BE7D7A1CC0C4498B6B3F00F8A4E1E (Accessed 14 November 2021)

16 Costa, Mia (2021) 'Ideology, Not Affect: What Americans Want from Political Representation'. *American Journal of Political Science*, 65(2), pp. 342–58. [online] Available from: https://onlinelibrary.wiley.com/doi/abs/10.1111/ajps.12571 (Accessed 23 August 2021)

17 Evans, Geoffrey and Tilley, James (2017) *The New Politics of Class: The Political Exclusion of the British Working Class*, First Edition, Oxford; New York, Oxford University Press.

18 Sloam, James and Henn, Matt (2019) *Youthquake 2017*, Cham, Springer International Publishing. [online] Available from: http://link.springer.com/10.1007/978-3-319-97469-9 (Accessed 29 December 2018)

19 Ibid.

20 Jungkunz, Sebastian and Marx, Paul (2021) 'Income Changes Do Not Influence Political Participation: Evidence from Comparative Panel Data'. *SSRN Electronic Journal*. [online] Available from: https://www.ssrn.com/abstract=3808461 (Accessed 27 December 2021)

21 Ferreira da Silva, Frederico, Garzia, Diego and De Angelis, Andrea (2021) 'From party to leader mobilization? The personalization of voter turnout'. *Party Politics*, 27(2), pp. 220–33. [online] Available from: https://doi.org/10.1177/1354068819855707 (Accessed 23 August 2021)

22 Marcus, George E. and MacKuen, Michael B. (1993) 'Anxiety, Enthusiasm, and the Vote: The Emotional Underpinnings of Learning and Involvement During Presidential Campaigns'. *American Political Science Review*, 87(3), pp. 672–85. [online] Available from: https://www.cambridge.org/core/product/identifier/S0003055400100905/type/journal_article (Accessed 24 December 2021)

23 Cockfield, Arthur (1983) 'Letter to Robin Butler, with Annotations by Butler and Ferdinand Mount'. [online] Available from: https://www.margaretthatcher.org/document/131708 (Accessed 25 November 2021)

24 Robinson, Emily (2017) *The Language of Progressive Politics in Modern Britain*, London, Palgrave Macmillan UK. [online] Available from: http://link.springer.com/10.1057/978-1-137-50664-1 (Accessed 28 September 2017)

25 Jones, Morgan (2021) 'Exiting Hogwarts Castle'. *Renewal*. [online] Available from: https://renewal.org.uk/exiting-hogwarts-castle/ (Accessed 29 December 2021)

26 Hadley, Katherine (1979) 'My Face, My Figure, My Diet'. *The Sun*, 16 March.

[online] Available from: https://www.margaretthatcher.org/document/103811 (Accessed 27 October 2022)

27 Hawkes, Steve and Cole, Harry (2016) 'New PM Theresa May can reunite Tories as she vows "Brexit means Brexit" before starting new job tomorrow'. *The Sun*. [online] Available from: https://www.thesun.co.uk/news/1429005/new-pm-theresa-may-can-reunite-tories-and-deliver-brexit/ (Accessed 1 September 2023)

28 Adu, Aletha and correspondent, Aletha Adu Political (2023) 'Former Tory chairman says Liz Truss interventions should be less frequent'. *The Guardian*, 17 February. [online] Available from: https://www.theguardian.com/politics/2023/feb/17/conservative-party-chairman-says-liz-truss-interventions-should-be-less-frequent (Accessed 1 September 2023)

29 Lords Hansard (2005) 'Written Answers: Thursday 21 July 2005'. *Hansard.* [online] Available from: https://publications.parliament.uk/pa/ld200506/ldhansrd/vo050721/text/50721w01.htm (Accessed 23 January 2020)

30 Vigor, Anthony (2004) 'Exposed by his sandwich'. *New Statesman*. [online] Available from: https://web.archive.org/web/20160814035625/http://www.newstatesman.com/node/159535 (Accessed 21 November 2022)

31 Streeting, Wes (2023) 'False hope is worse than no hope. Labour won't make promises it can't keep'. *The Observer*, 9 July. [online] Available from: https://www.theguardian.com/politics/2023/jul/09/labour-promises-tory-mismanagement-public-finances (Accessed 9 July 2023)

32 Webber, Esther (2022) 'The vindication of Rishi Sunak'. *POLITICO*. [online] Available from: https://www.politico.eu/article/the-vindication-of-rishi-sunak-new-uk-prime-minister-tory-leadership/ (Accessed 25 October 2022)

33 Quinn, Ben, Sparrow, Andrew and Sullivan, Helen (2022) 'Rishi Sunak warns Tories party faces "existential threat" and rules out early general election after winning race to be PM – live'. *The Guardian*, 24 October. [online] Available from: https://www.theguardian.com/politics/live/2022/oct/24/uk-politics-live-rishi-sunak-penny-mordaunt-boris-johnson-withdrawal-nominations-deadline-tory-leadership-contest-race (Accessed 24 October 2022)

34 Barber, Lionel (2022) 'Britain enjoys its "Obama moment": Rishi Sunak wins Tory leadership race and will be next prime minister. A British-Asian of Punjabi descent, pukka English public school boy and Goldman alumnus. Let's give him a break and not pigeon hole him. He'll need some luck!' *@lionelbarber*. [online] Available from: https://twitter.com/lionelbarber/status/1584533321169526785 (Accessed 24 October 2022)

35 Murphy, Anna (2023) 'Yes, Rishi Sunak is the best-dressed prime minister'. *The Times*, 1 September. [online] Available from: https://www.thetimes.co.uk/article/yes-rishi-sunak-is-the-best-dressed-prime-minister-r5sxxqccd (Accessed 1 September 2023)

36 Ferrier, Morwenna (2023) 'Derek Guy: the notorious fashion tweeter on Sunak's short trousers'. *The Guardian*. [online] Available from: https://www.theguardian.com/fashion/2023/aug/05/derek-

guy-the-notorious-fashion-tweeter-on-sunaks-short-trousers (Accessed 1 September 2023)

37 Greene, Steven (2004) 'Social Identity Theory and Party Identification'. *Social Science Quarterly*, 85(1), pp. 136–53. [online] Available from: https://onlinelibrary.wiley.com/doi/10.1111/j.0038-4941.2004.08501010.x (Accessed 27 December 2021)

38 Allegretti, Aubrey (2023) 'Tory MPs try to oust Tobias Ellwood from defence role for praising Taliban'. *The Guardian*, 20 July. [online] Available from: https://www.theguardian.com/politics/2023/jul/20/tory-mp-tobias-ellwood-apologises-video-praising-taliban (Accessed 1 September 2023)

39 Kowert, Rachel and Daniel, Emory (2021) 'The one-and-a-half sided parasocial relationship: The curious case of live streaming'. *Computers in Human Behavior Reports*, 4, p. 100150. [online] Available from: https://www.sciencedirect.com/science/article/pii/S2451958821000981 (Accessed 28 December 2021)

40 Andrews, Phoenix (2019) 'AOC's Anti-Fans'. *Los Angeles Review of Books*. [online] Available from: https://lareviewofbooks.org/article/aocs-antifans/ (Accessed 16 October 2021)

41 Ocasio-Cortez, Alexandria (2020) 'Anyone want to play Among Us with me on Twitch to get out the vote? (I've never played but it looks like a lot of fun)'. *@AOC*. [online] Available from: https://twitter.com/AOC/status/1318276809977434112 (Accessed 18 December 2021)

42 Perry, David M. (2018) 'Alexandria Ocasio-Cortez Has Mastered the Politics of Digital Intimacy'. *Pacific Standard*. [online] Available from: https://psmag.com/social-justice/alexandria-ocasio-cortez-has-mastered-the-politics-of-digital-intimacy (Accessed 28 December 2021)

43 Walsh, Kathleen N. (2021) 'AOC knew she'd face a backlash for talking about her trauma. There's a reason she told us anyway'. *The Independent*. [online] Available from: https://www.independent.co.uk/voices/aoc-instagram-live-capitol-sexual-assault-backlash-trauma-b1796545.html (Accessed 28 December 2021)

44 Institute of Politics at Harvard Kennedy School (2021) 'Spring 2021 Harvard Youth Poll'. *The Institute of Politics at Harvard University*. [online] Available from: https://iop.harvard.edu/youth-poll/spring-2021-harvard-youth-poll (Accessed 29 December 2021)

45 Free, Marcus and Hughson, John (2006) 'Common culture, commodity fetishism and the cultural contradictions of sport'. *International Journal of Cultural Studies*, 9(1), pp. 83–104. [online] Available from: https://doi.org/10.1177/1367877906061166 (Accessed 17 October 2021)

46 Waterson, Jim (2019) 'Brexit boost for BBC Parliament as channel briefly outrates MTV'. *The Guardian*, 23 January. [online] Available from: https://www.theguardian.com/media/2019/jan/23/brexit-boost-for-bbc-parliament-as-channel-briefly-outrates-mtv (Accessed 31 August 2023)

47 Durkheim, Emile (1912) *The Elementary Forms of the Religious Life*. [online] Available from: https://www.gutenberg.org/files/41360/41360-h/41360-h.htm (Accessed 26 October 2023)

48 Priestley, J.B. (1935) *English Journey*, London, Heinemann. [online] Available from: http://archive.org/details/in.ernet.dli.2015.175896 (Accessed 26 October 2022)

49 Kierkegaard, Søren (2015) *Papers and Journals*, London, Penguin.

50 Kierkegaard, Søren (2013) 'Upbuilding Discourses in Various Spirits (March 13, 1847)', in Hong, Howard V. and Hong, Edna H. (eds), *The Essential Kierkegaard*, Princeton, Princeton University Press, pp. 269–76. [online] Available from: https://doi.org/10.1515/9781400847198-019 (Accessed 18 October 2021)

51 Le Bon, Gustave (2009) *The Crowd: A Study of the Popular Mind*, Auckland, NZ, Floating Press.

52 McPhail, Clark (1991) *The Myth of the Madding Crowd*, New York, A. de Gruyter.

53 Hsiao, Yuan and Radnitz, Scott (2021) 'Allies or Agitators? How Partisan Identity Shapes Public Opinion about Violent or Nonviolent Protests'. *Political Communication*, 38, pp. 479–97. [online] Available from: https://doi.org/10.1080/10584609.2020.1793848 (Accessed 25 October 2023)

54 Thomson, Irene Taviss (2005) 'The Theory That Won't Die: From Mass Society to the Decline of Social Capital'. *Sociological Forum*, 20(3), pp. 421–48. [online] Available from: http://link.springer.com/10.1007/s11206-005-6596-3 (Accessed 10 July 2023)

55 Arendt, Hannah (2017) *The origins of totalitarianism*, London, Penguin Classics.

56 Katsiaficas, George N. (1987) *The imagination of the New Left: a global analysis of 1968*, Boston, MA, South End Press.

57 Hertog, James K. and McLeod, Douglas M. (2001) 'A Multiperspectival Approach to Framing Analysis: A Field Guide', in Reese, Stephen D. et al. (eds), *Framing Public Life: Perspectives on Media and Our Understanding of the Social World*, Abingdon, Routledge.

58 McLeod, Douglas M. and Hertog, James K. (1992) 'The manufacture of "public opinion" by reporters: informal cues for public perceptions of protest groups'. *Discourse & Society*, 3, pp. 259–75. [online] Available from: https://doi.org/10.1177/0957926592003003001 (Accessed 25 October 2023)

59 Masullo, G.M., Brown, D.K. and Harlow, S. (2021) 'A Better Way to Tell Protest Stories'. Center for Media Engagement. [online] Available from: https://mediaengagement.org/research/a-better-way-to-tell-protest-stories/ (Accessed 29 October 2021)

60 Wall, Tom (2022) '"Kill the bill": surge in Bristol riot charges prompts alarm over civil liberties'. *The Observer*, 12 February. [online] Available from: https://www.theguardian.com/uk-news/2022/feb/12/kill-the-bill-surge-in-bristol-riot-charges-prompts-alarm-over-civil-liberties (Accessed 1 September 2023)

61 Masullo, G.M., Brown, D.K. and Harlow, S. (2021) 'A Better Way to Tell Protest Stories'. Center for Media Engagement. [online] Available from: https://mediaengagement.org/research/a-better-way-to-tell-protest-stories/ (Accessed 29 October 2021)

62 Harlow, S., Kilgo, D.K., Salaverría, R. and García-Perdomo, V. (2020) 'Is the Whole World Watching? Building

a Typology of Protest Coverage on Social Media From Around the World'. *Journalism Studies*, 21, pp. 1590–608. [online] Available from: https://doi.org/10.1080/1461670X.2020.1776144 (Accessed 25 October 2023)

63 Righetti, Nicola (2021) 'The Anti-Gender Debate on Social Media. A Computational Communication Science Analysis of Networks, Activism, and Misinformation'. *Comunicazione politica*, pp. 223–50. [online] Available from: https://doi.org/10.3270/101610 (Accessed 6 September 2021)

64 Robertson, D.L., Pow, A.M., Hunt, D., Hudson, B. and Mickelsen, R. (2019) 'We are Just People: Transgender Individuals' Experiences of a Local Equal Rights Debate'. *Journal of LGBTQ Issues in Counseling*, 13(3), pp. 178–97. [online] Available from: https://doi.org/10.1080/15538605.2019.1627974 (Accessed 27 July 2021)

65 Yglesias, Matthew (2023) 'The two kinds of progressives'. [online] Available from: https://www.slowboring.com/p/the-two-kinds-of-progressives (Accessed 1 September 2023)

66 Ketelaars, Pauline (2016) 'What Strikes the Responsive Chord? The Effects of Framing Qualities on Frame Resonance among Protest Participants'. *Mobilization: An International Quarterly*, 21(3), pp. 341–60. [online] Available from: https://doi.org/10.17813/1086-671X-21-3-341 (Accessed 25 October 2023)

67 Ibid.

68 Wodak, Ruth (2015) *The Politics of Fear: What Right-Wing Populist Discourses Mean*, London, Sage.

69 Frischlich, Lena, Schatto-Eckrodt, Tim, Boberg, Svenja and Wintterlin, Florian (2021) 'Roots of Incivility: How Personality, Media Use, and Online Experiences Shape Uncivil Participation'. *Media and Communication*, 9, pp. 195–208. [online] Available from: https://www.cogitatiopress.com/mediaandcommunication/article/view/3360 (Accessed 25 October 2021)

70 Gervais, Bryan T. (2017) 'More than Mimicry? The Role of Anger in Uncivil Reactions to Elite Political Incivility', *International Journal of Public Opinion Research*, 29(3), pp. 384–405. [online] Available from: https://doi.org/10.1093/ijpor/edw010 (Accessed 25 October 2023)

71 Luther King Jr, Martin (1992) 'Letter from Birmingham Jail', *UC Davis Law Review*, 26(4), pp. 835–52. [online] Available from: https://lawreview.law.ucdavis.edu/issues/26/4/articles/DavisVol26No4_King.pdf (Accessed 25 October 2023)

72 Ketelaars, Pauline (2016) 'What Strikes the Responsive Chord? The Effects of Framing Qualities on Frame Resonance among Protest Participants'. *Mobilization: An International Quarterly*, 21(3), pp. 341–60. [online] Available from: https://doi.org/10.17813/1086-671X-21-3-341 (Accessed 25 October 2023)

73 Jost, John T. (2017) 'Ideological Asymmetries and the Essence of Political Psychology'. *Political Psychology*, 38(2), pp. 167–208. [online] Available from: https://onlinelibrary.wiley.com/doi/abs/10.1111/pops.12407 (Accessed 9 August 2021)

3. The uses (and abuses) of fandom

1 Bender, Michael C. and Haberman, Maggie (2022) 'Trump Under Fire From Within G.O.P. After Midterms'. *The New York Times*, 10 November. [online] Available from: https://www.nytimes.com/2022/11/09/us/politics/trump-republicans-midterms.html (Accessed 1 September 2023)

2 Gilbert, David (2023) 'QAnon Is Absolutely Melting Down Over Trump's Mugshot and Return to Twitter'. *Vice*. [online] Available from: https://www.vice.com/en/article/93kd8p/qanon-trump-mugshot-arrest-twitter (Accessed 1 September 2023)

3 Truss, Liz (2022) 'Growth is the best way to make everyone's lives better. It means more money in people's pockets, more money for businesses to create jobs, and more funding for world-class public services including the NHS and the Armed Forces. My piece in @ Telegraph 👇 https://telegraph.co.uk/politics/2022/10/03/abolishing-45p-tax-rate-tiny-part-big-plans-get-britain-moving/' *@trussliz*. [online] Available from: https://twitter.com/trussliz/status/1577230455237025793 (Accessed 25 October 2023)

4 Bright, Sam (2022) 'Kemi Badenoch Carries on Liz Truss' Tufton Street Traditions'. *Byline Times*. [online] Available from: https://bylinetimes.com/2022/11/14/kemi-badenoch-carries-on-liz-truss-tufton-street-traditions/ (Accessed 1 September 2023)

5 Hunte, Ben (2022) 'Exclusive: UK Government Pushed City Watchdog to Cancel Trans Inclusion Policy'. *Vice*. [online] Available from: https://www.vice.com/en/article/n7zbmd/kemi-badenoch-fca (Accessed 28 September 2022)

6 Balls, Katy (2022) 'Kemi Badenoch: the curriculum does not need "decolonising"'. [online] Available from: https://www.spectator.co.uk/article/kemi-badenoch-defends-the-government-s-new-race-strategy (Accessed 28 September 2022)

7 Ipsos (2021) 'Boris Johnson's net favourability score lowest since the 2019 election, meanwhile Conservative voters unhappy with party's immigration policies'. *Ipsos*. [online] Available from: https://www.ipsos.com/en-uk/boris-johnsons-net-favourability-score-lowest-2019-election (Accessed 13 June 2023)

8 Ford, Robert, Bale, Tim, Jennings, Will and Surridge, Paula (2021) *The British General Election of 2019*, Cham, Springer International Publishing. [online] Available from: https://link.springer.com/10.1007/978-3-030-74254-6 (Accessed 13 June 2023)

9 Ipsos (2022) 'Boris Johnson's likeability ratings fall to his lowest score as PM'. *Ipsos*. [online] Available from: https://www.ipsos.com/en-uk/boris-johnsons-likeability-ratings-fall-his-lowest-score-pm (Accessed 13 June 2023)

10 Dowd, Maureen (1992) 'THE 1992 CAMPAIGN: Political Memo; Of Knights and Presidents: Race of Mythic Proportions'. *The New York Times*, 10 October. [online] Available from: https://www.nytimes.com/1992/10/10/us/1992-campaign-political-memo-knights-presidents-race-mythic-proportions.html (Accessed 16 May 2022)

11 Morris, Joanna (2022) 'As rail workers prepare for Christmas strikes, what do Britons think of trade unionist Mick Lynch?' [online] Available from: https://yougov.co.uk/topics/politics/articles-reports/2022/12/20/rail-workers-prepare-christmas-strikes-what-do-bri (Accessed 1 September 2023)

12 Williams, Zoe (2022) '"You don't think strikes are the answer? What is?" RMT's Mick Lynch on work, dignity and union power'. *The Guardian*, 23 August. [online] Available from: https://www.theguardian.com/uk-news/2022/aug/23/mick-lynch-rmt-work-dignity-union-power (Accessed 25 October 2023)

13 Ramaswamy, Chitra (2023) '"Social mobility is a fairytale": Faiza Shaheen on fighting for Labour and hating Oxford'. *The Guardian*, 29 May. [online] Available from: https://www.theguardian.com/lifeandstyle/2023/may/29/social-mobility-is-a-fairytale-faiza-shaheen-on-fighting-for-labour-and-hating-oxford (Accessed 20 June 2023)

14 Shaheen, Faiza (2019) 'As a Labour candidate, I know we are the real "new politics" in Britain'. *The Guardian*, 25 February. [online] Available from: https://www.theguardian.com/commentisfree/2019/feb/25/labour-new-politics-mps-independent-group (Accessed 8 July 2023)

15 Neicho, Joshua (2019) 'Election 2019: Has mass campaigning in Chingford & Woodford Green helped or hindered Labour?' *OnLondon*. [online] Available from: https://www.onlondon.co.uk/election-2019-has-mass-campaigning-in-chingford-woodford-green-helped-or-hindered-labour/ (Accessed 20 June 2023)

16 Lothian-McLean, Moya (n.d.) 'General election: Greggs vegan sausage rolls keep selling out in this key marginal seat as Labour canvassers flood the area'. *indy100*. [online] Available from: https://www.indy100.com/news/labour-greggs-vegan-sausage-roll-faiza-shaheen-chingford-9242776 (Accessed 8 July 2023)

17 Bale, Tim, Webb, Paul and Poletti, Monica (2018) *Grassroots – Britain's party members: who they are, what they think and what they do*, London, QMUL. [online] Available from: https://www.qmul.ac.uk/media/qmul/media/publications/Grassroots,-Britain's-Party-Members.pdf (Accessed 25 October 2023)

18 Rainsford, Emily (2017) 'Exploring youth political activism in the United Kingdom: What makes young people politically active in different organisations?' *The British Journal of Politics and International Relations*, 19(4). [online] Available from: https://doi.org/10.1177/1369148117772866 (Accessed 25 October 2023)

19 Kale, Sirin (2015) 'Blackmail, Threats, and Fear: Young Tories Discuss the UK Conservative Party Bullying Scandal'. *Vice*. [online] Available from: https://www.vice.com/en/article/vdxj7j/young-conservatives-bullying-scandal-734 (Accessed 7 July 2023)

20 BBC News (2017) 'No charges over 2015 Conservative battle bus cases'. *BBC News*, 9 May. [online] Available from: https://www.bbc.com/news/uk-politics-39865801 (Accessed 1 September 2023)

21 Clarke, Mark (2014) 'Mark Clarke: Come to Newark this Saturday with RoadTrip2015'. *Conservative Home*.

[online] Available from: https://conservativehome.com/2014/05/28/mark-clarke-come-to-newark-this-saturday-with-roadtrip2015/ (Accessed 7 July 2023)

22 Kember, Billy (2015) '"It was all a big game at first, but that changed"'. *The Times*, 19 December. [online] Available from: https://www.thetimes.co.uk/article/it-was-all-a-big-game-at-first-but-that-changed-9tpwjf2tj (Accessed 9 July 2023)

23 Walters, Simon (2015) 'Secret tape of "Tatler Tory" bullying suicide victim'. *Mail Online*. [online] Available from: https://www.dailymail.co.uk/news/article-3259016/Secret-tape-Tatler-Tory-bullying-suicide-victim-Menacing-blackmail-threats-young-activist-kangaroo-court-revenge-adultery-rumours.html (Accessed 7 July 2023)

24 Butterworth, Benjamin (2023) 'Man groped by Tory MP Chris Pincher says Westminster is "not safe" for young aides'. *inews.co.uk*. [online] Available from: https://inews.co.uk/news/chris-pincher-man-groped-tory-mp-westminster-not-safe-young-aides-2459958 (Accessed 7 July 2023)

25 Watt, Nicholas (2007) 'The welcome party'. *The Guardian*, 11 May. [online] Available from: https://www.theguardian.com/politics/2007/may/11/tonyblair.labour9 (Accessed 25 October 2022)

26 Crick, Michael (2017) 'Corbyn says voters should choose hope over fear'. *Channel 4 News*. [online] Available from: https://www.channel4.com/news/corbyn-says-voters-should-choose-hope-over-fear (Accessed 1 September 2023)

27 Tocqueville, Alexis de (2012) *Democracy in America*, English edition, Nolla, E. (ed.), Indianapolis, Liberty Fund.

4. Grassroots fandom

1 Chester for Europe #FBPE (2019) 'Do you want to make some new friends and share your pro EU passion? Why not volunteer for your local #PeoplesVote Campaign group. More info here #FBPE https://peoples-vote.uk/volunteer https://t.co/9PkBzT2MFJ'. *@chesterforeu*. [online] Available from: https://twitter.com/chesterforeu/status/1138147194224218114 (Accessed 18 November 2021)

2 Seregina, Anastasia and Schouten, John W. (2017) 'Resolving identity ambiguity through transcending fandom'. *Consumption Markets and Culture*, 20(2), pp. 107–30.

3 Busch, Peter André, Hausvik, Geir Inge, Ropstad, Odd Karsten and Pettersen, Daniel (2021) 'Smartphone usage among older adults'. *Computers in Human Behavior*, 121, p. 106783. [online] Available from: https://www.sciencedirect.com/science/article/pii/S0747563221001060 (Accessed 1 September 2023)

4 Statista (2023) 'U.K.: smartphone usage by age 2012-2022'. *Statista*. [online] Available from: https://www.statista.com/statistics/300402/smartphone-usage-in-the-uk-by-age/ (Accessed 10 July 2023)

5 Chen, Brian X. (2023) 'The Future of Social Media Is a Lot Less Social'.

The New York Times, 19 April. [online] Available from: https://www.nytimes.com/2023/04/19/technology/personaltech/tiktok-twitter-facebook-social.html (Accessed 1 September 2023)

6 Doctorow, Cory (2023) 'Tiktok's enshittification'. *Pluralistic*. [online] Available from: https://pluralistic.net/2023/01/21/potemkin-ai/ (Accessed 10 July 2023)

7 Manthorpe, Rowland (2018) 'The UK's left is scrambling to adapt to Facebook's algorithm change'. *Wired UK*. [online] Available from: https://www.wired.co.uk/article/facebook-algorithm-changes-engagement-labour (Accessed 10 July 2023)

8 Saner, Emine (2022) '"This is fascism – we're all being attacked": "Stop Brexit Man" Steve Bray on lies, police powers and free speech'. *The Guardian*, 26 July. [online] Available from: https://www.theguardian.com/world/2022/jul/26/stop-brexit-man-steve-bray-on-lies-police-powers-and-free-speech (Accessed 10 July 2023)

9 Pridmore, Oliver (2023) 'Notts MP in scuffle after taking "Stop Brexit" man's hat'. *NottinghamshireLive*. [online] Available from: https://www.nottinghampost.com/news/local-news/nottinghamshire-mp-scuffle-after-taking-8024335 (Accessed 10 July 2023)

10 Evans, Geoffrey and Mellon, Jonathan (2019) 'Immigration, Euroscepticism, and the rise and fall of UKIP'. *Party Politics*, 25(1), pp. 76–87. [online] Available from: https://doi.org/10.1177/1354068818816969 (Accessed 17 May 2022)

11 Packham, Peter (2021) 'Brexit isn't working: pro-EU protest rally in Leeds'. *Yorkshire Bylines*. [online] Available from: https://yorkshirebylines.co.uk/politics/brexit-isnt-working-protest-rally-leeds/ (Accessed 4 January 2022)

12 Fiadotava, Anastasiya (2021) '"We came for the Sluts, but stayed for the Slutsk": FK Slutsk Worldwide Facebook page between ironic and genuine football fandom'. *HUMOR*, 34(2), pp. 259–82. [online] Available from: https://www.degruyter.com/document/doi/10.1515/humor-2021-0007/html (Accessed 17 August 2021)

13 Kumari, Shringi, Deterding, Sebastian and Freeman, Jonathan (2019) 'The Role of Uncertainty in Moment-to-Moment Player Motivation: A Grounded Theory', in *Proceedings of the Annual Symposium on Computer-Human Interaction in Play*, CHI PLAY '19, New York, NY, USA, Association for Computing Machinery, pp. 351–63. [online] Available from: https://doi.org/10.1145/3311350.3347148 (Accessed 18 August 2022)

14 Smith, Ian (2023) 'Just Stop Oil protesters storm Wimbledon court and throw confetti'. *euronews*. [online] Available from: https://www.euronews.com/green/2023/07/05/im-here-for-my-grandchildren-two-pensioners-storm-wimbledon-court-to-demand-climate-action (Accessed 10 July 2023)

15 Shepard, Benjamin, Bogad, L.M. and Duncombe, Stephen (2008) 'Performing vs. the Insurmountable: Theatrics, Activism, and Social Movements'. *Liminalities: A Journal of Performance Studies*, 4(3), p. 30.

16 Khomami, Nadia (2021) 'Michael Sheen declares himself a "not-for-profit actor"'. *The Guardian*, 6 December. [online]

Available from: https://www.theguardian.com/film/2021/dec/06/michael-sheen-not-for-profit-actor-activist (Accessed 3 January 2022)

17 Hay, Katharine (2020) '"I love JK Rowling" billboard at Edinburgh Waverley station removed for being "too political"'. *The Scotsman*. [online] Available from: https://www.scotsman.com/news/politics/jk-rowling-billboard-at-edinburgh-waverley-station-in-support-of-author-removed-2928241 (Accessed 1 September 2023)

18 Pawson, Chad (2020) 'I Love J.K. Rowling sign makes brief, controversial appearance in Vancouver'. *CBC*. [online] Available from: https://www.cbc.ca/news/canada/british-columbia/i-love-j-k-rowling-sign-makes-brief-controversial-appearance-in-vancouver-1.5722244 (Accessed 1 September 2023)

19 Minkel, Elizabeth (2017) 'The Year of Loving Things Again'. *Fansplaining*. [online] Available from: https://www.fansplaining.com/articles/the-year-of-loving-things-again (Accessed 22 December 2021)

20 Podilchak, Walter (1985) 'The Social Organisation of Fun'. *Loisir et Société / Society and Leisure*, 8(2), pp. 685–91. [online] Available from: http://www.tandfonline.com/doi/abs/10.1080/07053436.1985.10715235 (Accessed 22 November 2021)

21 Márquez, Xavier (2020) 'The mechanisms of cult production: An overview', in *Ruler Personality Cults from Empires to Nation-States and Beyond*, London, Routledge.

22 Traber, Denise, Hänni, Miriam, Giger, Nathalie and Breunig, Christian (n.d.) 'Social status, political priorities and unequal representation'. *European Journal of Political Research*, n/a(n/a). [online] Available from: https://onlinelibrary.wiley.com/doi/abs/10.1111/1475-6765.12456 (Accessed 22 November 2021)

23 Abts, Koen and Baute, Sharon (2021) 'Social resentment, blame attribution and Euroscepticism: the role of status insecurity, relative deprivation and powerlessness'. *Innovation: The European Journal of Social Science Research*, 0(0), pp. 1–26. [online] Available from: https://doi.org/10.1080/13511610.2021.1964350 (Accessed 23 August 2021)

24 BBC News (2016) 'Tom Watson hits back at Corbyn in "Trotskyist entryist" row'. *BBC News*, 15 August. [online] Available from: https://www.bbc.com/news/uk-politics-37082534 (Accessed 18 November 2021)

25 Bale, Tim, Webb, Paul and Poletti, Monica (2018) *Grassroots – Britain's party members: who they are, what they think and what they do*, London, QMUL. [online] Available from: https://esrcpartymembersprojectorg.files.wordpress.com/2018/01/grassroots-pmp_final.pdf (Accessed 16 August 2023)

26 HireHeels (2008) 'We adore shoes, but we LOVE HILLARY'. *HireHeels*. [online] Available from: https://web.archive.org/web/20080403180616/http://hireheels.com/ (Accessed 2 December 2021)

27 Silver, Nate (2008) 'How (not) to win over Clinton supporters'. *FiveThirtyEight*. [online] Available from: https://fivethirtyeight.com/features/how-not-to-win-over-clinton-supporters/ (Accessed 2 December 2021)

28 Tomasic, John (2008) 'Hell No: P.U.M.A. Spokesman Will Bower on Post-Clinton Party Unity'. *HuffPost.* [online] Available from: https://www.huffpost.com/entry/hell-no-puma-spokesman-wi_b_108581 (Accessed 2 December 2021)

29 Bower, Will (2008) 'My Evening With Harriet Christian'. *HuffPost.* [online] Available from: https://www.huffpost.com/entry/my-evening-with-harriet-c_b_104594 (Accessed 2 December 2021)

30 Gray, Rosie (2012) 'Hillary Clinton's 2008 Dead-Enders Fight On'. *BuzzFeed News.* [online] Available from: https://www.buzzfeednews.com/article/rosiegray/hillary-clintons-2008-dead-enders-fight-on (Accessed 2 December 2021)

31 Williams, Vanessa (2015) 'They were Hillary Clinton's die-hard loyalists. Here's where they are now.' *Washington Post.* [online] Available from: https://www.washingtonpost.com/politics/they-were-hillary-clintons-die-hard-loyalists-heres-where-they-are-now/2015/05/02/82025cf2-e92a-11e4-aae1-d642717d8afa_story.html (Accessed 2 December 2021)

32 *Newsweek* (2009) 'Will Bower interviewed by Newsweek. . .'. *Hillary Unleashed.* [online] Available from: https://hillaryunleashed.wordpress.com/2009/01/25/will-bower-interviewed-by-newsweek/ (Accessed 2 December 2021)

33 Schäfer, Armin (undefined/ed) 'Cultural Backlash? How (Not) to Explain the Rise of Authoritarian Populism'. *British Journal of Political Science*, pp. 1–17. [online] Available from: https://www.cambridge.org/core/journals/british-journal-of-political-science/article/cultural-backlash-how-not-to-explain-the-rise-of-authoritarian-populism/FFE9742798D8CC4BF6ED325FDBAFA251 (Accessed 6 October 2021)

34 Jewell, Hannah (2015) 'Ed Miliband Has Developed A Small But Growing Fandom Of Teen Girls'. *BuzzFeed.* [online] Available from: https://www.buzzfeed.com/hannahjewell/the-milifandom (Accessed 24 December 2021)

35 Bock, Pauline (2020) 'March of the "Milifans": Ed Miliband's female groupies are back and we mean business (and energy)'. *The Telegraph*, 8 April. [online] Available from: https://www.telegraph.co.uk/women/politics/march-milifans-ed-milibands-female-groupies-back-mean-business/ (Accessed 4 January 2022)

36 Cohen, Libby (2020) 'Inside the "Markeyverse," the passionate online fandom for Sen. Ed Markey'. *The Daily Dot.* [online] Available from: https://www.dailydot.com/debug/ed-markey-markeyverse-twitter-tiktok/ (Accessed 15 December 2021)

37 Kashinsky, Lisa (2021) 'Why the Wuniverse isn't the Markeyverse'. *POLITICO.* [online] Available from: https://politi.co/3kMQOQb (Accessed 15 December 2021)

38 Oladipo, Gloria (2021) 'Michelle Wu becomes Boston's first woman and person of color to be elected mayor'. *The Guardian*, 3 November. [online] Available from: https://www.theguardian.com/us-news/2021/nov/03/michelle-wu-boston-mayor-first-woman-person-of-color (Accessed 15 December 2021)

39 Alarcón G., Maximiliano, Fossa, Lisette and Solis, Camilo (2021) 'Poblaciones,

memes y K-Pop: el esfuerzo de la ciudadanía independiente por levantar una campaña paralela por Boric y derrotar a Kast'. *Interferencia.* [online] Available from: https://interferencia.cl/articulos/poblaciones-memes-y-k-pop-el-esfuerzo-de-la-ciudadania-independiente-por-levantar-una (Accessed 20 December 2021)

40 Ibid.

41 Bankoff, Caroline (n.d.) 'Hillary Clinton Is Just Trying to Chill'. *Intelligencer.* [online] Available from: https://nymag.com/intelligencer/2015/07/hillary-clinton-is-just-trying-to-chill.html (Accessed 3 January 2022)

42 Nuzzi, Olivia (2014) 'Inside the World of Rand Paul Swag'. *The Daily Beast,* 20 August. [online] Available from: https://www.thedailybeast.com/articles/2014/08/20/inside-the-world-of-rand-paul-swag (Accessed 21 September 2021)

43 Friedman, Vanessa (2015) 'Presidential Hopefuls Sell Swag and Collect Data'. *The New York Times.* [online] Available from: https://www.nytimes.com/2015/06/25/fashion/presidential-campaign-stores-voter-data.html (Accessed 3 January 2022)

5. Fan creativity

1 O'Neill, Lauren (2017) 'This GIF Site of Corbyn Set to "Rock DJ" Is the Future Liberals Want'. *Vice.* [online] Available from: https://www.vice.com/en/article/ywm9jb/jeremy-corbyn-robbie-williams-rock-dj-cans4corbyn (Accessed 22 June 2023)

2 Turk, Tisha (2014) 'Fan work: Labor, worth, and participation in fandom's gift economy'. *Transformative Works and Cultures,* 15. [online] Available from: https://journal.transformativeworks.org/index.php/twc/article/view/518 (Accessed 10 July 2023)

3 Abse, Leo (1996) *The Man Behind the Smile: Tony Blair and the Politics of Perversion,* London, Robson Books.

4 Abse, Leo (1989) *Margaret, Daughter of Beatrice: A Politician's Psycho-biography of Margaret Thatcher,* London, J. Cape.

5 Abse, Leo (1973) *Private Member,* London, Macdonald.

6 Abse, Leo (2000) *Fellatio, Masochism, Politics and Love,* London, Robson Books.

7 Associated Press (2008) 'Leo Abse, Labor Party Stalwart From Wales, Is Dead at 91'. *The New York Times,* 25 August. [online] Available from: https://www.nytimes.com/2008/08/25/world/europe/25abse.html (Accessed 29 October 2022)

8 Hansard Society (2019) 'Audit of Political Engagement 16'. *Hansard Society.* [online] Available from: https://www.hansardsociety.org.uk/publications/reports/audit-of-political-engagement-16 (Accessed 30 October 2021)

9 Flanagan, Padraic (2023) 'Line of Duty's Adrian Dunbar admits voicing Cressida Dick spoof'. *The Times,* 10 July. [online] Available from: https://www.thetimes.co.uk/article/line-of-dutys-adrian-dunbar-admits-voicing-cressida-dick-spoof-jdz3rmnct (Accessed 10 July 2023)

10 Mayonnaise, Betty (2018) 'The Iain Duncan Smiths. Politically correct'. *is this music?*, 7 September. [online] Available from: https://www.isthismusic.com/the-iain-duncan-smiths-ten-with-betty-qa (Accessed 10 July 2023)

11 Burkeman, Oliver (2010) 'Nick Clegg – the British Obama?' *The Guardian*, 19 April. [online] Available from: https://www.theguardian.com/politics/2010/apr/19/nick-clegg-obama (Accessed 24 December 2021)

12 Oliver, Jonathan and Smith, David (2010) 'Nick Clegg is nearly as popular as Winston Churchill'. *The Times*, 18 April. [online] Available from: https://www.thetimes.co.uk/article/nick-clegg-is-nearly-as-popular-as-winston-churchill-t9gn20hnmbm (Accessed 24 December 2021)

13 Carvalho, Edzia and Winters, Kristi (2015) '"I Went with What I Always Do. . .": A Qualitative Analysis of "Cleggmania" and Vote Choice in the 2010 British General Election'. *Parliamentary Affairs (2015)*, 68, pp. 423–46.

14 Guest, Nat (2010) 'Catch-up Blog: Cleggmania, Timey-Wimey Stuff & The Whedonverse'. *@unfortunatalie*. [online] Available from: https://nothingbutawordbag.wordpress.com/2010/05/04/catch-up-cleggmania-timey-wimey-stuff-the-whedonverse/ (Accessed 4 November 2021)

15 dirtypoliticsconfessions (n.d.) 'Playing Dirty'. *Because someone had to. How: You send in your confessions via ask and I create the graphics for you. . .* [online] Available from: https://dirtypoliticsconfessions.tumblr.com/ (Accessed 4 November 2021)

16 Le Conte, Marie (2020) 'Members in Parliament: the ups and downs of political porn'. *The Face*. [online] Available from: https://theface.com/society/uk-parliament-political-porn-prime-ministers?token=322 (Accessed 4 November 2021)

17 Belam, Martin (2013) '"The who, what and why of UsVsTh3m" – Martin Belam at Hacks/Hackers London'. *martinbelam.com*. [online] Available from: https://martinbelam.com/2013/hacks_hackers_usvsth3m/ (Accessed 4 November 2021)

18 Young, Michael (2017) 'The Art of the Plausible and the Aesthetics of Doubt'. *Log*, (41), pp. 37–44. [online] Available from: https://www.jstor.org/stable/26323714 (Accessed 22 November 2021)

19 Lambert-Beatty, Carrie (2009) 'Make-Believe: Parafiction and Plausibility'. *October*, (129), pp. 51–84. [online] Available from: https://doi.org/10.1162/octo.2009.129.1.51 (Accessed 23 December 2021)

20 McLeod, Kembrew (2020) 'Pranksters on a Mission: An Interview With the Yes Men'. *MIT Press Reader*. [online] Available from: https://thereader.mitpress.mit.edu/an-interview-with-the-yes-men/ (Accessed 23 December 2021)

21 Gibson, Lydialyle (2020) 'Carrie Lambert-Beatty: What Happens When an Artwork Deceives Its Audience?' *Harvard Magazine*. [online] Available from: https://www.harvardmagazine.com/2020/carrie-lambert-beatty (Accessed 23 December 2021)

22 Whyman, Tom (2020) 'The Trevor Bastard Extended Universe is modern art'. *The Outline*. [online] Available from: https://theoutline.com/post/8466/trevor-bastard-extended-universe-twitter-art (Accessed 22 November 2021)

23 Öpik, Lembit (2015) 'Specsavers Employee of the month for me: rebecca. With Mark on right – these guys shine'. *@lembitopik*. [online] Available from: https://twitter.com/lembitopik/status/614517489884614656 (Accessed 1 September 2023)

24 Koshy, Yohann (2017) 'The New Wave of Satire for Our Morbid Political Landscape'. *Vice*. [online] Available from: https://www.vice.com/en/article/53n9v8/the-new-wave-of-satire-for-our-morbid-political-landscape (Accessed 13 December 2021)

25 Magee, Will (2019) 'How a fake football club exposed Twitter's hypocrisy'. *Huck Magazine*. [online] Available from: https://www.huckmag.com/art-and-culture/tech/how-a-fake-football-club-exposed-twitters-hypocrisy/ (Accessed 22 November 2021)

26 Streatham Rovers Football Club (2019) 'We've had the ongoing issue of the dog muck outside the clubhouse ignored by local MPs from three different political parties but within days of announcing his candidacy for London mayor Rory Stewart has shown he's not afraid to get his hands dirty. Absolutely first class 👏👏👏'. *@StreathamRovers*. [online] Available from: https://twitter.com/StreathamRovers/status/1181272337381023745 (Accessed 23 December 2021)

27 Stewart, Rory (2019) 'So so sorry. Our fault entirely. Unfortunately my staff member defected to Venezuela last night – apparently his extradition vehicle was not mobile friendly – but he assures me is sending another team member with a pooper scooper to @StreathamRovers tonight. Thanks again'. *@RoryStewartUK*. [online] Available from: https://twitter.com/RoryStewartUK/status/1181623302411948032 (Accessed 24 December 2021)

28 Stewart, Rory (2019) 'So so sorry. Our fault entirely. Unfortunately my staff member defected to Venezuela last night – apparently his extradition vehicle was not mobile friendly – but he assures me is sending another team member with a pooper scooper to @Streatham Rovers tonight. Thanks again'. *@RoryStewartUK*. [online] Available from: https://twitter.com/RoryStewartUK/status/1181623302411948032? (Accessed 25 October 2023)

29 Whyman, Tom (2020) 'The problem with complaining that "everyone's an Iran expert now"'. *The Guardian*, 9 January. [online] Available from: https://www.theguardian.com/commentisfree/2020/jan/09/experts-social-media-middle-east-crisis-twitter (Accessed 13 December 2021)

30 Stone, Jon (2019) 'Jo Swinson forced to deny shooting stones at squirrels with slingshot'. *The Independent*. [online] Available from: https://www.independent.co.uk/news/uk/politics/jo-swinson-squirrels-shooting-stones-lib-dems-slingshot-fake-news-a9209196.html (Accessed 24 December 2021)

31 Hallin, Daniel (1986) *The 'Uncensored War': The Media and Vietnam*, Oxford, Oxford University Press.

32 Mayhew, Freddy (2021) 'Daily Star editor: Cummings mask and other front pages'. *Press Gazette*. [online] Available from: https://pressgazette.co.uk/daily-star-editor-says-dominic-cummings-taking-the-piss-front-pages/ (Accessed 29 October 2022)

33 Davis, Paul (2019) 'The Purist/Partisan Spectator Discourse: Some Examination and Discrimination'. *Sport, Ethics and Philosophy*, 13(2), pp. 247–58. [online] Available from: https://doi.org/10.1080/17511321.2018.1498116 (Accessed 6 December 2021)

34 The Policy Institute (2021) 'Liberals have most difficulty getting along with opponents on "culture war" issues'. *King's College London.* [online] Available from: https://www.kcl.ac.uk/news/liberals-have-most-difficulty-getting-along-with-opponents-on-culture-war-issues (Accessed 26 October 2022)

6. The sensibles are not sensible

1 Cohen, Daniel (2019) '"Loud, obsessive, tribal": the radicalisation of remain'. *The Guardian.* [online] Available from: https://www.theguardian.com/politics/2019/aug/13/brexit-remain-radicalisation-fbpe-peoples-vote (Accessed 18 November 2021)

2 Anon (1996) 'UK's Mr Sensible'. *POLITICO.* [online] Available from: https://www.politico.eu/article/uks-mr-sensible/ (Accessed 28 June 2023)

3 Clarke, Ken (2023) 'I'm not known for being tough on immigration – but we must give the Rwanda plan a chance'. *The Telegraph*, 9 July. [online] Available from: https://www.telegraph.co.uk/news/2023/07/09/mps-must-give-the-rwanda-plan-a-chance/ (Accessed 10 July 2023)

4 Dunt, Ian (2022) 'But what we really need in the British political system, and what we sorely lack, is deliberation, evidence-assessment, cautious policy formulation and effective delivery systems. Not a bunch of stick-thin politics nerds shouting: FUCK YOU LOOK AT THE SIZE OF MY DEATH COCK'. *@IanDunt.* [online] Available from: https://twitter.com/IanDunt/status/1552595568102342657 (Accessed 28 July 2022)

5 Judah, Ben (2022) 'With Rishi Sunak's elevation to Prime Minister a long period of populist chaos in British politics – defined by Brexit, Boris and Corbyn – draws to a close. The next chapter belongs to Sunak, Starmer and their "sensibles."' *@b_judah.* [online] Available from: https://twitter.com/b_judah/status/1584546012278198272 (Accessed 25 October 2022)

6 Maitlis, Emily (2022) 'Sunak tone spot on – talked about "compassion" in his decisions – we haven't heard that word for a long long time. And bold enough to say he was there to clean up Truss mistakes. No hiding from that.' *@emilymaitlis.* [online] Available from: https://twitter.com/maitlis/status/1584864075770888194 (Accessed 25 October 2022)

7 Rhodes, R.A.W. (1994) 'THE HOLLOWING OUT OF THE STATE: THE CHANGING NATURE OF THE PUBLIC SERVICE IN BRITAIN'. *The Political Quarterly*, 65(2), pp. 138–51. [online] Available from: https://onlinelibrary.wiley.com/doi/10.1111/j.1467-923X.1994.tb00441.x (Accessed 28 June 2023)

8 Goodier, Michael (2022) 'NHS hospital trusts paying hundreds of millions in

interest to private firms'. *The Guardian*, 25 October. [online] Available from: https://www.theguardian.com/politics/2022/oct/25/nhs-hospital-trusts-paying-hundreds-of-millions-in-interest-to-private-firms (Accessed 1 September 2023)

9 Thiel, Peter (2009) 'The Education of a Libertarian'. *Cato Unbound*. [online] Available from: https://www.cato-unbound.org/2009/04/13/peter-thiel/education-libertarian (Accessed 17 November 2021)

10 Miles, Alice (2010) 'I love elections. I love the massive, mad, manic effort'. *The Independent*. [online] Available from: https://www.independent.co.uk/voices/commentators/alice-miles-i-love-elections-i-love-the-massive-mad-manic-effort-of-it-all-1943081.html (Accessed 14 November 2021)

11 AFP News Agency (2019) *ToniBler and Klinton: Love for West lives on in Kosovar names*. [online] Available from: https://www.youtube.com/watch?v=BNln7bBp974 (Accessed 2 November 2021)

12 Richards, Steve (2004) 'Tony Blair could have been a great leader, but he was too young and inexperienced'. *The Independent*. [online] Available from: https://www.independent.co.uk/voices/commentators/steve-richards/tony-blair-could-have-been-a-great-leader-but-he-was-too-young-and-inexperienced-59772.html (Accessed 2 January 2022)

13 Blair, Tony (2010) *A Journey*, London, Random House.

14 Hinsliff, Gaby (2019) 'The end of the liberal Tory'. *Prospect Magazine*. [online] Available from: https://www.prospectmagazine.co.uk/magazine/the-end-of-the-liberal-tory-conservative-party-boris-johnson-rory-stewart (Accessed 27 July 2022)

15 Robinson, Emily (2017) *The Language of Progressive Politics in Modern Britain*, London, Palgrave Macmillan UK. [online] Available from: http://link.springer.com/10.1057/978-1-137-50664-1 (Accessed 22 December 2021)

16 Hopkin, Jonathan and Rosamond, Ben (2018) 'Post-truth Politics, Bullshit and Bad Ideas: "Deficit Fetishism" in the UK'. *New Political Economy*, 0(6), pp. 641–55. [online] Available from: https://www.tandfonline.com/doi/full/10.1080/13563467.2017.1373757 (Accessed 10 October 2020)

17 McSmith, Andy (2013) 'Ed Miliband urged to bring back "grown-ups" to Labour front bench'. *The Independent*. [online] Available from: https://www.independent.co.uk/news/uk/politics/ed-miliband-urged-to-bring-back-grownups-to-labour-front-bench-8760157.html (Accessed 26 July 2022)

18 Parker, George (2023) 'Michael Heseltine: "The adults are back in charge"'. *Financial Times*, 17 March. [online] Available from: https://www.ft.com/content/cd91db6f-e9d6-45dc-b92f-404dc8f2724e (Accessed 10 July 2023)

19 Badenoch, Kemi (2023) 'Topical Questions – Hansard – UK Parliament'. *Hansard*. [online] Available from: https://hansard.parliament.uk/Commons/2023-06-29/debates/50840133-BC73-4FD1-B441-0AA52F30BDA0/TopicalQuestionshighlight=%22grown+ups%22 (Accessed 30 June 2023)

20 Blair, Tony (1996) 'Ideological blurring'. *Prospect Magazine*. [online] Available from: https://www.prospectmagazine.co.uk/magazine/ideologicalblurring-labour-ideology-polarising (Accessed 29 December 2021)

21 Abse, Leo (1996) *The Man Behind the Smile: Tony Blair and the Politics of Perversion*, London, Robson Books.

22 Marsan, Eddie (2018). 'If I was running a GE campaign for a new centrist party, the Party political broadcast would just be a re run of the 2012 Olympic opening ceremony, with the words "Make Britain Great Again" at the end.' *@eddiemarsan*. [online] Available from: https://twitter.com/eddiemarsan/status/1028632653698883584 (Accessed 25 October 2023)

23 Rose, Steve (2022) '"A Jerusalem for everyone": was the 2012 Olympics the last gasp of liberal Britain?' *The Guardian*, 16 July. [online] Available from: https://www.theguardian.com/culture/2022/jul/16/danny-boyle-2012-london-olympic-opening-ceremony-feelgood-factor (Accessed 25 October 2023)

24 Watt, Nicholas (2012) 'Olympics opening ceremony was "multicultural crap", Tory MP tweets'. *The Guardian*, 27 July. [online] Available from: https://www.theguardian.com/politics/2012/jul/28/olympics-opening-ceremony-multicultural-crap-tory-mp (Accessed 2 January 2022)

25 Kircher, Madison Malone (2019) 'Sorry But Your Favorite Viral Story is Probably Fake'. *The Cut*. [online] Available from: https://www.thecut.com/2019/06/how-to-spot-a-fake-viral-story.html (Accessed 1 September 2023)

26 Graham, Timothy, Bruns, Axel, Angus, Daniel, Hurcombe, Edward and Hames, Sam (2021) '#IStandWithDan versus #DictatorDan: the polarised dynamics of Twitter discussions about Victoria's COVID-19 restrictions'. *Media International Australia*, 179(1), pp. 127–48. [online] Available from: https://doi.org/10.1177/1329878X20981780 (Accessed 27 November 2021)

27 Wahlquist, Calla (2020) 'Questioning Daniel Andrews: how reporters came under attack in Victoria'. *The Guardian*, 2 October. [online] Available from: https://www.theguardian.com/australia-news/2020/oct/03/questioning-daniel-andrews-how-reporters-came-under-attack-in-victoria (Accessed 27 November 2021)

28 Alex – Fold Up Toy Designer ✂️📦 (2021) 'I decided to check back with the account that I linked to, only to find a wall of "Tweet unavailable" messages. 🙄 Luckily I took screenshots last night. 🙄 They QTed people using the tags, adding the tags themselves EIGHTY TWO (82) times between 8:00pm & 10:30pm. https://t.co/EAtDhlIJL1'. *@FoldUpToys*. [online] Available from: https://twitter.com/FoldUpToys/status/1429015781266821121 (Accessed 7 December 2021)

29 Allsopp, David (2021) '"Ask Rape Crisis Scotland" – a manufactured trend'. *Trans Safety Network*. [online] Available from: https://transsafety.network/posts/ask-rape-crisis-scotland (Accessed 7 December 2021)

30 Allsopp. David (2021) 'The usual suspects are artificially boosting the transphobic "IStandWith. . ." hashtag, with the top account tweeting it over

60 times, and the top RT account retweeting it over 220 times today'. @ *doublehelix*. [online] Available from: https://mobile.twitter.com/doublehelix/status/1442145230703243265 (Accessed 7 December 2021)

31 Cherry, Joanna (2021) 'Thank you to everyone who has tweeted or messaged their support overnight. I promise I will continue to stand up for the rights of women & girls & same sex attracted people & I won't give into bullying, harassment or intimidation. #IStandWithJoannaCherry'. *Twitter*. [online] Available from: https://twitter.com/joannaccherry/status/1460525832821264384 (Accessed 7 December 2021)

32 Richards, Xander (2021) 'SNP groups call for Joanna Cherry to have whip removed amid conversion therapy row'. *The National*. [online] Available from: https://www.thenational.scot/news/19723577.joanna-cherry-lose-whip-amid-conversion-therapy-row-snp-groups-say/ (Accessed 7 December 2021)

33 Allsopp, David (2021) '@joannaccherry Cheerleading your own hashtag now? People may be interested to know that 1000 of the tweets on that hashtag are actually retweets from just 8 accounts, some retweeting over 200 times each. Not quite the grassroots support that it might appear.' @ *doublehelix*. [online] Available from: https://twitter.com/doublehelix/status/1460545650861518858 (Accessed 7 December 2021)

34 Chung, Frank (2021) 'What's behind the rise of the "Dan Stans"?' *news.com.au*,17 February. [online] Available from: https://www.news.com.au/technology/online/social/whats-behind-the-rise-of-the-dan-stans/news-story/2a428b7a9bee322c63ebe0fd34174f09 (Accessed 7 December 2021)

35 Mance, Henry (2020) 'How the People's Vote fell apart'. *Financial Times*, 7 August. [online] Available from: https://www.ft.com/content/e02992f6-cf9e-46b3-8d45-325fb183302f (Accessed 3 November 2021)

36 Carras, Christi (2020) 'Gov. Andrew Cuomo approves of people who identify as "Cuomosexuals"'. *Los Angeles Times*. [online] Available from: https://www.latimes.com/entertainment-arts/story/2020-04-28/andrew-cuomo-sexual-ellen-degeneres-youtube (Accessed 6 August 2021)

37 Jong-Fast, Molly (2020) 'America's Governor? Why We Are Crushing on Andrew Cuomo Right Now'. *Vogue*. [online] Available from: https://www.vogue.com/article/andrew-cuomo-why-we-love-him-now-coronavirus (Accessed 2 December 2021)

38 Wong, Ashley (2021) 'What to Do With All Those "Cuomosexual" Tees?' *The New York Times*. [online] Available from: https://www.nytimes.com/2021/08/10/style/cuomosexual-shirts-designs.html (Accessed 2 December 2021)

39 Jost, John T. (2020) *A theory of system justification*, Cambridge, MA, Harvard University Press.

40 Taylor, Ros (2016) 'Resistance to cultural change drove Trump's support – just as with Brexit'. *LSE BREXIT*. [online] Available from: https://blogs.lse.ac.uk/brexit/2016/11/11/resistance-to-cultural-change-drove-trumps-support-just-as-with-brexit/ (Accessed 1 September 2023)

41 Hobbes, Michael (2021) 'Reactionary centrism consists of exactly one principle, to wit: The leftists made us do it. https://persuasion.community/p/the-collapse-of-liberal-internationalism https://t.co/9hN2LVaZ7t'. *@RottenInDenmark*. [online] Available from: https://twitter.com/RottenInDenmark/status/1469569468925894657 (Accessed 12 December 2021)

42 Huertas, Aaron (2018) 'We Need to Talk About Reactionary Centrists'. *Medium*. [online] Available from: https://medium.com/s/story/we-need-to-talk-about-reactionary-centrists-f0e6f8c4d58 (Accessed 7 December 2021)

43 Anon (1919) 'REDS TRY TO STIR NEGROES TO REVOLT; Widespread Propaganda on Foot Urging Them to Join I.W.W. and "Left Wing" Socialists. ATTACK COLORED LEADERS Publications Circulated Among Uneducated Classes in Southern States.' *The New York Times*, 28 July. [online] Available from: https://www.nytimes.com/1919/07/28/archives/reds-try-to-stir-negroes-to-revolt-widespread-propaganda-on-foot.html (Accessed 16 December 2021)

44 Special to *The New York Times* (1919) 'REDS ARE WORKING AMONG NEGROES; Widespread Propaganda by Radical Leaders Known to the Government. TAKES BOLSHEVIST FORM Two of the Negro Propagandists Said to be Harvard Graduates.' *The New York Times*, 19 October. [online] Available from: https://www.nytimes.com/1919/10/19/archives/reds-are-working-among-negroes-widespread-propaganda-by-radical.html (Accessed 16 December 2021)

45 Thiessen, Marc A. (2017) 'Yes, antifa is the moral equivalent of neo-Nazis'. *Washington Post*, 30 August. [online] Available from: https://www.washingtonpost.com/opinions/yes-antifa-is-the-moral-equivalent-of-neo-nazis/2017/08/30/9a13b2f6-8d00-11e7-91d5-ab4e4bb76a3a_story.html (Accessed 31 December 2021)

7. When fans go bad

1 Moraine, Sunny (2022) 'I honestly wonder if part of the reason why we're so eager to do pile-ons is that we are STARVED for any sort of consequences for bad behavior on the elite level so we're inclined to go for what we feel is attainable'. *@dynamicsymmetry*. [online] Available from: https://twitter.com/dynamicsymmetry/status/1554884771557285894 (Accessed 30 October 2022)

2 Marwick, Alice E. (2021) 'Morally Motivated Networked Harassment as Normative Reinforcement'. *Social Media + Society*, 7(2), p. 205630512110213. [online] Available from: http://journals.sagepub.com/doi/10.1177/20563051211021378 (Accessed 7 June 2021)

3 Brady, William J., McLoughlin, Killian, Doan, Tuan Nguyen and Crockett, Molly (2021) 'How social learning amplifies moral outrage expression in online social networks'. [online] Available from: https://psyarxiv.com/gf7t5/ (Accessed 24 August 2021)

4 Wagner, Kyle (2014) 'The Future Of The Culture Wars Is Here, And It's Gamergate'. *Deadspin.* [online] Available from: https://deadspin.com/the-future-of-the-culture-wars-is-here-and-its-gamerga-1646145844 (Accessed 19 November 2021)

5 McCormick, Rich (2014) 'Intel buckles to anti-feminist campaign by pulling ads from gaming site'. *The Verge.* [online] Available from: https://www.theverge.com/2014/10/2/6886747/intel-buckles-to-anti-feminist-campaign-by-pulling-ads-from-gaming (Accessed 25 August 2023)

6 Wagner, Kyle (2014) 'The Future Of The Culture Wars Is Here, And It's Gamergate'. *Deadspin.* [online] Available from: https://deadspin.com/the-future-of-the-culture-wars-is-here-and-its-gamerga-1646145844 (Accessed 19 November 2021)

7 Stop Funding Hate (2017) 'Stop Funding Hate'. *Stop Funding Hate.* [online] Available from: https://stopfundinghate.info/ (Accessed 25 August 2023)

8 Skinner, Anna (2023) 'Jesus TV show actors defend Pride flag on set after calls to boycott'. *Newsweek.* [online] Available from: https://www.newsweek.com/jesus-tv-show-actors-defend-pride-flag-set-after-calls-boycott-1803895 (Accessed 25 August 2023)

9 Associated Press (2023) 'Bud Light sales plunged after boycott over campaign with transgender influencer, company reveals'. *NBC News.* [online] Available from: https://www.nbcnews.com/business/business-news/bud-light-sales-plunged-boycott-campaign-transgender-influencer-compan-rcna97944 (Accessed 25 August 2023)

10 Murrer, Sally (2021) 'Popular Milton Keynes restaurant says "matter is with the police" following deluge of bad reviews after refusing to serve Tommy Robinson'. *MK Citizen.* [online] Available from: https://www.miltonkeynes.co.uk/news/people/popular-milton-keynes-restaurant-says-matter-is-with-the-police-following-deluge-of-bad-reviews-after-refusing-to-serve-tommy-robinson-3442401 (Accessed 21 December 2021)

11 Robinson, Tommy (2021) 'So "wing kingz" refused to serve me food for my children'. Telegram. [online] Available from: https://t.me/TommyRobinsonNews/28056 (Accessed 24 August 2023)

12 Cheng, Li-Keng and Toung, Chung-Lin (n.d.) 'Are celebrities accountable for the misconduct of their fans?' *Psychology & Marketing*, n/a(n/a). [online] Available from: http://onlinelibrary.wiley.com/doi/abs/10.1002/mar.21604 (Accessed 6 November 2021)

13 BBC News (2017) 'McDonald's Rick and Morty Szechuan sauce stunt backfires'. *BBC News*, 8 October. [online] Available from: https://www.bbc.com/news/world-us-canada-41543636 (Accessed 7 November 2021)

14 Not Dan Harmon (2017) *Rick and Morty Szechuan Sauce 'Riot' in LA.* [online] Available from: https://www.youtube.com/watch?v=7_HboVYEkWw (Accessed 7 November 2021)

15 Hibberd, James (2017) 'Rick and Morty co-creator slams trolls attacking their female writers'. *Entertainment Weekly.* [online] Available from: http://ew.com/tv/2017/09/21/rick-morty-dan-harmon-female-writers/ (Accessed 5 October 2017)

16 Epstein, Reid J. (2021) 'Wisconsin Republicans Push to Take Over the State's Elections'. *The New York Times*. [online] Available from: https://www.nytimes.com/2021/11/19/us/politics/wisconsin-republicans-decertify-election.html?referringSource=articleShare (Accessed 19 November 2021)

17 Marley, Patrick and Glauber, Bill (2021) 'Ron Johnson calls for having Republican lawmakers take over federal elections in Wisconsin'. *Milwaukee Journal Sentinel*. [online] Available from: https://www.jsonline.com/story/news/politics/elections/2021/11/10/ron-johnson-calls-gop-wisconsin-lawmakers-take-over-elections/6376079001/ (Accessed 19 November 2021)

18 Owen, Tess, Lamoureux, Mack and Hamilton, Keegan (2022) 'Man Accused of Attacking Nancy Pelosi's Husband Left Trail of Far-Right Hate'. *Vice*. [online] Available from: https://www.vice.com/en/article/m7gkey/david-depape-paul-pelosi-attack (Accessed 29 October 2022)

19 Trump, Donald J. (2016) 'TRANSCRIPT: Donald Trump's Speech Responding To Assault Accusations'. *NPR*, 13 October. [online] Available from: https://www.npr.org/2016/10/13/497857068/transcript-donald-trumps-speech-responding-to-assault-accusations (Accessed 2 January 2022)

20 Freyd, Jennifer J. (1997) 'Violations of Power, Adaptive Blindness and Betrayal Trauma Theory'. *Feminism & Psychology*, 7(1), pp. 22–32. [online] Available from: http://journals.sagepub.com/doi/10.1177/0959353597071004 (Accessed 31 October 2021)

21 Torres, Ignacio, Riegle, Ashley, Karar, Hana and Valiente, Alexa (2016) 'Meet the Trumpettes: Donald Trump's Loyal High Society Female Supporters'. *ABC News*. [online] Available from: https://abcnews.go.com/Politics/meet-trumpettes-donald-trumps-loyal-high-society-female/story?id=42888751 (Accessed 28 August 2023)

22 Center for Countering Digital Hate (2022) 'Social Media's Role in Amplifying Dangerous Lies About LGBTQ+ People'. *Center for Countering Digital Hate*. [online] Available from: https://counterhate.com/research/digital-hate-lgbtq/ (Accessed 26 August 2023)

23 Gogarty, Kayla (2022) 'Anti-LGBTQ Twitter account "Libs of TikTok" seemingly inspired attacks from Florida governor's press secretary'. *Media Matters for America*. [online] Available from: https://www.mediamatters.org/twitter/anti-lgbtq-twitter-account-libs-tiktok-seemingly-inspired-attacks-florida-governors-press (Accessed 26 August 2023)

24 euronews (2022) '"Libs of Tiktok": Twitter account targets LGBT+ teachers in the U.S.' *euronews*, 2 May. [online] Available from: https://www.euronews.com/2022/05/02/libs-of-tiktok-twitter-account-is-targeting-lgbtq-teachers-in-the-u-s (Accessed 26 August 2023)

25 Lorenz, Taylor, Dwoskin, Elizabeth and Jamison, Peter (2022) 'Twitter account Libs of TikTok blamed for harassment of children's hospitals'. *Washington Post*, 7 September. [online] Available from: https://www.washingtonpost.com/technology/2022/09/02/lgbtq-threats-hospitals-libs-of-tiktok/ (Accessed 15 August 2023)

26 Levinson, Jonathan (2023) 'Bomb threat shuts down OHSU clinic after anti-trans information posted online'. *Oregon Public Broadcasting*. [online] Available from: https://www.opb.org/article/2023/08/05/ohsu-bomb-threat-lgbtq/ (Accessed 15 August 2023)

27 Reduxx Team (2023) 'Oregon Breast Cancer Patient Dropped From Family Health Provider After Objecting to Trans Pride Flag'. *Reduxx*. [online] Available from: https://reduxx.info/oregon-breast-cancer-patient-dropped-from-family-health-provider-after-objecting-to-trans-pride-flag/ (Accessed 26 August 2023)

28 Farrow, Ronan (2023) 'Elon Musk's Shadow Rule'. *The New Yorker*. [online] Available from: https://www.newyorker.com/magazine/2023/08/28/elon-musks-shadow-rule (Accessed 23 August 2023)

29 Thalen, Mikael (2022) 'Elon Musk fans get an antisemitic trope to trend after Twitter user criticizes him'. *The Daily Dot*. [online] Available from: https://www.dailydot.com/debug/elon-musk-twitter-rothschild-conspiracy/ (Accessed 4 June 2022)

30 Ibid.

31 McCann, Charlie (2023) 'The Musk superfans who want to live on Mars with Elon'. *The Economist*, 21 April. [online] Available from: https://www.economist.com/1843/2023/04/21/the-musk-superfans-who-want-to-live-on-mars-with-elon (Accessed 25 August 2023)

32 Tufekci, Zeynep (2018) 'How social media took us from Tahrir Square to Donald Trump'. *MIT Technology Review*. [online] Available from: https://www.technologyreview.com/2018/08/14/240325/how-social-media-took-us-from-tahrir-square-to-donald-trump/ (Accessed 21 November 2021)

33 Wilson, Anne E., Parker, Victoria A. and Feinberg, Matthew (2020) 'Polarization in the contemporary political and media landscape'. *Current Opinion in Behavioral Sciences*, 34, pp. 223–28. [online] Available from: https://www.sciencedirect.com/science/article/pii/S2352154620301078 (Accessed 21 September 2021)

34 Ismail, Aymann (2021) 'How the Far-Right Deep Web Is Talking About Kyle Rittenhouse Now'. Slate. [online] Available from: https://slate.com/news-and-politics/2021/11/kyle-rittenhouse-trial-verdict-far-right-reaction.html (Accessed 27 November 2021)

35 Mackey, Robert (2021) 'As Kyle Rittenhouse Walks Free, Republican Lawmakers Fight Over Who Loves Him the Most'. *The Intercept*. [online] Available from: https://theintercept.com/2021/11/19/kyle-rittenhouse-walks-free-republican-lawmakers-fight-loves/ (Accessed 28 November 2021)

36 Weingarten, Ben (2021) 'Kyle Rittenhouse's crime was standing up to the woke mob'. *Newsweek*. [online] Available from: https://www.newsweek.com/kyle-rittenhouses-crime-was-standing-woke-mob-opinion-1652737 (Accessed 28 November 2021)

37 Nyhan, Brendan and Reifler, Jason (2010) 'When Corrections Fail: The Persistence of Political Misperceptions'. *Political Behavior*, 32(2), pp. 303–30. [online] Available from: http://link.springer.com/10.1007/s11109-010-9112-2 (Accessed 8 October 2021)

38 Nyhan, Brendan and Reifler, Jason (2019) 'The roles of information deficits

and identity threat in the prevalence of misperceptions'. *Journal of Elections, Public Opinion and Parties*, 29(2), pp. 222–44. [online] Available from: https://www.tandfonline.com/doi/full/10.1080/17457289.2018.1465061 (Accessed 8 October 2021)

39 Freiling, Isabelle, Krause, Nicole M., Scheufele, Dietram A. and Brossard, Dominique (2021) 'Believing and sharing misinformation, fact-checks, and accurate information on social media: The role of anxiety during COVID-19'. *New Media & Society*, p. 14614448211011451. [online] Available from: https://doi.org/10.1177/14614448211011451 (Accessed 23 August 2021)

8. Moral panics and radicalization

1 Associated Press (2023) 'Toddlers can't get gender-affirming surgeries, despite claims'. *AP News*. [online] Available from: https://apnews.com/article/fact-check-transgender-surgery-medicine-legislation-LGBTQ-491630629027 (Accessed 10 July 2023)

2 Jost, John T., Stern, Chadly, Rule, Nicholas O. and Sterling, Joanna (2017) 'The Politics of Fear: Is There an Ideological Asymmetry in Existential Motivation?' *Social Cognition*, 35(4), pp. 324–53. [online] Available from: http://guilfordjournals.com/doi/10.1521/soco.2017.35.4.324 (Accessed 30 December 2021)

3 Bleakley, Paul (2023) 'Panic, pizza and mainstreaming the alt-right: A social media analysis of Pizzagate and the rise of the QAnon conspiracy'. *Current Sociology*, 71(3), pp. 509–25. [online] Available from: https://doi.org/10.1177/00113921211034896 (Accessed 21 August 2023)

4 Patriotic Alternative (2023) 'Telegram channel "Patriotic Alternative Official" – @PatrioticAlternativeOfficial – TGStat'. *TGStat.com*. [online] Available from: https://tgstat.com/channel/@PatrioticAlternativeOfficial (Accessed 21 August 2023)

5 Taylor, Diane (2023) 'Police arrest 15 people after violence outside hotel housing asylum seekers'. *The Guardian*, 11 February. [online] Available from: https://www.theguardian.com/uk-news/2023/feb/11/merseyside-violence-outside-hotel-housing-asylum-seekers-arrests (Accessed 23 August 2023)

6 Andrews, Phoenix (2023) 'Covid has created a host of online stars each with a dedicated fanbase'. *The Times*, 22 August. [online] Available from: https://www.thetimes.co.uk/article/covid-has-created-a-host-of-online-stars-each-with-a-dedicated-fanbase-dml85m322 (Accessed 22 August 2023)

7 Ibid.

8 Hu, Jane C. (2020) 'Covid's Cassandra: The Swift, Complicated Rise of Eric Feigl-Ding'. *Undark Magazine*. [online] Available from: https://undark.org/2020/11/25/complicated-rise-of-eric-feigl-ding/ (Accessed 23 August 2023)

9 Linker, Damon (2019) 'What if Karl Rove was right about the reality-based community?' *The Week*, 26 July. [online] Available from: https://theweek.com/

articles/854892/what-karl-rove-right-about-realitybased-community (Accessed 20 May 2022)

10 Lorenz, Taylor (2022) 'Johnny Depp trial gives rise to a new breed of content creators'. *Washington Post.* [online] Available from: https://www.washingtonpost.com/technology/2022/06/02/johnny-depp-trial-creators-influencers/ (Accessed 4 June 2022)

11 Smith, Hannah (2022) 'Amber Heard did not quote The Talented Mr Ripley during trial'. *Full Fact.* [online] Available from: https://fullfact.org/online/amber-heard-film-quote/ (Accessed 10 July 2023)

12 Weiss, Geoff (2022) 'YouTube channel LegalBytes has surged by livestreaming the Depp vs. Heard trial – and earned $5,000 in a week'. *Business Insider.* [online] Available from: https://www.businessinsider.com/law-youtuber-legalbytes-streaming-johnny-depp-amber-heard-trial-2022-4 (Accessed 23 August 2023)

13 Lorenz, Taylor (2022) 'Johnny Depp trial gives rise to a new breed of content creators'. *Washington Post.* [online] Available from: https://www.washingtonpost.com/technology/2022/06/02/johnny-depp-trial-creators-influencers/ (Accessed 4 June 2022)

14 Winkie, Luke (2022) 'Johnny Depp's Online Army Is Certain He's Innocent. I Asked Them Why.' Slate. [online] Available from: https://slate.com/culture/2022/05/johnny-depp-amber-heard-trial-explained.html (Accessed 10 July 2023)

15 Wood, Poppy (2021) 'Justice warriors or troll army? Meet the "Deppheads", Johnny Depp's diehard superfans'. *The Times,* 14 March. [online] Available from: https://www.thetimes.co.uk/article/justice-warriors-or-troll-army-meet-the-deppheads-johnny-depps-diehard-superfans-5b5x0pmn7 (Accessed 10 July 2023)

16 Lemon, Katherine N. and Verhoef, Peter C. (2016) 'Understanding Customer Experience Throughout the Customer Journey'. *Journal of Marketing,* 80(6), pp. 69–96. [online] Available from: http://journals.sagepub.com/doi/10.1509/jm.15.0420 (Accessed 30 December 2021)

17 Khalfallah, Badis (2021) 'Funnel Marketing: Our Illustrated Guide'. *Implement.* [online] Available from: https://www.join-implement.com/posts/funnel-marketing-our-illustrated-guide (Accessed 30 December 2021)

18 Citarella, Joshua (2019) 'Irony Politics & Gen Z'. *New Models.* [online] Available from: https://newmodels.io/editorial/issue-1/14-irony-politics-gen-z-2019-citarella (Accessed 26 August 2023)

19 Citarella, Joshua (2021) *Radical Content,* [online] Available from: https://www.patreon.com/file?h=46548075&i=7230091 (Accessed 20 March 2021)

20 Rogers, Richard (2020) 'Deplatforming: Following extreme Internet celebrities to Telegram and alternative social media'. *European Journal of Communication,* p. 026732312092206. [online] Available from: http://journals.sagepub.com/doi/10.1177/0267323120922066 (Accessed 19 June 2020)

21 Citarella, Joshua (2020) 'Marxist memes for TikTok teens: can the internet radicalize teenagers for the left?' *The Guardian,* 12 September. [online] Available from: https://www.theguardian.

com/commentisfree/2020/sep/12/marxist-memes-tiktok-teens-radical-left (Accessed 30 December 2021)

22 Citarella, Joshua (2021) 'There's a new tactic for exposing you to radical content online: the "slow red-pill"'. *The Guardian*. [online] Available from: http://www.theguardian.com/commentisfree/2021/jul/15/theres-a-new-tactic-for-exposing-you-to-radical-content-online-the-slow-red-pill (Accessed 16 July 2021)

23 Case, Mary Anne (2019) 'Trans Formations in the Vatican's War on "Gender Ideology"'. *Signs: Journal of Women in Culture and Society*, 44(3), pp. 639–64. [online] Available from: https://www.journals.uchicago.edu/doi/abs/10.1086/701498 (Accessed 25 October 2021)

24 Saul, Heather (2015) 'Pope Francis compares arguments for transgender rights to nuclear arms'. *The Independent*, 21 February. [online] Available from: https://www.independent.co.uk/news/people/pope-francis-compares-arguments-for-transgender-rights-to-nuclear-arms-race-10061223.html (Accessed 31 December 2021)

25 BBC News (2020) 'Polish election: Andrzej Duda says LGBT "ideology" worse than communism'. *BBC News*, 14 June.[online] Available from: https://www.bbc.com/news/world-europe-53039864 (Accessed 27 December 2021)

26 lslan, Helen (2022) 'Transphobia: How the trans-hostile media coverage began in the UK'. *Medium*. [online] Available from: https://medium.com/@mimmymum/transphobia-how-the-trans-hostile-media-coverage-began-in-the-uk-429dc76bf0ac (Accessed 10 July 2023)

27 Dickinson, Tim (2021) 'How the Anti-Vaxxers Got Red-Pilled'. *Rolling Stone*. [online] Available from: https://www.rollingstone.com/culture/culture-features/qanon-anti-vax-covid-vaccine-conspiracy-theory-1125197/ (Accessed 12 December 2021)

28 Hopkin, Jonathan (2020) *Anti-System Politics: The Crisis of Market Liberalism in Rich Democracies*, Oxford, Oxford University Press.

29 Imrie, Matt (2022) 'The Bookstart Bear and Tala the Storyteller'. *Teen Librarian*. [online] Available from: http://teenlibrarian.co.uk/2022/10/04/the-bookstart-bear-and-tala-the-storyteller/ (Accessed 6 October 2022)

30 Citarella, Joshua (2021) 'There's a new tactic for exposing you to radical content online: the "slow red-pill"'. *The Guardian*. [online] Available from: http://www.theguardian.com/commentisfree/2021/jul/15/theres-a-new-tactic-for-exposing-you-to-radical-content-online-the-slow-red-pill (Accessed 16 July 2021)

31 Brown, Rivkah (2022) 'How I Deradicalised My Terf Mum'. *Novara Media*. [online] Available from: https://novaramedia.com/2022/12/24/how-i-deradicalised-my-terf-mum/ (Accessed 10 July 2023)

Conclusion

1 Sedgman, Kirsty (2023) *On Being Unreasonable: Being Unreasonable and Making Things Better*, London, Faber & Faber.

2 Berlant, Lauren and Greenwald, Jordan (2012) 'Affect in the End Times'. *Qui Parle*, 20(2), pp. 71–89. [online] Available from: https://read.dukeupress.edu/qui-parle/article/20/2/71/10223/Affect-in-the-End-TimesA-Conversation-with-Lauren (Accessed 30 June 2023)

3 Jacob Stolworthy (2023) 'Rod Stewart explains why he's "still a fan" of disgraced Boris Johnson'. *The Independent*, 16 June. [online] Available from: https://www.independent.co.uk/arts-entertainment/music/news/rod-stewart-boris-johnson-partygate-report-b2358673.html (Accessed 10 July 2023)

4 Walsh, Calla (2021) 'Stan Politics, Ed Markey, and Palestine'. *Mondoweiss*. [online] Available from: https://mondoweiss.net/2021/12/stan-politics-ed-markey-and-palestine/ (Accessed 3 January 2022)

5 Poe, Andrew (2021) 'Un-represent: theorizing the reason of political fanaticism'. *Distinktion: Journal of Social Theory*, 0(0), pp. 1–18. [online] Available from: https://doi.org/10.1080/1600910X.2021.1946116 (Accessed 17 November 2021)

6 Berger, John (1999) 'Against the great defeat of the world'. *Race & Class*, 40(2–3), pp. 1–4. [online] Available from: https://doi.org/10.1177/030639689904000201 (Accessed 30 October 2022)

7 Berger, John (1999) 'Welcome to the abyss'. *The Guardian*, 20 November. [online] Available from: https://www.theguardian.com/books/1999/nov/20/books.guardianreview (Accessed 31 October 2022)

INDEX